Logistics and
Supply Chain
Management

Logistics and Supply Chain Management

Strategies for Reducing Cost and Improving Service

Second Edition

MARTIN CHRISTOPHER

PEARSON EDUCATION LIMITED

Head Office:
Edinburgh Gate
Harlow CM20 2JE
Tel: +44 (0)1279 623623
Fax: +44 (0)1279 431059

London Office:
128 Long Acre, London WC2E 9AN
Tel: +44 (0)171 447 2000
Fax: +44 (0)171 240 5771

First published in Great Britain 1992
Second edition 1998

© Financial Times Professional Limited 1998

The right of Martin Christopher to be identified as
Author of this Work has been asserted by him in accordance
with the Copyright, Designs and Patents Act 1988.

ISBN 0 273 63049 0

British Library Cataloguing in Publication Data
A CIP catalogue record for this book can be obtained
from the British Library.

5 7 9 10 8 6

Typeset by Pantek Arts, Maidstone, Kent
Printed and bound in Great Britain by
Biddles Ltd, Guildford and King's Lynn

*The Publishers' policy is to use paper manufactured
from sustainable forests.*

About the Author

Martin Christopher is Professor of Marketing and Logistics at Cranfield School of Management, one of Europe's leading Business Schools, which is itself a part of Cranfield University. His work in the field of logistics and supply chain management has gained international recognition. He has published widely and his recent books include *Logistics and Supply Chain Management* and *Marketing Logistics*. Martin Christopher is also co-editor of the *International Journal of Logistics Management* and is a regular contributor to conferences and workshops around the world.

At Cranfield, Martin Christopher chairs the Centre for Logistics and Transportation, the largest activity of its type in Europe. The work of the centre covers all aspects of transportation and logistics and offers both full-time and part-time Masters degree courses as well as extensive management development programmes. Research plays a key role in the work of the Centre and contributes to its international standing.

Martin Christopher is an Emeritus Fellow of the Institute of Logistics on whose Council he sits. In 1988 he was awarded the Sir Robert Lawrence Gold Medal for his contribution to logistics education.

Dedicated to the memory of Jim Cooper

Contents

Preface

In today's highly competitive, global marketplace the pressure on organizations to find new ways to create and deliver value to customers grows ever stronger. Gradually, in emerging economies as well as mature markets, the power of the buyer has overtaken that of the customer.

The rules are different in a buyers' market. In particular customer service becomes a key differentiator as the sophistication and demands of customers continually increase.

At the same time, market maturity combined with new sources of global competition has led to over-capacity in many industries leading to an inevitable pressure on price. Price has always been a critical competitive variable in many markets and the signs are that it will become even more of an issue as the 'commoditization' of markets continues.

It is against this backdrop that the discipline and philosophy of logistics and supply chain management has moved to the centre stage over the last two decades. The concept of integration within the business and between businesses is not new, but the acceptance of its validity by managers is. There has been a growing recognition that it is through logistics and supply chain management that the twin goals of cost reduction and service enhancement can be achieved. Better management of the 'pipeline' means that customers are served more effectively and yet the costs of providing that service are reduced.

This is the focus of this second edition of *Logistics and Supply Chain Management*. The basic themes and underlying structure of the book have not changed from the first edition but as ideas progress and best practice gets even better, the need for revision and up-dating becomes inevitable.

In preparing this new edition I have been considerably assisted by Helen Peck who has researched and contributed many of the case examples and by Tracy Brawn who skillfully created order out of chaos in producing the finished manuscript. I am grateful to them both.

Martin Christopher
Professor of Marketing & Logistics
Cranfield School of Management

Logistics and competitive strategy

This chapter:

Introduces the concept of logistics with a brief review of its origins in military strategy and its subsequent adoption within industry.

●

Highlights the principles of competitive strategy and the pursuit of differentiation through the development of productivity and value advantage.

●

Explains the concept of the value chain and the integrative role of logistics within the organization.

●

Describes the emerging discipline of supply chain management, defining it and explaining how and why it takes the principles of logistics forward.

●

Explains the rise of the virtual organization and the factors which have precipitated the emergence of supply chain management.

In the early part of 1991 the world was given a dramatic example of the importance of logistics. As a precursor to the Gulf War it had been necessary for the United States and its allies to move huge amounts of material great distances in what were thought to be impossibly short time-frames. Half a million people and over half a million tonnes of material and supplies were airlifted 12,000 kilometres with a further 2.3 million tonnes of equipment moved by sea – all of this achieved in a matter of months.

Throughout the history of mankind wars have been won and lost through logistics strengths and capabilities – or the lack of them. It has been argued that the defeat of the British in the American War of Independence can largely be attributed to logistics failure. The British Army in America depended almost entirely upon Britain for supplies. At the height of the war there were 12,000 troops overseas and for the most part they had not only to be equipped, but fed from Britain. For the first six years of the war the administration of these vital supplies was totally inadequate, affecting the course of operations and the morale of the troops. An organization capable of supplying the army was not developed until 1781 and by then it was too late.[1]

> It is only in the recent past that business organizations have come to recognize the vital impact that logistics management can have in the achievement of competitive advantage.

In the Second World War logistics also played a major role. The Allied Forces' invasion of Europe was a highly skilled exercise in logistics, as was the defeat of Rommel in the desert. Rommel himself once said that '... before the fighting proper, the battle is won or lost by quartermasters'.

However whilst the Generals and Field Marshals from the earliest times have understood the critical role of logistics, strangely it is only in the recent past that business organizations have come to recognize the vital impact that logistics management can have in the achievement of competitive advantage. This lack of recognition partly springs from the

3

relatively low level of understanding of the benefits of integrated logistics. Arch Shaw, writing in 1915, pointed out that:

> 'The relations between the activities of demand creation and physical supply ... illustrate the existence of the two principles of interdependence and balance. Failure to co-ordinate any one of these activities with its group-fellows and also with those in the other group, or undue emphasis or outlay put upon any one of these activities, is certain to upset the equilibrium of forces which means efficient distribution.
>
> ... The physical distribution of the goods is a problem distinct from the creation of demand ... Not a few worthy failures in distribution campaigns have been due to such a lack of co-ordination between demand creation and physical supply ...
>
> Instead of being a subsequent problem, this question of supply must be met and answered before the work of distribution begins.'[2]

It has taken a further 70 years or so for the basic principles of logistics management to be clearly defined.

What is logistics management in the sense that it is understood today? There are many ways of defining logistics but the underlying concept might be defined as follows:

> *Logistics is the process of strategically managing the procurement, movement and storage of materials, parts and finished inventory (and the related information flows) through the organization and its marketing channels in such a way that current and future profitability are maximized through the cost-effective fulfilment of orders.*

This basic definition will be extended and developed as the book progresses, but it makes an adequate starting point.

Competitive advantage

A central theme of this book is that effective logistics management can provide a major source of competitive advantage – in other words a position of enduring superiority over competitors in terms of customer preference may be achieved through logistics.

The bases for success in the marketplace are numerous, but a simple model is based around the triangular linkage of the company, its customers and its competitors – the 'Three C's'. The 'Three C's' in question are: the customer, the competition and the company. Figure 1.1. illustrates the three-way relationship.

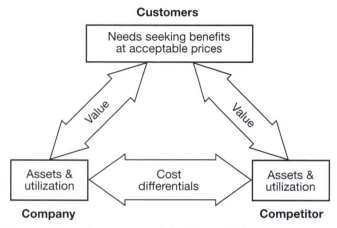

Fig. 1.1 Competitive advantage and the 'three C's'
Source: Ohmae, K., *The Mind of the Strategist*, Penguin Books, 1983

The source of competitive advantage is found firstly in the ability of the organization to differentiate itself, in the eyes of the customer, from its competition and secondly by operating at a lower cost and hence at greater profit.

Seeking a sustainable and defensible competitive advantage has become the concern of every manager who is alert to the realities of the marketplace. It is no longer acceptable to assume that good products will sell themselves, neither is it advisable to imagine that success today will carry forward into tomorrow.

Let us consider the bases of success in any competitive context. At its most elemental, commercial success derives either from a cost advantage or a value advantage or, ideally, both. It is as simple as that – the most profitable competitor in any industry sector tends to be the lowest cost producer or the supplier providing a product with the greatest perceived differentiated values.

Put very simply, successful companies either have a productivity advantage or they have a 'value' advantage or a combination of the two. The productivity advantage gives a lower cost profile and the value advantage gives the product or offering a differential 'plus' over competitive offerings.

Let us briefly examine these two vectors of strategic direction.

1 Productivity advantage

In many industries there will typically be one competitor who will be the low cost producer and, more often than not, that competitor will have the greatest sales volume in the sector. There is substantial evidence to suggest that 'big is beautiful' when it comes to cost advantage. This is partly due to economies of scale which enable fixed costs to be spread over a greater volume but more particularly to the impact of the 'experience curve'.

The experience curve is a phenomenon which has its roots in the earlier notion of the 'learning curve'. Researchers discovered during the last war that it was possible to identify and predict improvements in the rate of output of workers as they became more skilled in the processes and tasks on which they were working. Subsequent work by Bruce Henderson, founder of the Boston Consulting Group, extended this concept by demonstrating that all costs, not just production costs, would decline at a given rate as volume increased (see Figure 1.2). In fact, to be precise, the relationship that the experience curve describes is between real unit costs and cumulative volume. Further it is generally recognized that this cost decline applies only to 'value added', i.e. costs other than bought in supplies.

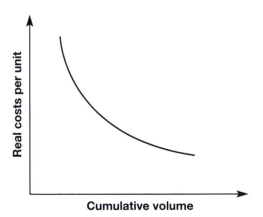

Fig. 1.2 The experience curve

Traditionally it has been suggested that the main route to cost reduction was by gaining greater sales volume and there can be no doubt about the close linkage between relative market share and relative costs. However it must also be recognized that logistics management can provide a multitude of ways to increase efficiency and productivity and hence contribute significantly to reduced unit costs. How this can be achieved will be one of the key themes of this book.

> **Logistics management can provide a multitude of ways to increase efficiency and productivity and hence contribute significantly to reduced unit costs.**

2 Value advantage

It has long been an axiom in marketing that 'customers don't buy products, they buy benefits'. Put another way the product is purchased not for itself but for the promise of what it will 'deliver'. These benefits may be intangible, i.e. they relate not to specific product features but rather to such things as image or reputation. Alternatively the delivered offering may be seen to out-perform its rivals in some functional aspect.

Unless the product or service we offer can be distinguished in some way from its competitors there is a strong likelihood that the marketplace will view it as a 'commodity' and so the sale will tend to go to the cheapest supplier. Hence the importance of seeking to add additional values to our offering to mark it out from the competition.

What are the means by which such value differentiation may be gained? Essentially the development of a strategy based upon added values will normally require a more segmented approach to the market. When a company scrutinizes markets closely it frequently finds that there are distinct 'value segments'. In other words different groups of customers within the total market attach different importance to different benefits. The importance of such benefit segmentation lies in the fact that often there are substantial opportunities for creating differentiated appeals for specific segments. Take the motor car as an example. A model such as the Ford Mondeo is not only positioned in the middle range of European cars but within that broad category specific versions are aimed at defined segments. Thus we find the basic, small engine, two-door model at one end of the spectrum and the four-door, high performance version at the other extreme. In between are a whole variety of options each of which seeks to satisfy the needs of quite different 'benefit segments'. Adding value through differentiation is a powerful means of achieving a defensible advantage in the market.

Equally powerful as a means of adding value is service. Increasingly it is the case that markets are becoming more service sensitive and this of course poses particular challenges for logistics management. There is a trend in many markets towards a decline in the strength of the 'brand' and a consequent move towards 'commodity' market status. Quite simply this means it is becoming progressively more difficult to compete purely on the basis of brand or corporate image. Additionally, there is increasingly a convergence of technology within product categories which means that it is no longer possible to compete effectively on the basis of product differences. Thus the need to seek differentiation through means other than technology. A number of companies have responded to this by focusing upon service as a means of gaining a competitive edge. Service in this context relates to the process of developing relationships with customers through the provision of an augmented offer. This augmentation can take many forms including delivery service, after-sales services, financial packages, technical support and so forth.

In practice what we find is that the successful companies will often seek to achieve a position based upon both a productivity advantage and a value advantage. A useful way of examining the available options is to present them as a simple matrix. Let us consider these options in turn.

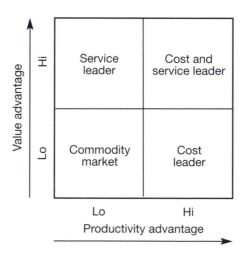

Fig. 1.3 Logistics and competitive advantage

For companies who find themselves in the bottom left hand corner of our matrix (Figure 1.3) the world is an uncomfortable place. Their products are indistinguishable from their competitors' offerings and they have no cost advantage. These are typical commodity market situations and ultimately the only strategy is either to move to the right on the matrix, i.e. to cost leadership, or upwards towards service leadership. Often the cost leadership route is simply not available. This particularly will be the case in a mature market where substantial market share gains are difficult to achieve. New technology may sometimes provide a window of opportunity for cost reduction but in such situations the same technology is often available to competitors.

Cost leadership strategies have traditionally been based upon the economies of scale, gained through sales volume. This is why market share is considered to be so important in many industries. However, if volume is to be the basis for cost leadership then it is preferable for that volume to be gained early in the market life cycle. The 'experience curve' concept, briefly described earlier, demonstrates the value of early market share gains – the higher your share relative to your competitors the lower your costs should be. This cost advantage can be used strategically to assume a position of price leader and, if appropriate, to make it impossible for higher cost competitors to survive. Alternatively, price may be maintained enabling above average profit to be earned which potentially is available to further develop the position of the product in the market.

An increasingly powerful route to achieving a cost advantage comes not necessarily through volume and the economies of scale but instead through logistics management. In many industries logistics costs represent such a significant proportion of total costs that it is possible to make major cost reductions through fundamentally reengineering logistics processes. Various means of achieving this will be discussed later in this book.

The other way out of the 'commodity' quadrant of the matrix is to seek a strategy of differentiation through service excellence. We have already commented on the fact that markets have become more 'service-sensitive'. Customers in all industries are seeking greater responsiveness and reliability from suppliers; they are looking for reduced lead times, just-in-time delivery and value-added services that enable them to do a better job of serving their customers. In Chapter 2 we will examine the specific ways in which superior service strategies, based upon enhanced logistics management, can be developed.

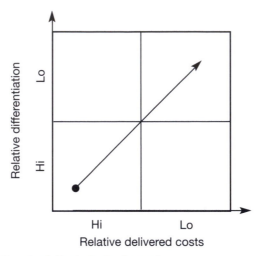

Fig. 1.4 Marketing logistics' strategic goal

One thing is for sure: there is no middle ground between cost leadership and service excellence. Indeed the challenge to management is to identify appropriate logistics strategies to take the organization to the top right hand corner of the matrix. Companies who occupy that position have offers that are distinctive in the value they deliver and are also cost competitive. Clearly it is a position of some strength, occupying 'high ground' which is extremely difficult for competitors to attack. Figure 1.4 clearly presents the strategic challenge to logistics: it is to seek out strategies that will take the business away from the 'commodity' end of the market towards a securer position of strength based upon differentiation and cost advantage.

Gaining competitive advantage through logistics

Of the many changes that have taken place in management thinking over the last ten years or so perhaps the most significant has been the emphasis placed upon the search for strategies that will provide superior value in the eyes of the customer. To a large extent the credit for this must go to Michael Porter, the Harvard Business School Professor, who through his research and writing[3,4] has alerted managers and strategists to the central importance of competitive relativities in achieving success in the marketplace.

One concept in particular that Michael Porter has brought to a wider audience is the 'value chain':

> 'Competitive advantage cannot be understood by looking at a firm as a whole. It stems from the many discrete activities a firm performs in designing, producing, marketing, delivering, and supporting its product. Each of these activities can contribute to a firm's relative cost position and create a basis for differentiation ... The value chain disaggregates a firm into its strategically relevant activities in order to understand the behaviour of costs and the existing and potential sources of differentiation. A firm gains competitive advantage by performing these strategically important activities more cheaply or better than its competitors.'[4]

Value chain activities (shown in Figure 1.5) can be categorized into two types – primary activities (inbound logistics, operations, outbound logistics, marketing and sales, and service) and support activities (infrastructure, human resource management, technology development and procurement). These support activities are integrating functions that cut across the various primary activities within the firm. Competitive advantage is derived from the way in which firms organize and perform these discrete activities within the value chain. To gain competitive advantage over its rivals, a firm must deliver value to its customers through performing these activities more efficiently than its competitors or by performing the activities in a unique way that creates greater differentiation.

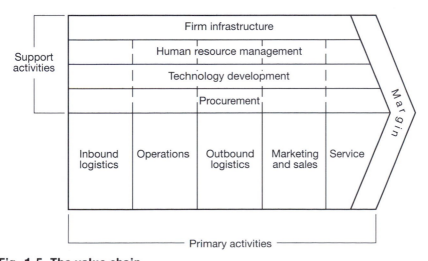

Fig. 1.5 The value chain
Source: Porter, M.E., *Competitive Advantage*, The Free Press, 1985

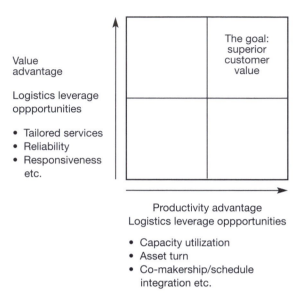

Value advantage

Logistics leverage oppportunities

- Tailored services
- Reliability
- Responsiveness
etc.

The goal: superior customer value

Productivity advantage
Logistics leverage oppportunities

- Capacity utilization
- Asset turn
- Co-makership/schedule integration etc.

Fig. 1.6 Gaining competitive advantage through logistics

Logistics management, it can be argued, has the potential to assist the organization in the achievement of both a cost/productivity advantage and a value advantage. As Figure 1.6 suggests, in the first instance there are a number of important ways in which productivity can be enhanced through logistics. Whilst these possibilities for leverage will be discussed in detail later in the book, suffice it to say that the opportunities for better capacity utilization, inventory reduction and closer integration with suppliers at a planning level, are considerable. Equally the prospects for gaining a value advantage in the marketplace through superior customer service should not be underestimated. It will be argued later that the way we service the customer has become a vital means of differentiation.

To summarize, those organizations that will be the leaders in the markets of the future will be those that have sought and achieved the twin peaks of excellence: they have gained both cost leadership and service leadership.

The underlying philosophy behind the logistics concept is that of planning and co-ordinating the materials flow from source to user as an integrated system rather than, as was so often the case in the past, managing the goods flow as a series of independent activities. Thus under a logistics management regime the goal is to link the marketplace, the distribution network, the manufacturing process and the procurement activity in such a way that customers are serviced at higher levels and yet at lower cost. In other words to achieve the goal of competitive advantage through both cost reduction and service enhancement.

The mission of logistics management

It will be apparent from the previous comments that the mission of logistics management is to plan and co-ordinate all those activities necessary to achieve desired levels of delivered service and quality at lowest possible cost. Logistics must therefore be seen as the link between the marketplace and the operating activity of the business. The scope of

> The scope of logistics spans the organization, from the management of raw materials through to the delivery of the final product.

logistics spans the organization, from the management of raw materials through to the delivery of the final product. Figure 1.7 illustrates this total systems concept.

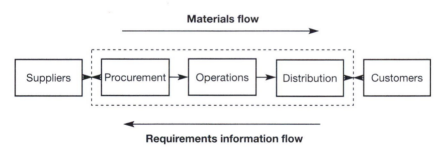

Fig. 1.7 Logistics management process

Logistics management, from this total systems viewpoint, is the means whereby the needs of customers are satisfied through the co-ordination of the materials and information flows that extend from the marketplace, through the firm and its operations and beyond that to suppliers. To achieve this company-wide integration clearly requires a quite different orientation than that typically encountered in the conventional organization.

For example, for many years marketing and manufacturing have been seen as largely separate activities within the organization. At best they have coexisted, at worst there has been open warfare.

Manufacturing priorities and objectives have typically been focused on operating efficiency, achieved through long production runs, minimized set-ups and change-overs and product standardization. On the other hand marketing has sought to achieve competitive advantage through variety, high service levels and frequent product changes.

In today's more turbulent environment there is no longer any possibility of manufacturing and marketing acting independently of each other. The internecine disputes between the 'barons' of production and marketing are clearly counter-productive to the achievement of overall corporate goals.

It is no coincidence that in recent years both marketing and manufacturing have become the focus of renewed attention. Marketing as a concept and a philosophy of customer orientation now enjoys a wider acceptance than ever in the western world. It is now generally accepted that the need to understand and meet customer requirements is a prerequisite for survival. At the same time, in the search for improved cost competitiveness, manufacturing management has been the subject of a massive renaissance. The last decade has seen the rapid introduction of flexible manufacturing systems (FMS), of new approaches to inventory based on materials requirements planning (MRP) and just-in-time (JIT) methods and, perhaps most important of all, a sustained emphasis on quality.

Equally there has been a growing recognition of the critical role that procurement plays in creating and sustaining competitive advantage as part of an integrated logistics process. Leading-edge organizations now routinely include supply-side issues in the development of their strategic plans. Not only is the cost of purchased materials and supplies a significant part of total costs in most organizations, but there is a major opportunity for leveraging the capabilities and competencies of suppliers through closer integration of the buyers' and the suppliers' logistics processes.

In this scheme of things, logistics is therefore essentially an integrative concept that seeks to develop a system-wide view of the firm. It is fundamentally a *planning* concept that seeks to create a framework through which the needs of the marketplace can be translated into a manufacturing strategy and plan, which in turn links into a strategy and plan for procurement. Ideally there should be a 'one-plan' mentality within the business which seeks to replace the conventional stand-alone and separate plans of marketing, distribution, production and procurement. This, quite simply, is the mission of logistics management.

The supply chain and competitive performance

Traditionally most organizations have viewed themselves as entities that exist independently from others and indeed need to compete with them in order to survive. There is almost a Darwinian ethic of the 'survival of the fittest' driving much of corporate strategy. However such a philosophy can be self-defeating if it leads to an unwillingness to co-operate in order to compete. Behind this seemingly paradoxical concept is the idea of supply chain integration.

The supply chain is the network of organizations that are involved, through upstream and downstream linkages, in the different processes and activities that produce value in the form of products and services in the hands of the ultimate consumer. Thus for example a shirt manufacturer is a part of a supply chain that extends upstream through the weavers of fabrics to the manufacturers of fibres, and downstream through distributors and retailers to the final consumer. Each of these organizations in the chain are dependent upon each other by definition and yet paradoxically by tradition do not closely co-operate with each other.

Supply chain management is not the same as 'vertical integration'. Vertical integration normally implies ownership of upstream suppliers and downstream customers. This was once thought to be a desirable strategy but increasingly organizations are now focusing on their 'core business' – in other words the things they do really well and where they have a differential advantage. Everything else is 'out-sourced' – in other words it is procured outside the firm. So, for example, companies that perhaps once made their own components now only assemble the finished product, e.g. automobile manufacturers. Other companies may also subcontract the manufacturing as well, e.g. Nike in footwear and sportswear. These companies have sometimes been termed 'virtual' or 'network' organizations. A typical example of this new type of business organization is provided by Apple Computers where over 90 per cent of the cost of sales of a typical Apple computer is purchased content.

Clearly this trend has many implications for logistics management, not the least being the challenge of integrating and co-ordinating the flow of materials from a multitude of suppliers, often offshore, and similarly managing the distribution of the finished product by way of multiple intermediaries.

15

In the past it was often the case that relationships with suppliers and downstream customers (such as distributors or retailers) were adversarial rather than co-operative. It is still the case today that some companies will seek to achieve cost reductions or profit improvement at the expense of their supply chain partners. Companies such as these do not realize that simply transferring costs upstream or downstream does not make them any more competitive. The reason for this is that ultimately all costs will make their way to the final marketplace to be reflected in the price paid by the end user. The leading-edge companies recognize the fallacy of this conventional approach and instead seek to make the supply chain as a whole more competitive through the value it adds and the costs that it reduces overall. They have realized that the real competition is not company against company but rather supply chain against supply chain.

It must be recognized that the concept of supply chain management whilst relatively new, is in fact no more than an extension of the logic of logistics. Logistics management is primarily concerned with optimizing flows within the organization whilst supply chain management recognizes that internal integration by itself is not sufficient. Figure 1.8 suggests that there is in effect an evolution of integration from the stage 1 position of complete functional independence where each business function such as production or purchasing does their own thing in complete isolation from the other business functions. An example would be where production seeks to optimize its unit costs of manufacture by long production runs without regard for the build-up of finished goods inventory and heedless of the impact it will have on the need for warehousing space and the impact on working capital.

Stage 2 companies have recognized the need for at least a limited degree of integration between adjacent functions, e.g. distribution and inventory management or purchasing and materials control. The natural next step to stage 3 requires the establishment and implementation of an 'end-to-end' planning framework that will be fully described later in this book.

Stage 4 represents true supply chain integration in that the concept of linkage and co-ordination that is achieved in stage 3 is now extended upstream to suppliers and downstream to customers. There is thus a crucial and important distinction to be made between *logistics* and *supply chain management*.

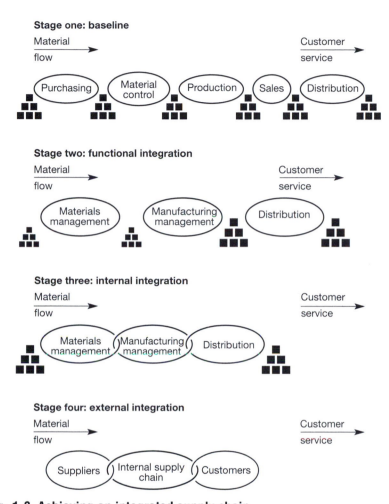

Stage one: baseline

Material flow →

Customer service →

Purchasing · Material control · Production · Sales · Distribution

Stage two: functional integration

Material flow →

Customer service →

Materials management · Manufacturing management · Distribution

Stage three: internal integration

Material flow →

Customer service →

Materials management · Manufacturing management · Distribution

Stage four: external integration

Material flow →

Customer service →

Suppliers · Internal supply chain · Customers

Fig. 1.8 Achieving an integrated supply chain

Source: Stevens, G.C. 'Integrating the supply chain', *International Journal of Physical Distribution and Materials Management*, Vol 19, No. 8, 1989.

Logistics is essentially a planning orientation and framework that seeks to create a single plan for the flow of product and information through a business. Supply chain management builds upon this framework and seeks to achieve linkage and co-ordination between *processes* of other entities in the pipeline, i.e. suppliers and customers, and the organization itself. Thus for example one goal of supply chain management might be to reduce or eliminate the buffers of inventory that exist between organizations in a chain through the sharing of information on demand and current stock levels. This is the concept of 'co-managed inventory' (CMI) that will be discussed in more detail later in the book.

It will be apparent that supply chain management involves a significant change from the traditional arms-length, even adversarial, relationships that so often typified buyer/supplier relationships in the past. The focus of supply chain management is on co-operation and trust and the recognition that properly managed 'the whole can be greater than the sum of its parts'.

The definition of supply chain management that is adopted in this book is:

The management of upstream and downstream relationships with suppliers and customers to deliver superior customer value at less cost to the supply chain as a whole.

Thus the focus of supply chain management is upon the management of *relationships* in order to achieve a more profitable outcome for all parties in the chain. This brings with it some significant challenges since there may be occasions when the narrow self-interest of one party has to be subsumed for the benefit of the chain as a whole.

Whilst the phrase 'supply chain management' is now widely used, it could be argued that it should really be termed *'demand chain management'* to reflect the fact that the chain should be driven by the market, not by suppliers. Equally the word 'chain' should be replaced by *'network'* since there will normally be multiple suppliers and, indeed, suppliers to suppliers as well as multiple customers and customers' customers to be included in the total system.

Figure 1.9 illustrates this idea of the firm being at the centre of a network of suppliers and customers.

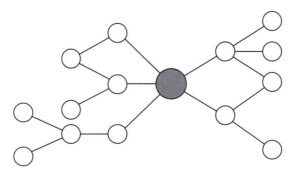

Fig. 1.9 The supply chain is a network

Extending this idea it has been suggested that a supply chain could more accurately be defined as:

A network of connected and interdependent organizations mutually and co-operatively working together to control, manage and improve the flow of materials and information from suppliers to end users.

Source: J. Aitken[5]

Dell Computers: using the supply chain to compete

The personal computer (PC) sector was still in its infancy when, in 1983, medical student Michael Dell began buying up remainder stocks of outdated IBM PCs from local retailers, upgrading them in his college dorm, then selling them on at bargain prices to eager consumers. Dell abandoned his studies soon afterwards to concentrate on his growing computer business. By 1985 his company, Dell Computers, had switched from upgrading old IBMs to building its own machines, but Dell was different from other computer manufacturers of its day. The machines themselves were technologically unremarkable, but it was the way in which they were sold – directly to the customer – that gave Dell a unique advantage over established, product-focused, PC makers.

While the industry leaders vied amongst themselves to introduce PCs with ever more impressive technology, little consideration was given to the mundane business of supply chain management. The computers they produced were invariably made-to-forecast and because of the way they were sold – through shops, resellers, and systems integrators – were then destined to languish for an average of two months in warehouses or on shop shelves before being purchased by the customer. Meanwhile Dell remained focused on the end user, thus avoiding the inherent double jeopardy created by the dynamics and economics of the industry. Firstly, around 80 per cent of the costs of manufacturing a PC are component costs, and component costs have been falling since the industry's inception, particularly the all-important processors that continue to fall in price by an average of 30 per cent per year.[1] The longer these components wait to be sold, the worse value they become. Secondly, there is the risk that a step-change in

▶

19

▶ technology may make millions of pounds' worth of finished PCs obsolete overnight, forcing manufacturers to either compensate resellers for unloading stocks at a loss, or incur the costs of shipping them to developing countries where they can be sold off cheaply.

By selling directly to the customer Dell was able to configure and assemble every PC to order, thus avoiding the risks associated with carrying finished inventory, which in turn enabled it to maintain its cost advantage over its conventional rivals. Dell's low priced machines with their bespoke configuration, became an attractive alternative for those customers who were confident enough to buy direct.

For many years, received wisdom in the industry considered Dell's position to be nothing more than that of a successful niche player. It was widely believed that the majority of business-to-business customers and indeed consumers buying PCs for the home, would always prefer to purchase their equipment through traditional channels, where help would be at hand should something go wrong and consumers could see and touch the products before purchase. In a bid to break out of its perceived niche, Dell embarked on a brief flirtation with conventional retail distribution channels. The move was a mistake. Retail sales plummeted as soon as Dell offered a new PC through its direct channels. Dell was obliged to compensate the retailers for their losses. As a result the company posted its first ever loss ($36m) in 1993.[2] The ill-judged foray was a salutary lesson in the perils of attempting to operate through conflicting distribution channels and a vindication of its original low-cost direct sales strategy.

Dell pulled out of the retail market in 1994 and retrenched with a vengeance, rebounding immediately with profits of $149m. From this point on Dell concentrated on finding ways to leverage the strengths of its original direct sales strategy, concentrating on minimizing inventory and increasing return on capital employed. Leanness, flexibility and above all time compression were the keys. Over the next three years Dell's operations were closely reexamined to squeeze every possible moment of non-value adding time out of its procurement and assembly processes. By 1997, Dell was not only a model of JIT manufacturing, but had applied its own exacting time standards to the rest of its supply chain. It had specified that the majority of components have to be warehoused within 15 minutes of Dell's three factories (in Austin, Texas; Limerick, Ireland; Penang, Malaysia), and many components are not ordered from a supplier before Dell receives a customer order. To achieve such levels of co-operation and integration, Dell has reduced its number of suppliers from 204 companies in 1992 to just 47. At the same time it has preferred to source from suppliers close to their plants rather than from more distant offshore suppliers, even though the local manufacturing costs may be higher.

For Dell's Limerick plant, at least 40 per cent of components are produced and supplied on a JIT basis, a further 45 per cent of components are held in supplier hubs, located close to Dell's factory. The suppliers restock their own warehouses and manage their own inventories, delivering to the factories on a consignment stock basis. Bulky finished subassemblies, such as monitors and speakers are treated differently. Instead of shipping them to Dell's factories, they are sent directly to the customer from the suppliers' hub (located close to the market rather than close to Dell's factory), saving Dell approximately $30 per item in freight costs. Dell is billed for the components only when they leave the suppliers' warehouse in response to a customer order, so that the components themselves are likely to spend only half a day as Dell's own inventory. The supplier receives payment approximately 45 days later.

Where the suppliers of essential components (such as disk drives) cannot be assembled as quickly as the computers can be bolted together, Dell is pressing the suppliers to shorten their own lead times, but in the meantime, their components must be built to forecast. Fortunately, demand for components is much more predictable than demand for finished goods, though shortages of some critical components (most noticeably microprocessors) continues to be a problem across the industry. Here again, the direct sales method places Dell at an advantage over those makers who use traditional routes to market. Because Dell communicates directly with its customers, it is able to shape demand through its telephone sales by steering customers towards configurations using readily available components.

Meanwhile Dell has forged ahead with Internet sales as an even more cost effective version of its direct-sales approach. Dell is not the first or the only PC retailer to venture into cyberspace, though by 1997 it was certainly the most successful, mainly because no other manufacturer was better placed to make such a move. Within six months of

▶

► opening for business through its Website, Dell was clocking up Internet sales of $1m per day, with sales through the channel growing by 20 per cent per month.[3] Far from remaining a small niche option, direct buyers now account for a third of all PC sales in the US, up from only 15 per cent in 1991. Internet sales have been slower to take-off in Europe and Asia, but they are rising and are set to climb higher in these increasingly computer literate societies.

To place an order customers simply dial into the Website and follow the on-screen instructions. The software allows them to monitor on-screen the price impact of each option as they configure their PC, then tap in their credit card or account payment details, before finally placing the order at the click of a mouse. The customer receives confirmation of the order within five minutes of its placement, not more than 36 hours later their bespoke PCs are trundling off the production lines and onto the delivery trucks. Most of this time is spent not assembling the machines, but testing the machines and loading software. Dell can expect to see payment for most sales within 24 hours of order placement, while rivals such as PC market leader, Compaq, must wait around 35 days for payment through primary dealers. Even other direct sellers are apt to take over a fortnight to convert an order in cash.

By the end of 1997, Dell was growing at a rate that was more than three times the industry average and had become the world's second biggest PC maker (by unit sales). Third quarter revenues were up 58 per cent to $3,188m, and profits for the quarter up 71 per cent on the previous year to $248m. Finished goods inventory and work in progress stood at a combined figure of just $57m, with a further $244m in raw material and other items, giving a total inventory of around 11 days of sales.[4] Dell's growth and return on investment are the envy of the industry and have been reflected in the staggering rise of Dell's stock price. Other established industry players have tried to emulate Dell's direct sales formula, but have retreated after running into the same channel conflicts as Dell had encountered in 1993 with its foray into retail sales. In the meantime, Dell is moving on to its next big growth opportunity – the network server business – where through its partnership with network equipment manufacturer 3Com Corp, it hopes to apply its PC and time-saving know-how to reduce the lengthy period needed to test the compatibility of each newly launched computer or networking device. By supplying 3Com with new computers as soon as they are introduced, the partners hope to slash the existing 60–90 days testing period for new equipment to just two weeks. Acting together to bring new solutions to the market more quickly, the partners were set to outpace their rivals and make a lasting impression on the network server business.

References
1. *The Economist*, 'Dell Computer: selling PCs like bananas', 5 October 1996, p. 99.
2. Serwer, Andrew E, 'Michael Dell turns the PC world inside out', *Fortune*, 8 September 1997, pp. 38–44.
3. McWilliams, Gary, 'Whirlwind on the web', *Business Week*, 7 April 1997, pp. 132, 134, 136.
4. Wheatley, Malcolm, 'Less means more', *Logistics Europe*, January 1998, pp. 36–39

The changing logistics environment

As the competitive context of business continues to change, bringing with it new complexities and concerns for management generally, it also has to be recognized that the impact of these changes on logistics can be considerable. Indeed, of the many strategic issues that confront the business organization today, perhaps the most challenging are in the area of logistics.

Much of this book will be devoted to addressing these challenges in detail but it is useful at this stage to highlight what are perhaps the most pressing currently. These are:

● The customer service explosion
● Time compression
● Globalization of industry
● Organizational integration

The customer service explosion

So much has been written and talked about service, quality and excellence that there is no escaping the fact that the customer in today's marketplace is more demanding, not just of product quality, but also of service.

As more and more markets become in effect 'commodity' markets, where the customer perceives little technical difference between competing offers, the need is for the creation of differential advantage through added value. Increasingly a prime source of this added value is through customer service.

Customer service may be defined as the consistent provision of time and place utility. In other words products don't have value until they are in the hands of the customer at the time and place required. There are clearly many facets of customer service, ranging from on-time delivery through to after-sales support. Essentially the role of customer service should be to enhance 'value-in-use', meaning that the product becomes worth more in the eyes of the customer because service has added value to the core product. In this way significant differentiation of the total offer (that is the core product plus the service package) can be achieved.

> The customer in today's marketplace is more demanding, not just of product quality, but also of service.

Those companies that have achieved recognition for service excellence, and thus have been able to establish a differential advantage over their competition are typically those companies where logistics management is a high priority. Companies like Xerox, BMW, Benetton and Dell Computers are typical of such organizations. The achievement of competitive advantage through service comes not from slogans or expensive so-called customer care programmes, but rather from a combination of a carefully thought out strategy for service, the development of appropriate delivery systems and commitment from people, from the Chief Executive down.

The attainment of service excellence in this broad sense can only be achieved through a closely integrated logistics strategy. In reality, the ability to become a world class supplier depends as much upon the effectiveness of one's operating systems as it does upon the presentation of the product, the creation of images and the influencing of consumer perceptions. In other words, the success of McDonald's, British Airways, or any of the other frequently-cited paragons of service excellence, is not due to their choice of advertising agency, but rather to their recognition that managing the logistics of service delivery on a consistent basis is the crucial source of differential advantage.

Time compression

One of the most visible features of recent years has been the way in which time has become a critical issue in management. Product life cycles are shorter than ever, industrial customers and distributors require just-in-time deliveries, and end users are ever more willing to accept a substitute product if their first choice is not instantly available.

In the case of new product introduction there are many implications for management resulting from this reduction of the time 'window' in which profits may be made. Many commentators have focused upon the need to seek out novel forms of managing the new product development process; venture teams along the lines pioneered by DuPont and 3M being one such approach. Others have highlighted the need to improve the quality of the feedback from the marketplace and to link this more directly into the firm's R & D effort.

All of these initiatives are indeed necessary if the business is to stay alive. However, amidst all the concern with the process of creating and managing innovation, there is one issue which perhaps is only now being given the attention it demands. That issue is the problem of extended logistics lead times.

The concept of logistics lead time is simple: How long does it take to convert an order into cash? Whilst management has long recognized the competitive impact of shorter order cycles, this is only a part of the total process whereby working capital and resources are committed to an order.

From the moment when decisions are taken on the sourcing and procurement of materials and components through the manufacturing subassembly process to the final distribution and after-market support, there are a myriad of complex activities that must be managed if customers are to be gained and retained. This is the true scope of logistics lead-time management.

As we have noted, one of the basic functions of logistics is the provision of 'availability'. However, in practice, what is so often the case is that the integration of marketing and manufacturing planning that is necessary to achieve this competitive requirement is lacking. Further problems are caused by limited co-ordination of supply decisions with the changing requirements of the marketplace and the restricted visibility that purchasing and manufacturing have of final demand, because of extended supply and distribution 'pipelines'.

To overcome these problems and to establish enduring competitive advantage by ensuring timely response to volatile demand, a new and fundamentally different approach to the management of lead times is required.

Globalization of industry

The third of the strategic issues that provide a challenge for logistics management is the trend towards globalization.

A global company is more than a multinational company. In the global business materials and components are sourced worldwide, manufactured offshore and sold in many different countries perhaps with local customization.

Such is the trend towards globalization that it is probably safe to forecast that before long most markets will be dominated by global companies. The only role left for national companies will be to cater for specific and unique local demands, for example in the food industry.

For global companies like Hewlett Packard, Philips and Caterpillar, the management of the logistics process has become an issue of central concern. The difference between profit and loss on an individual product can hinge upon the extent to which the global pipeline can be optimized, because the costs involved are so great. The global company seeks to achieve competitive advantage by identifying world markets for its products and then developing a manufacturing and logistics strategy to support its marketing strategy. So a company like Caterpillar, for example, has dispersed assembly operations to key overseas markets and uses global logistics channels to supply parts to offshore assembly plants and after-markets. Where appropriate, Caterpillar will use third party companies to manage distribution and even final finishing. So for example in the United States a third party company, in addition to providing parts inspection and warehousing, actually attaches options to fork lift trucks. Wheels, counterweights, forks and masts are installed as specified by Caterpillar. Thus local market needs can be catered for from a standardized production process.

Even in a geographically compact area like Europe we find that there is still a significant need for local customization. A frequently cited example is the different preferences for washing machines. The French prefer top-loading machines, the British go for front-loaders, the Germans prefer high-speed spins, the Italians prefer a lower speed! In addition there are differences in electrical standards and differences in distribution channels. In the United Kingdom, most washing machines are sold through national chains specializing in white goods. In Italy, white goods are sold through a profusion of small retailers and customers bargain over price.

The challenge to a global company like Whirlpool therefore is how to achieve the cost advantage of standardization whilst still catering for the local demand for variety. Whirlpool is responding to that challenge by seeking to standardize on parts, components and modules and then, through flexible manufacturing and logistics, to provide the specific products demanded by each market.

Organizational integration

Whilst the theoretical logic of taking a systems view of the business might be apparent, the reality of practical implementation is something else. The classical business organization is based upon strict functional divisions and hierarchies. It is difficult to achieve a closely integrated, customer-focused materials flow whilst the traditional territorial boundaries are jealously guarded by entrenched management with its outmoded priorities.

In these conventional organizations, materials managers manage materials, whilst production managers manage production, and market-ing managers manage marketing. Yet these functions are components of a system that needs some overall plan or guidance to fit together. Managing the organization under the traditional model is just like trying to complete a complex jigsaw puzzle without having the picture on the box cover in front of you.

The challenges that face the business organization in today's environment are quite different from those of the past. To achieve a position of sustainable competitive advantage, tomorrow's organiza-tion will be faced with the need to dispense with outmoded labels like marketing manager, manufacturing manager or purchasing manager. Instead we will need broad-based integrators who are oriented towards the achievement of marketplace success based upon managing processes and people that deliver service. Generalists rather than narrow specialists will increasingly be required to integrate materials management with operations management and delivery. Knowledge of systems theory and behaviour will become a prerequisite for this new type manager. As important will be the orientation of these managers: they will be market-orientated with a sharp focus upon customer service as the primary source of competitive advantage.

The new rules of competition

We are now entering the era of 'supply chain competition'. The fundamental difference from the previous model of competition is that an organization can no longer act as an isolated and independent entity in competition with other similarly 'stand-alone' organizations. Instead, the need to create value delivery systems that are more responsive to fast-changing markets and that are much more consistent and reliable in the delivery of that value requires that the supply chain as a whole be focused on the achievement of these goals.

In the past the ground rules for marketing success were obvious: strong brands, backed up by large advertising budgets and aggressive selling. This formula now appears to have lost its power. Instead, the argument is heard, companies must recognize that increasingly it is through their *capabilities* and *competencies* that they compete.[6,7]

Essentially, this means that organizations create superior value for customers and consumers by managing their *core processes* better than competitors manage theirs. These core processes encompass such activities as new product development, supplier development, order fulfilment and customer management. By performing these fundamental activities in a more cost-effective way than competitors, it is argued, organizations will gain the advantage in the marketplace.

One capability that is now regarded by many companies as fundamental to success in the marketplace is the management of inbound and outbound logistics. As product life cycles shorten, as customers adopt just-in-time practices and as sellers' markets become buyers' markets then the ability of the organization to respond rapidly and flexibly to demand can provide a powerful competitive edge.

A major contributing factor influencing the changed competitive environment has been the trend towards 'commoditization' in many markets. A commodity market is characterized by perceived product equality in the eyes of customers resulting in a high preparedness to substitute one make of product for another. Research increasingly suggests that consumers are less loyal to specific brands but instead will have a portfolio of brands within a category from which they make their choice. In situations such as this, actual product availability becomes a major determinant of demand. There is evidence that more and more decisions are being taken at the point of purchase and if there is a gap on the shelf where Brand X should be but Brand Y is there instead, then there is a strong probability that Brand Y will win the sale.

It is not only in consumer markets that the importance of logistics process excellence is apparent. In business-to-business and industrial markets it seems that product or technical features are of less importance in winning orders than issues such as delivery lead times and flexibility. This is not to suggest that product or technical features are

In today's marketplace the order-winning criteria are more likely to be service-based then product-based.

unimportant – rather it is that they are taken as a 'given' by the customer. Quite simply, in today's marketplace the order-winning criteria are more likely to be service-based then product-based.

A parallel development in many markets is the trend towards a consolidation of demand. In other words customers – as against consumers – are tending to grow in size whilst becoming fewer in number. The retail grocery industry is a good example in that in most Northern European countries a handful of large retailers account for over 50 per cent of all sales in any one country. This tendency to the concentration of buying power is being accelerated as a result of global competition and the fact that in most industries there is a worldwide over-capacity. The impact of these trends is that these more powerful customers are becoming more demanding in terms of their service requirements from suppliers.

At the same time as the power in the distribution channel continues to shift from supplier to buyer, there is a trend for customers to reduce their supplier base. In other words they want to do business with fewer suppliers and often on a longer-term basis. The successful companies in the coming years will be those that recognize these trends and seek to establish strategies which are based upon establishing closer relationships with key accounts. Such strategies will focus upon seeking innovative ways to create more value for these customers. These strategies will be 'vertical' rather than 'horizontal' in that the organization will seek to do more for fewer customers rather than looking for more customers to whom to sell the same product. The car industry provides a good example of this phenomenon with 'lead' suppliers taking on much greater responsibility for the delivery of entire systems or modules to the assembly line.

Such a transition from volume-based growth to value-based growth will require a much greater focus on managing the core processes that we referred to earlier. Whereas the competitive model of the past relied heavily on *product* innovation this will have to be increasingly supplemented by *process* innovation. The basis for competing in this new era will be:

Competitive advantage = Product excellence × process excellence

Figure 1.10 suggests that for many companies the investment has mainly concentrated on product excellence and less on process excellence.

This is not to suggest that product innovation should be given less emphasis – far from it – but rather that more emphasis needs to be placed on developing and managing processes that deliver greater value for key customers.

We have already commented that product life cycles are getting shorter. What we have witnessed in many markets is the effect of changes in technology and consumer demand combining to produce more volatile markets where a product can be obsolete almost as soon

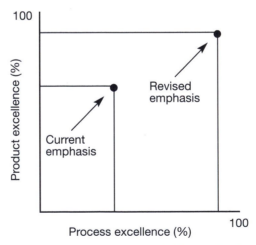

Fig. 1.10 Investing in process excellence yields greater benefits

as it reaches the market. There are many current examples of shortening life cycles but perhaps the personal computer symbolizes them all. In this particular case we have seen rapid developments in technology which have firstly created markets where none existed before and then almost as quickly have rendered themselves obsolete as the next generation of product is announced.

Such shortening of life cycles create substantial problems for logistics management. In particular, shorter life cycles demand shorter lead times – indeed our definition of lead time may well need to change. Lead times are traditionally defined as the elapsed period from receipt of customer order to delivery. However, in today's environment there is a wider perspective that needs to be taken. The real lead time is the time taken from the drawing board, through procurement, manufacture and assembly to the end market. This is the concept of strategic lead time and the management of this time span is the key to success in managing logistics operations.

There are already situations arising where the life cycle is shorter than the strategic lead time. In other words the life of a product on the market is less than the time it takes to design, procure, manufacture and distribute that same product! The implications of this are considerable both for planning and operations. In a global context the problem is exacerbated by the longer transportation times involved.

Ultimately, therefore, the means of achieving success in such markets is to accelerate movement through the supply chain and to make the entire logistics system far more flexible and thus responsive to these fast-changing markets.

Whilst there are many implications of these pressures for the way we manage logistics there are three key issues which will be recurring themes throughout the book: responsiveness, reliability and relationships.

1 Responsiveness

In today's just-in-time world the ability to respond to customers' requirements in ever-shorter time-frames has become critical. Not only do customers want shorter lead times, they are also looking for flexibility and, increasingly, solutions to their problems. In other words the supplier has to be able to meet the precise needs of customers in less time than ever before. The key word in this changed environment is *agility*. Agility implies the ability to move quickly and to meet customer demand sooner. In a fast-changing marketplace agility is actually more important than long-term strategy in a traditional business planning sense. Because future demand patterns are uncertain by definition this makes planning more difficult and, in a sense, hazardous.

In the future, organizations must be much more *demand-driven* than *forecast-driven*. The means of making this transition will be through the achievement of agility, not just within the company but across the supply chain.

2 Reliability

One of the main reasons why any company carries safety stock is because of uncertainty. It may be uncertainty about future demand or uncertainty about a supplier's ability to meet a delivery promise, or about the quality of materials or components. Significant improvements in reliability can only be achieved through reengineering the processes that impact performance. Manufacturing managers long ago realized that the best way to improve product quality is not by quality control through inspection but rather to focus on process control. The same is true for logistics reliability.

A key to improving reliability in logistics processes is enhanced *pipeline visibility*. It is often the case that there is limited visibility of downstream demand at the end of the pipeline. This problem is exacerbated the further removed from final demand the organization or supply chain entity is. Thus the manufacturer of synthetic fibres may have little awareness of current demand for the garments that incorporate those fibres in the material from which they are made.

If a means can be found of opening up the pipeline so that there is clear end-to-end visibility then reliability of response will inevitably improve.

3 Relationships

The trend towards customers seeking to reduce their supplier base has already been commented upon. In many industries the practice of 'single sourcing' is widespread. It is suggested that the benefits of such practices include improved quality, innovation sharing, reduced costs and integrated scheduling of production and deliveries. Underlying all of this is the idea that buyer/supplier relationships should be based upon partnership. More and more companies are discovering the advantages that can be gained by seeking mutually beneficial, long-term relationships with suppliers. From the suppliers' point of view, such partnerships can prove a formidable barrier to entry for competitors. The more processes are linked between the supplier and the customer the more the mutual dependencies and hence the more difficult it is for competitors to break in.

Supply chain management by definition is about the management of relationships across complex networks of companies that whilst legally independent are in reality interdependent. Successful supply chains will be those which are governed by a constant search for win-win solutions based upon mutuality and trust. This is not a model of relationships that has typically prevailed in the past. It is one that will have to prevail in the future as supply chain competition becomes the norm.

These three themes of responsiveness, reliability and relationships provide the basis for successful logistics and supply chain management. They are themes that will be explored in greater detail later in this book. As we enter the 21st century the need for a greater focus on the logistics processes that underpin supply chain effectiveness becomes ever more apparent.

Summary

This chapter familiarizes the reader with the tenets of competitive strategy and within them the vectors of strategic direction, productivity and value advantages. Managers are urged to look beyond the traditional touchstones of the experience curve and the link between relative costs and market share. They are encouraged to seek out and develop logistics strategies which exploit numerous latent opportunities to increase efficiency and productivity which deliver significant advances in customer service. They may include efforts to realize better capacity utilization, inventory reduction and/or service improvements through closer co-operation with suppliers. Behind every enduring example of differentiation through service excellence is an example of a well thought through strategy for managing the logistics of service delivery.

Vertically integrated businesses continue to be dismembered, refocused and transformed into virtual ones held together not by ownership and financial engineering, but by closely integrated core business processes. Where once vertical integration produced rivalry and mistrust within the supply chain, new competitive pressures are demanding speed and flexibility, which themselves require greater openness and trust. In fact the ability to manage process innovation and integration are becoming as important capabilities as product innovation.

References

1. Bowler, R.A., *Logistics and the Failure of the British Army in America 1775–1783*, Princeton University Press, 1975.
2. Shaw, A.W., *Some Problems in Market Distribution*, Harvard University Press, 1915.
3. Porter, M.E., *Competitive Strategy*, The Free Press, 1980.
4. Porter, M.E., *Competitive Advantage*, The Free Press, 1985.
5. Aitken, J., *Supply Chain Integration within the Context of a Supplier Association*, Cranfield University, Ph.D. Thesis, 1998.
6. Stalk, G., Evans, P. and Shulman, L.E., 'Competing on Capabilities: The New Rules of Corporate Strategy', *Harvard Business Review*, March–April 1992.
7. Prahalad, C. and Hamel, G., 'The Core Competence of the Corporation', *Harvard Business Review*, May–June 1990.

2

The customer service dimension

This chapter:

Highlights the importance of managing the marketing and logistics interface on an integrated basis.

●

Emphasizes the need to understand the multiple elements of service from the customers' perspective.

●

Explains the importance of customer retention and the lifetime value of a customer.

●

Outlines the idea of a service-driven logistics system based upon identified service priorities and a customer base segmented according to service requirements.

●

Introduces the idea of the 'perfect order' as the basis for measuring service performance.

Earlier in Chapter 1 the mission of logistics management was defined simply in terms of providing the means whereby customers' service requirements are met. In other words the ultimate purpose of any logistics system is to satisfy customers. It is a simple idea that is not always easy to recognize if you are a manager involved in activities such as production scheduling or inventory control which may seem to be some distance away from the marketplace. The fact is of course that everybody in the organization has a stake in customer service. Indeed many successful companies have started to examine their internal service standards in order that everyone who works in the business understands that they must service someone – if they don't, why are they on the payroll?

The objective should be to establish a chain of customers that links people at all levels in the organization directly or indirectly to the marketplace.[1] Xerox is a company that has worked hard to implement the idea of the internal customer. They have even extended the idea to the point of linking the pay of head office staff to an index of customer satisfaction. Managing the customer service chain through the business and onwards through distribution and intermediaries in organizations like Xerox is the central concern of logistics management.

The marketing and logistics interface

Even though the textbooks describe marketing as the management of the 'Four P's' – product, price, promotion and place – it is probably true to say that in practice, most of the emphasis has always been placed on the first three. 'Place', which might better be described in the words of the old cliché: 'the right product, in the right place at the right time', was rarely considered part of mainstream marketing.

There are signs that this view is rapidly changing, however, as the power of customer service as a potential means of differentiation is increasingly recognized. In more and more markets the power of the brand has declined and customers are willing to accept substitutes; even technology differences between products have been removed so that it is harder to maintain a competitive edge through the product itself. In situations like this it is customer service that can provide the distinctive difference between one company's offer and that of its competitors.

One of the best selling management books of recent years, *In Search of Excellence*,[2] has alerted managers and others to the simple truth that customers create sales and the most successful companies are those that win the most customers and keep them.

It may seem strange that such obvious axioms should provide the basis for a book that appeared on executives' desks around the world. Nevertheless it has taken a major recession to focus many organizations' attention upon the customer more sharply than was often the case in the past. The lessons of *In Search of Excellence* extended beyond a concern for customer relations, but it is perhaps in this field that the greatest scope for improvement lies in the 'non-excellent' company. Two factors have perhaps contributed more than anything else to the growing importance of customer service as a competitive weapon. One is the continual development of customer expectations; in almost every market the customer is now more demanding, more 'sophisticated' than he or she was, say, 30 years ago. Likewise, in industrial purchasing situations we find that buyers expect higher levels of service from vendors, particularly as more manufacturers convert to just-in-time manufacturing systems.

The second factor is the slow but inexorable transition towards 'commodity' type markets. By this is meant that increasingly the power of the 'brand' is diminishing as technologies of competing products converge, thus making product differences difficult to perceive – at least to the average buyer. Take, for example, the current state of the personal computer market. There are so many competing models which in reality are substitutable as far as most would-be purchasers are concerned. Unless one is particularly expert it is difficult to use product features as the basis for choice.

Faced with a situation such as this the customer may be influenced by price or by 'image' perceptions but overriding these aspects may well be 'availability' – in other words, is the product in stock, can I have it now? Since availability is clearly an aspect of customer service, we are in effect saying that the power of customer service is paramount in a situation such as this. Nor is it only in consumer markets that we are encountering the force of customer service as a determinant of purchase, there is much evidence from industrial markets of the same phenomenon.

On top of all this we have seen the growth of the 'service' sector in many Western economies. Over 75 per cent of the GNP of the United Kingdom is derived from the non-manufacturing sector, and every year the percentage increases. The marketing of services should not call for any different philosophy than that underlying the marketing of physical products. Rather it calls for possibly an even greater emphasis upon availability, particularly given the 'perishability' of the service product. Nevertheless, both service products and tangible products are increasingly dependent for their success upon the supplier's ability to enhance their appeal through the 'added value' of customer service.

What is customer service?

It was suggested in Chapter 1 that the role of customer service is to provide 'time and place utility' in the transfer of goods and services between buyer and seller. Put another way, there is no value in the product or service until it is in the hands of the customer or consumer. It follows that making the product or service 'available' is what, in essence, the distribution function of the business is all about. 'Availability' is in itself a complex concept, impacted upon by a galaxy of factors which together constitute customer service. These factors might include delivery frequency and reliability, stock levels and order cycle time, for example. Indeed it could be said that ultimately customer service is determined by the interaction of all those factors that affect the process of making products and services available to the buyer.

In practice, we see that many companies have varying views of customer service. LaLonde and Zinszer[3] in a major study of customer service practices suggested that customer service could be examined under three headings:

1. Pre-transaction elements
2. Transaction elements
3. Post-transaction elements

The pre-transaction elements of customer service relate to corporate policies or programmes, e.g. written statements of service policy, adequacy of organizational structure and system flexibility. The transaction elements are those customer service variables directly involved in performing the physical distribution function, e.g. product and delivery reliability. The post-transaction elements of customer service are generally supportive of the product while in use, for instance, product warranty, parts and repair service, procedures for customer complaints and product replacement.

Table 2.1 indicates some of the many elements of customer service under these three headings.

In any particular product/market situation, some of these elements will be more important than others and there may be factors other than those listed above which have a significance in a specific market. Indeed the argument that will be developed is that it is essential to understand customer service in terms of the differing requirements of different market segments and that no universally appropriate list of elements exists; each market that the company services will attach different importance to different service elements.

It is because of the multivariate nature of customer service and because of the widely differing requirements of specific markets that it is essential for any business to have a clearly identified policy towards customer service. It is surprising perhaps that so few companies have defined policies on customer service, let alone an organization flexible enough to manage and control that service, when it is considered that service can be the most important element in the company's marketing mix. A considerable body of evidence exists which supports the view that if the product or service is not available at the time the customer requires it and a close substitute is available then the sale will be lost to the competition. Even in markets where brand loyalty is strong a stock-out might be sufficient to trigger off brand switching.

> It is because of the multivariate nature of customer service and because of the widely differing requirements of specific markets that it is essential for any business to have a clearly identified policy towards customer service.

Table 2.1 The components of customer service

Pre-transaction elements

For example:

- *Written customer service policy*
  (Is it communicated internally and externally, is it understood, is it specific and quantified where possible?)
- *Accessibility*
  (Are we easy to contact/do business with? Is there a single point of contact?)
- *Organization structure*
  (Is there a customer service management structure in place? What level of control do they have over their service process?)
- *System flexibility*
  (Can we adapt our service delivery systems to meet particular customer needs?)

Transaction elements

For example:

- *Order cycle time*
  (What is the elapsed time from order to delivery? What is the reliability/variation?)
- *Inventory availability*
  (What percentage of demand for each item can be met from stock?)
- *Order fill rate*
  (What proportion of orders are completely filled within the stated lead time?)
- *Order status information*
  (How long does it take us to respond to a query with the required information? Do we inform the customer of problems or do they contact us?)

Post-transaction elements

For example:

- *Availability of spares*
  (What are the in-stock levels of service parts?)
- *Call-out time*
  (How long does it take for the engineer to arrive and what is the 'first call fix rate'?)
- *Product tracing/warranty*
  (Can we identify the location of individual products once purchased? Can we maintain/extend the warranty to customers' expected levels?)
- *Customer complaints, claims etc.*
  (How promptly do we deal with complaints and returns? Do we measure customer satisfaction with our response?)

A recent study[4] identified that a significant cost penalty is incurred by both manufacturers and retailers when a stock-out occurs on the shelf. The research, conducted in the United States, found that on a typical afternoon a shopper in the average supermarket will face stock-outs on 8.2 per cent of items in the categories studied. Those same shoppers failed to buy an alternative 34 per cent of the time. They postponed the purchase or took their business elsewhere. The net effect of this is that the retailer lost 46 per cent of the potential sales dollars that would have been spent on those out-of-stock items.

Figure 2.1 shows how the profit impact of an out-of-stock can become significant for the retailer. For the manufacturer the cost can be even greater as an out-of-stock may well encourage the shopper to choose an alternative and, as a result, to stay with that alternative.

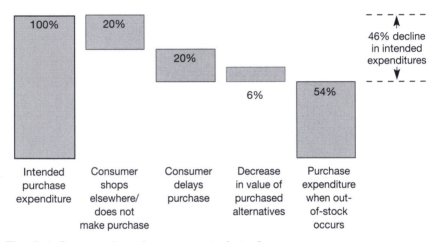

Fig. 2.1 Revenue loss due to an out-of-stock
Source: Andersen Consulting

In industrial markets, too, the same pressures on purchasing source loyalty seem to be at work. It is perhaps not surprising that as more and more companies adopt 'just-in-time' strategies, with minimal inventories, they require even higher levels of response from suppliers. The demand is for ever-shorter delivery lead times and reliable delivery. The pressure on suppliers is further increased as these same customers seek to rationalize their supplier base and to do business with fewer suppliers. Becoming a preferred supplier in any industry today inevitably means that a high priority must be placed on delivering superior customer service.

Many companies have suffered in this new competitive environment because in the past they have focused on the traditional aspects of marketing – product development, promotional activities and price competition, and, whilst these are still necessary dimensions of a marketing strategy, they are not sufficient. Equally damaging has been the focus on cost reduction that has driven many companies' operational and logistics strategy – particularly as a result of recession. Cost reduction is a worthy goal as long as it is not achieved at the expense of value creation. Low cost strategies may lead to *efficient* logistics but not to *effective* logistics. More often than not today the order-winning criteria are those elements of the offer that have a clearly identifiable positive impact upon the customers' own value-creating process.

One powerful way of highlighting the impact that customer service and logistics management can have on marketing effectiveness is outlined in Figure 2.2. The suggestion here is that customer service impacts not only on the ultimate end user but also on intermediate customers such as distributors. Traditionally marketing has focused on the end customer – or consumer – seeking to promote brand values and to generate a 'demand pull' on the marketplace for the company's products. More recently we have come to recognize that this by itself is not sufficient. Because of the swing in power in many marketing channels away from manufacturers and towards the distributor (e.g. the large concentrated retailers) it is now vital to develop the strongest possible relations with such intermediaries – in other words to create a customer franchise as well as a consumer franchise.

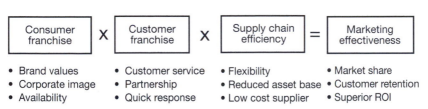

Fig. 2.2 The impact of logistics and customer service on marketing

The impact of both a strong consumer franchise and a customer franchise can be enhanced or diminished by the efficiency of the suppliers' logistics system. It is only when all three components are working optimally that marketing effectiveness is maximized. To stress the interdependence of these three components of competitive performance it is suggested that the relationship is multiplicative. In other words the combined impact depends upon the product of all three.

Customer service and customer retention

It will be apparent from what has been said that organizations which compete only on the product's features will find themselves at a severe disadvantage to those companies that augment the basic product with added-value services. It was one of the leading thinkers in marketing, Theodore Levitt, who first said that 'people don't buy products, they buy benefits'. The idea behind this statement is that it is the totality of the 'offer' which delivers customer value. A simple example would be that a finished product in a warehouse is the same as a finished product in the hands of the customer in terms of its tangible features. Clearly however the product in the hands of the customer has far more value than the product in the warehouse. Distribution service in this case has been the source of added value. Figure 2.3 develops this idea with the concept of the 'service surround'.

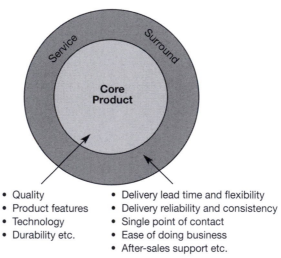

- Quality
- Product features
- Technology
- Durability etc.

- Delivery lead time and flexibility
- Delivery reliability and consistency
- Single point of contact
- Ease of doing business
- After-sales support etc.

Fig. 2.3 Using service to augment the core product

At the centre is the core product which is the basic product as it leaves the factory. The outer 'halo' represents all the added values that customer service and logistics provide. Clearly it is not only customer service and logistics activity that add value; in many cases advertising, branding and the packaging can all enhance the perceived value of the product to the customer. However it is increasingly evident, as we have seen, that it takes more than branding to differentiate the product.

What impact does the service surround have on the customer?

One of the classic definitions of marketing is that it is concerned with 'getting and keeping customers'. In practice if we look at where most organizations' marketing effort focuses, it is on the 'getting' of customers, rather than on the 'keeping' of them. Thus an examination of the typical marketing plan will show a bias towards increasing market share rather than towards customer retention. Whilst new customers are always welcome in any business it has to be realized that an existing customer provides a higher profit contribution and has the potential to grow in terms of the value and frequency of purchases.

The importance of customer retention is underlined by the concept of the 'lifetime value' of a customer. The lifetime value of a customer is calculated as follows:

Lifetime value = Average transaction value × yearly frequency of purchase × customer 'life expectancy'

One study of the car market in the United States found that a satisfied customer is likely to stay with the same supplier for a further 12 years after the first satisfactory purchase and, during that period, will buy four more cars of the same make. The study estimated that to a car manufacturer, this level of customer retention is worth $400m in new car sales annually.

A simple measure of customer retention is to ask the question: 'How many of the customers that we had 12 months ago do we still have today?'. This measure is the real test of customer retention. It can be extended to include the value of purchases made by the retained customer base to assess how successful the company has been in increasing the level of purchasing from these accounts (see Figure 2.4).

Furthermore there is evidence to suggest that retained customers are more profitable than new customers. In the first case a retained customer typically costs less to sell to and to service. Also as the relationship develops there is a greater likelihood that they will give a

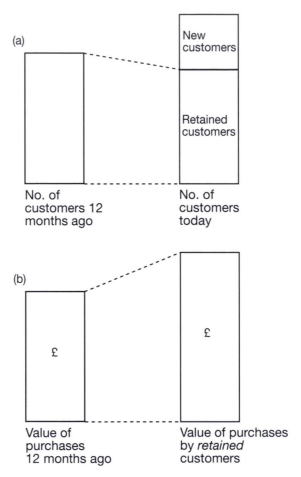

Fig. 2.4 Customer retention indicators

greater part of their business to a supplier whom they are prepared to treat as a partner. Furthermore, satisfied customers tell others and thus the chance increases that further business from new customers will be generated through this source.

A prime objective of any customer service strategy should be to enhance customer retention. Whilst customer service obviously also plays a role in winning new customers it is perhaps the most potent weapon in the marketing armoury for the keeping of customers.

There is rapidly emerging a new focus in marketing and logistics on the creation of 'relationships' with customers. The idea is that we should seek to create such a level of satisfaction with customers that they do not feel it necessary even to consider alternative offers or suppliers. Many markets are characterized by a high level of volatility or 'promiscuity' amongst the customer base. In these markets customers will buy one brand on one occasion and then are just as likely to buy another on the next occasion.

The principle behind *Relationship Marketing* is that the organization should consciously strive to develop marketing strategies to maintain and strengthen customer loyalty. So, for example, an airline might develop a frequent-flyer programme, or a credit card company might award points based upon the value of purchases made with the card that can then be redeemed for prizes. At the other extreme a company like IBM will consciously seek to develop long-term relationships with its customers through training programmes, client seminars, frequent customer communication and so on.

Service-driven logistics systems

The role of logistics can be seen as the development of systems and the supporting co-ordination processes to ensure that customer service goals are met. This is the idea of the service-driven logistics system – a system that is designed to meet defined service goals.

So often we find that organizations design and manage systems which have internally-focused objectives rather than external goals. For example many companies with a strong production-orientation have developed 'mega-plants' which can produce world volumes of product with great economies of scale – yet

> So often we find that organizations design and manage systems which have internally-focused objectives rather than external goals.

paradoxically this strategy could reduce flexibility and lengthen lead times because of greater distance from markets. A far more effective starting point for logistics system design is the marketplace; in other words we must fully understand the service needs of the various markets that we address and then seek to develop low cost logistics solutions.

Ideally all logistics strategies and systems should be devised in the following sequence:

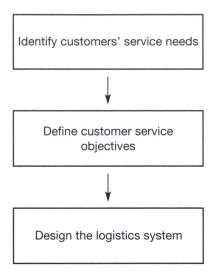

Hence it would be wrong to launch straight in, as so many companies do, and seek to reengineer an existing logistics system (or design a new one) purely to achieve internal requirements such as cost reduction. Instead the sequence has to be that a detailed understanding of customers' needs – and how these needs might differ by market segment – leads to a definition of customer service objectives. In turn, this statement of customer service objectives then becomes the focal point around which logistics systems must be designed.

It would be appropriate at this point to look briefly at the first two stages of this process: identifying customers' service needs and the development of customer service objectives.

Identifying customers' service needs

It is important to remember that no two customers will ever be exactly the same in terms of their service requirements. However it will often be the case that customers will fall into groups or 'segments' which are characterized by a broad similarity of service needs. These groupings might be thought of as 'service segments'. The logistics planner needs therefore to know just what the service issues are that differentiate customers. Market research can be of great assistance in understanding this service segmentation and it is often surprising to see how little formal research is conducted in this crucial area.

How might such a research programme be implemented?

The first point to emphasize is that customer service is perceptual. Whatever our own 'hard' internal measures of service might say our service performance is, perceptions are the reality. We might use measures which, whilst providing useful measures of productivity, do not actually reflect the things the customer values. For example whilst 'stock availability' is a widespread internal measure of performance, a more appropriate external measure from the customer's viewpoint could be 'on-time delivery'. Hence it is critical that we develop a set of service criteria that are meaningful to customers.

The approach to service segmentation suggested here follows a three-stage process:

1 Identify the key components of customer service as seen by customers themselves.
2 Establish the relative importance of those service components to customers.
3 Identify 'clusters' of customers according to similarity of service preferences.

1 Identifying the key components of customer service

A common failing in business is to assume that 'we know what our customers want'. However, the truth is that it is so easy to become divorced from the reality of the marketplace when management is consumed with the day-to-day pressures of running a business. How should we know which aspects of service are most highly rated by the customer? Given the complexity of the market that the typical company serves, how might it better understand the segmentation of those markets in terms of service requirements? What does it take for a company to become the supplier of choice?

Clearly it is important to develop an understanding of the service needs of customers through detailed research.

The first step in research of this type is to identify the key sources of influence upon the purchase decision. If, for example, we are selling components to a manufacturer, who will make the decision on the choice of supplier? This is not always an easy question to answer as in many cases there will be several people involved. The purchasing manager of the company to which we are selling may only be acting as an agent for others within the firm. In other cases his influence will be much greater. Alternatively if we are manufacturing products for sale through retail outlets, is the decision to stock made centrally by a retail chain or by individual store managers? The answers can often be supplied by the sales force. The sales representative should know from experience who are the decision makers.

Given that a clear indication of the source of decision-making power can be gained, the customer service researcher at least knows who to research. The question remains as to which elements of the vendor's total marketing offering have what effect upon the purchase decision.

Ideally once the decision-making unit in a specific market has been identified, an initial, small-scale research programme should be initiated based upon personal interviews with a representative sample of buyers. The purpose of these interviews is to elicit, in the language of the customers, firstly the importance they attach to customer service *vis-à-vis* the other marketing mix elements such as price, product quality, promotion etc, and secondly, the specific importance they attach to the individual components of customer service.

The importance of this initial step in measuring customer service is that relevant and meaningful measures of customer service are generated by the customers themselves. Once these dimensions are defined we can identify the relative importance of each one and the extent to which different types of customer are prepared to trade-off one aspect of service for another.

2 Establishing the relative importance of customer service components

One of the simplest ways of discovering the importance a customer attaches to each element of customer service is to take the components generated by means of the process described in step 1 and to ask a representative sample of customers to rank order them from the 'most important' to the 'least important'. In practice this is difficult, particularly with a large number of components and would not give any insight into the relative importance of each element. Alternatively a form of rating scale could be used. For example, the respondents could be asked to place a weight from 1 to 10 against each component according to how much importance they attached to each element. The problem here is that respondents will tend to rate most of the components as highly important, especially since those components were generated on the grounds of importance to customers anyway. A partial solution is to ask the respondent to allocate a total of 100 points amongst all the elements listed, according to perceived importance. However, this is a fairly daunting task for the respondent and can often result in an arbitrary allocation.

Fortunately a relatively recent innovation in consumer research technology now enables us to evaluate very simply the implicit importance that a customer attaches to the separate elements of customer service. The technique is based around the concept of trade-off and can best be illustrated by an example from everyday life. In considering, say, the purchase of a new car we might desire specific attributes, e.g. performance in terms of speed and acceleration, economy in terms of petrol consumption, size in terms of passenger and luggage capacity and, of course, low price. However, it is unlikely that any one car will meet all of these requirements so we are forced to trade-off one or more of these attributes against the others.

The same is true of the customer faced with alternative options of distribution service. The buyer might be prepared to sacrifice a day or two on lead time in order to gain delivery reliability, or to trade-off order completeness against improvements in order entry etc. Essentially the trade-off technique works by presenting the respondent with feasible combinations of customer service elements and asking for a rank order of preference for those combinations. Computer analysis then determines the implicit importance attached by the respondent to each service element.[5]

3 Identifying customer service segments

Now that we have determined the importance attached by different respondents to each of the service attributes previously identified, the final step is to see if any similarities of preference emerge. If one group of respondents for example has a clearly distinct set of priorities from another then it would be reasonable to think of them both as different service segments.

How can these customer service segments be identified? One technique that has been successfully used in this connection is cluster analysis. Cluster analysis is a computer-based method for looking across a set of data and seeking to 'match' respondents across as many dimensions as possible. Thus if two respondents completed the stage 2 trade-off analysis in a similar way their importance scores on the various service dimensions would be similar and hence the cluster analysis would assign them to the same group.

One study in an industrial market suggested that the traditional way of segmenting customers according to 'Standard Industrial Classification' (SIC) had little relevance to purchasing behaviour. The classic categorization of customers according to industry sector did not correlate with the attributes they sought from suppliers. Instead it seemed that some companies were very time-sensitive in terms of delivery reliability – a 'just-in-time' segment – regardless of the industry they were in. In the same way there was a very clear 'price' segment which also cut across conventional industrial classifications. A further segment was much more responsive to a 'relationship' approach, valuing technical support and close supplier liaison much more highly. As a result of this research the supplier was better able to focus its marketing efforts and to reengineer its supply chain strategy to achieve a better match with customer requirements.

Defining customer service objectives

The whole purpose of logistics strategy is to provide customers with the level and quality of service that they require and to do so at less cost to the total supply chain. In developing a market-driven logistics strategy the aim is to achieve 'service excellence' in a consistent and cost-effective way.

> The whole purpose of logistics strategy is to provide customers with the level and quality of service that they require and to do so at less cost to the total supply chain.

The definition of appropriate service objectives is made easier if we adopt the concept of the *perfect order*. The perfect order is achieved when the customer's service requirements are met in full. Clearly such a definition is specific to individual customers, but it is usually possible to group customers into segments and then to identify, along the lines described earlier, the key service needs of those segments. The perfect order is achieved only when each of those service needs are met to the customer's satisfaction.

The measure of service is therefore defined as the percentage of occasions on which the customer's requirements are met in full. Normally this percentage would be measured across all customers over a period of time. However, it can also be used to measure service performance at the individual customer level and indeed at any level, e.g. segment, country or by distribution centre.

One frequently encountered measure of the perfect order is 'on-time, in-full' (OTIF). An extension of this is on-time, in-full and error-free. This latter element relates to documentation, labelling and damage to the product or its packaging. To calculate the actual service level using the perfect order concept requires performance on each element to be monitored and then the percentage achievement on each element is multiplied together.

For example, if the actual performance across all orders for the last 12 months was as follows:

On-time   : 90%
In-full   : 80%
Error-free : 70%

the actual perfect order achievement would be:

$$90\% \times 80\% \times 70\% = 50.4\%$$

In other words the likelihood that a perfect order was achieved during the period under review was only 50.4 per cent!

The cost benefit of customer service

All companies have to face a basic fact: there will be significant differences in profitability between customers. Not only do different customers buy different quantities of different products, but the cost to service these customers will typically vary considerably. This issue will be explored more fully in Chapter 3.

The 80/20 rule will often be found to hold: that is 80 per cent of the profits of the business come from 20 per cent of the customers. Furthermore 80 per cent of the total costs to service will be generated from 20 per cent of the customers (but probably not the same 20 per cent!). Whilst the proportion may not be exactly 80/20 it will generally be in that region. (This is the so-called Pareto Law, named after a 19th century Italian economist.)

The challenge to customer service management therefore is firstly to identify the real profitability of customers and then secondly to develop strategies for service that will improve the profitability of all customers.

What has to be recognized is that there are costs as well as benefits in providing customer service and that therefore the appropriate level and mix of service will need to vary by customer type.

The basic relationship between the level of service and the cost is often depicted as a steeply rising curve (Figure 2.5).

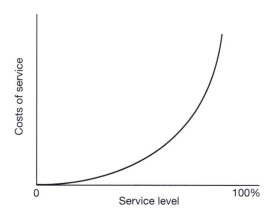

Fig. 2.5 The costs of service

This phenomenon is largely due to the high costs of additional inventory required to cover against unexpectedly high levels of demand.

However if it is possible to find alternative service strategies for servicing customers, say for example by speeding up the flow of information about customer requirements and by using faster modes of transport, then the same level of service can be achieved with less inventory – in effect pushing the curve to the right (Figure 2.6). This is the idea of substituting information and responsiveness for inventory.

At the same time as the costs of service are being considered it is also appropriate to seek to understand what the benefits of service are. If improved levels of service cost more to achieve than they produce by way of long-term sales revenue then clearly those costs are not justified. Similarly it must also be recognized that different segments in the total market may respond in quite different ways to higher or lower levels of service.

Identifying customer response to service level changes is not easy. It is rather like trying to quantify the effects of advertising. Because there are so many variables impinging upon customer behaviour, including

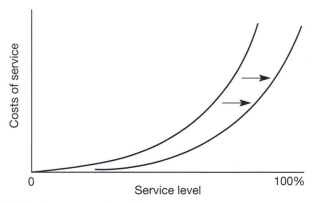

Fig. 2.6 Shifting the costs of service

competitors' marketing activities, it would take a fairly complex exper-
imental design to conduct rigorous empirical research into this issue.

As far as the absolute level of service is concerned then clearly there
must be a finite limit to the impact that service improvements can have
upon customers' purchasing behaviour. In other words, after some
point diminishing returns will set in (see Figure 2.7).

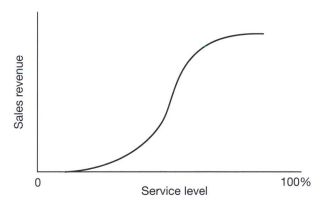

Fig. 2.7 The returns to service

It is suggested that the service response curve is S-shaped for several reasons. Firstly in most markets there will be a minimum level of service that
is deemed acceptable – this is the 'service threshold'. If we do not make it
to this point then returns to additional service expenditure will be minimal. For example in a competitive retail market, offering to double stock
availability from 5 per cent to 10 per cent would clearly be ineffectual!

55

Once the threshold is passed, increasing returns to service improvements should be achieved – if there is any degree of service sensitivity in the market. Inevitably, however, there will come a point where diminishing returns will set in – beyond this point we are in the region of service overkill where additional expenditure on service does not pay back.

Putting these two curves together, as in Figure 2.8, highlights the nature of the cost/benefit trade-off in service level decisions.

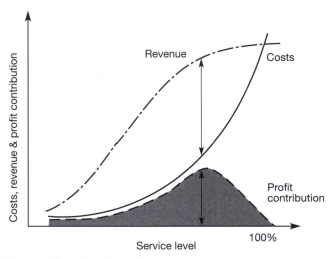

Fig. 2.8 The cost/benefit of service

One thing is clear from this model: no matter what the shape of the service response curve or where the point of diminishing returns sets in, if the cost curve can be 'pushed to the right' then profits at all levels of service will be improved.

Setting customer service priorities

Whilst it should be the objective of any logistics system to provide all customers with the level of service they require it must be recognized that because no budget is unlimited there will inevitably need to be service priorities. In this connection the Pareto, or 80/20 rule, can provide us with the basis for developing a more cost-effective service strategy. Fundamentally, the service issue is that since not all our customers are equally profitable nor are our products equally profitable, should not the highest service be given to key customers and key products? Since we can assume that money spent on service is a scarce resource then we should look upon the service decision as a resource allocation issue.

Figure 2.9 shows how a typical company might find its profits varying by customer and by product.

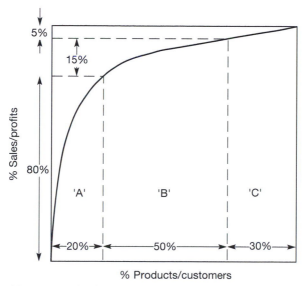

Fig. 2.9 The 'Pareto' or 80/20 rule

The curve is traditionally divided into three categories: the top 20 per cent of products and customers by profitability are the 'A' category; the next 50 per cent or so are labelled 'B' and the final 30 per cent are category 'C'. The precise split between the categories is arbitrary as the shape of the distribution will vary from business to business and from market to market.

The appropriate measure should be profit rather than sales revenue or volume. The reason for this is that revenue and volume measures might disguise considerable variation in costs. In the case of customers this cost is the 'cost to serve' and we will later suggest an approach to measuring customer profitability. In the case of product profitability we must also be careful that we are identifying the appropriate service-related costs as they differ by product. One of the problems here is that conventional accounting methods do not help in the identification of these costs. Typically accounting systems will focus upon factory costs and will use some method of full-cost allocation to deal with the problem of fixed costs.

What we should be concerned to do at this stage in the analysis is to identify the contribution to profit that each product (at the individual stock-keeping unit (SKU) level) makes. By contribution we mean the difference between total revenue accruing and the directly attributable costs that attach as the product moves through the logistics system.

Looking first at differences in product profitability, what use might be made of the A,B,C categorization? Firstly it can be used as the basis for classic inventory control whereby the highest level of service (as represented by safety stock) is provided for the 'A' products, a slightly lower level for the 'B' products and lower still for the 'C's'. Thus we might seek to follow the stock-holding policy shown below:

Product category	Stock availability
A	99%
B	97%
C	90%

Alternatively, and probably to be preferred, we might differentiate the stock holding by holding the 'A' items as close as possible to the customer and the 'B' and 'C' items further back up the supply chain. The savings in stock-holding costs achieved by consolidating the 'B' and 'C' items as a result of holding them at fewer locations would normally cover the additional cost of despatching them to the customer by a faster means of transportation (e.g. overnight delivery).

Perhaps the best way to manage product service levels is to take into account both the profit contribution and the individual product demand.

We can bring both these measures together in the form of a simple matrix in Figure 2.10. The matrix can be explained as follows:

Quadrant 1: Seek cost reductions

Because these products have high volume it would suggest that they are in frequent demand. However they are also low in profit contribution and the priority should be to re-examine product and logistics costs to see if there is any scope for enhancing profit.

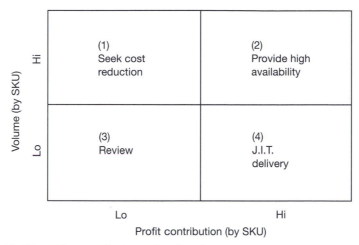

Fig. 2.10 Managing product service levels

Quadrant 2: Provide high availability

These products are frequently demanded and they are more profitable. We should offer the highest level of service on these items by holding them as close to the customer as possible and with high availability. Because there will be relatively few of these items we can afford to follow such a strategy.

Quadrant 3: Review

Products in this category should be regularly appraised with a view to deletion from the range. They do not contribute to profits (or at least only marginally) and they are slow movers from a sales point of view. Unless they play a strategic role in the product portfolio of the firm then there is probably a strong case for dropping them.

Quadrant 4: J.I.T. delivery

Because these products are highly profitable but only sell at a relatively slow rate they are candidates for J.I.T. delivery. In other words they should be kept in some central location, as far back up the supply chain as possible in order to reduce the total inventory investment, and then shipped by express transport direct to customers.

This concept of service prioritization by product can be extended to include customer priorities. Because the same 80/20 rule applies to customers as it does to products, it makes sense to focus resources on key accounts as well as key products.

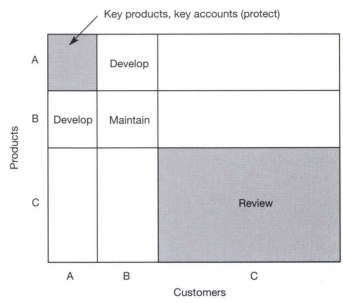

Fig. 2.11 Customer service and the 80/20 rule

Figure 2.11 shows that if the 80/20 rule applies both to products and customers then all businesses are actually very dependent upon a very few customers buying a few high profit lines. Indeed the arithmetic is easy:

20% of customers buying 20% of the products
= 4% of all customer/product transactions

Which provides:

80% of 80% of total profit = 64%

In other words just 4 per cent of transactions (measured order-line by order-line) gives us 64 per cent of all our profit!

How can we make use of this important fact? The first thing is obviously to offer the highest levels of service and availability to key customers ordering key products. At the other end of the spectrum we should constantly review the less profitable customers and the less profitable products. In between there is scope for a degree of pragmatism perhaps based upon the 'critical value' of an item to the customer. This is particularly relevant when developing a service strategy for spare parts. The idea is that if certain items are essential for, say, the operation of a machine where the down-time costs are high then those parts would be accorded a high critical value. If appropriate a 'weight' could be assigned on the basis of criticality and the 80/20 ranking based on profit could be adjusted accordingly. Table 2.2 provides an example:

Table 2.2 Critical value analysis

Products	Profitability rank order	Critical value to customers			Rank × critical	Order of priority for service
		1	2	3		
C	1			x	3	1
P	2		x		4	2 =
R	3		x		6	5
B	4	x			4	2 =
X	5	x			5	4
Y	6			x	18	8
Z	7		x		14	7
H	8	x			8	6
J	9			x	27	10
K	10		x		20	9

Critical values: 1 = Sale lost
2 = Slight delay acceptable
3 = Longer delay acceptable

Setting service standards

Obviously if service performance is to be controlled then it must be against pre-determined standards.

Ultimately the only standard to be achieved is 100 per cent conformity to customer expectations. This requires a clear and objective understanding of the customers' requirements and at the same time places an obligation upon the supplier to shape those expectations. In other words there must be a complete match between what the customer expects and what we are willing and able to provide. This may require negotiation of service standards since clearly it is in neither party's interest to provide service levels which would lead to a long-term deterioration in profitability – either for the supplier or the customer.

What are the customer service elements for which standards should be set?

Firstly there are the internal service standards. In many respects these mirror the standards that our external customers place upon us. As far as these external standards are concerned they must be defined by the customers themselves. This requires customer research and competitive benchmarking studies to be conducted so that an objective definition of customer service for each market segment may be identified.

However for the moment we can indicate some of the key areas where standards are essential:

- Order cycle time
- Stock availability
- Order-size constraints
- Ordering convenience
- Frequency of delivery
- Delivery reliability
- Documentation quality
- Claims procedure
- Order completeness
- Technical support
- Order status information

Let us examine each of these in turn:

Order cycle time

This is the elapsed time from customer order to delivery. Standards should be defined against customer's stated requirements.

Stock availability

This relates to the percentage of demand for a given line item (stock-keeping unit, or SKU) that can be met from available inventory.

Order-size constraints

More and more customers seek just-in-time deliveries of small quantities. Do we have the flexibility to cope with the range of customer demands likely to be placed upon us?

Ordering convenience

Are we accessible and easy to do business with? How are we seen from the customers' viewpoint? Do our systems talk to their systems?

Frequency of delivery

A further manifestation of the move to just-in-time is that customers require more frequent deliveries within closely specified time-windows. Again it is flexibility of response that should be the basis for the performance standard.

Delivery reliability

What proportion of total orders are delivered on time? It is a reflection not just of delivery performance but also of stock availability and order processing performance.

Documentation quality

What is the error rate on invoices, delivery notes and other customer communications? Is the documentation 'user friendly'? A surprisingly large number of service failures are from this source.

Claims procedure

What is the trend in claims? What are their causes? How quickly do we deal with complaints and claims? Do we have procedures for 'service recovery'?

Order completeness

What proportion of orders do we deliver complete, i.e. no back-orders or part shipments?

Technical support

What support do we provide customers with after the sale? If appropriate do we have standards for call-out time and first-time fix rate on repairs?

Order status information

Can we inform customers at any time on the status of their order? Do we have 'hot lines' or their equivalent? Do we have procedures for informing customers of potential problems on stock availability or delivery?

All of these issues are capable of quantification and measurement against customer requirements. Similarly they are all capable of comparison against competitive performance.

It must be recognized that from the customer's perspective there are only two levels of service – either 100 per cent or 0 per cent. In other words either the customer gets exactly what he/she ordered at the time and place required or they don't. It must also be remembered that 100 per cent order fill rates are extremely difficult to achieve – the laws of probability see to that! If there are ten items on a particular order and each item is carried in stock at the 95 per cent level of availability then the probability that the complete order can be filled is $(0.95)^{10}$ which is 0.599. In other words, just over a 50/50 chance that we can satisfy the complete order.

Table 2.3 shows how the probability of order fill diminishes as the number of items on the customer order increases:

Table 2.3 Probability of a complete order

Number of lines in order	Line item availability			
	90%	92%	94%	95%
1	.900	.920	.940	.950
2	.810	.846	.884	.903
3	.729	.779	.831	.857
4	.656	.716	.781	.815
5	.590	.659	.734	.774
6	.531	.606	.690	.735
7	.478	.558	.648	.698
8	.430	.513	.610	.663
9	.387	.472	.573	.630
10	.348	.434	.538	.599
11	.314	.399	.506	.569
12	.282	.368	.476	.540
13	.254	.338	.447	.513
14	.225	.311	.400	.488
15	.206	.286	.395	.463
16	.195	.263	.372	.440
17	.167	.243	.349	.418
18	.150	.223	.328	.397
19	.135	.205	.309	.377
20	.122	.185	.290	.358

Ideally organizations should establish standards and monitor performance across a range of customer service measures. For example, using the pre-transaction, transaction and post-transaction framework, the following measures provide valuable indicators of performance.

Pre-transaction
- Stock availability
- Target delivery dates
- Response times to queries

Transaction
- Order fill rate
- On-time delivery
- Back-orders by age
- Shipment delays
- Product substitutions

Post-transaction
- First call fix rate
- Customer complaints
- Returns/claims
- Invoice errors
- Service parts availability

It is possible to produce a composite index based upon multiple service measures and this can be a useful management tool particularly for communicating service performance internally. Such an index is shown in Table 2.4 where the weight attached to each service element reflects the importance that the customers attach to those elements.

Table 2.4 Composite service index

Service element	Importance weight (i)	Performance level (ii)	Weighted score (i) × (ii)
Order fill rate	30%	70%	.21
On-time delivery	25%	60%	.15
Order accuracy	25%	80%	.20
Invoice accuracy	10%	90%	.09
Returns	10%	95%	.095
		Index =	0.745

Customer service is one of the most powerful elements available to the organization in its search for competitive advantage and yet it is often the least well managed. The key message of this chapter has been that the quality of customer service performance depends in the main upon the skill with which the logistics system is designed and managed. Put very simply, the output of all logistics activity is customer service.

British Steel: creating customer value through logistics and supply chain management

There was a time, not so long ago, when the suggestion that British Steel might be held up as a shining example of industrial efficiency and innovation would have met with a level of disbelief. But having survived the traumas of privatization and worldwide recession, British Steel has reemerged in the 1990s as a powerful force in the global steel business. The company is the largest steel manufacturer in the Western hemisphere, and among the most efficient.[1] Until an overvalued Sterling began to take its toll in 1997, it was also one of the most profitable, exporting around half of its 16m tonnes annual production, mostly to other parts of Europe.[2]

In the late 1990s (exchange rates aside), British Steel's greatest competitive challenge comes from two distinct quarters. Firstly, from the new breed of US-style 'mini-mill' operators, whose small, flexible and highly efficient plants are threatening to make large-scale integrated works obsolete. And secondly, from encroachment by alternative materials manufacturers - most noticeably the growing use of aluminium in the automotive sector - to which steel manufacturers are responding with the development of lighter, more sophisticated, higher performance steels.

The automotive industry is a vitally important market for British Steel, consuming approximately 20 per cent of its total output.[3] Most of the major European vehicle manufacturers are supplied by British Steel through one of its largest operating businesses, British Steel Strip Products (BSSP). BSSP supplies materials to third-party pressworkers, via steel service centres, which process the steel to meet their customers' requirements. There are however, structural changes underway throughout the automotive supply chain. The motor manufacturers themselves continue to reduce the number of direct first tier presswork suppliers, while increasing the proportion of work outsourced to those remaining. As a result, these first tier suppliers are increasingly likely to find themselves responsible for the development of entire systems, engaging them in all aspects of product design, material specification and selection. They in turn are outsourcing much of the work to second tier suppliers, or upstream to stockholders or service centres. Meanwhile, reduced lead times mean that the first tier suppliers must also find ways to integrate themselves (and their suppliers) into the vehicle manufacturers' ever more sophisticated, syncronized, logistics systems.

To secure British Steel's position within this shifting marketplace, BSSP is investing heavily in supply chain partnership development activities with selected indirect pressworkers, creating a range of value-adding products and services, each designed to support them in fulfilling the demands of the vehicle manufacturers. The activities include: specialist seminars aimed to ease cross-functional and interorganizational working; fostering co-operation across the whole supply chain through process or supply chain mapping and logistics integration; and encouraging the use of a simultaneous engineering approach to new product design and development. On the services side, BSSP offers its customers access to specialist expertise and technologies which could not be developed cost-effectively in-house. These include a team of consultants providing advice on strategic and operational issues, and access to Finite Element Analysis (FEA) technology. FEA is an emerging technology which reduces development costs and lead times by assessing the in-press performance of steels and their coatings, optimizing material specifications and blank shapes ahead of tool completion, thus reducing press try-out time and initial production problems.

Working alongside BSSP, is British Steel's distribution and services arm, BSD. In 1996, BSD opened the first steel service and processing centre to be designed, built, and located specifically to meet the needs of its automotive industry customers. BSD was already operating two other steel service centres in the UK, but the £13.5m facility at Wednesfield, near Wolverhampton, was the first to be dedicated to a single industry sector.[4] Its facilities are designed to enable BDS to work more closely than ever before with its presswork customers and their subcontractors, through each stage of product development, from design through to full manufacture.

The moves towards industry-dedicated processing and the development of value-adding customer support services are demonstrations of British Steel's long-term commitment to the motor industry. They form the core of a unique three-year programme designed to strengthen

▶

▶ British Steel's own position within the industry by improving the competitiveness of its service centre and presswork customers, and through them its whole motor industry supply chain. Importantly, the programme brings together the first fully co-ordinated network of these three key tiers of automotive suppliers.[5]

References

1. Lorenz, Andrew (1997) 'The Squeeze is On', *Management Today*, August 1997, pp. 34–37.
2. *Yorkshire Post* (1997), 'Forging a New Identity', 22 April, *Yorkshire Post/FT McCarthy* (Q1:110).
3. Butterworth, Chris (1996) 'Supplier-driven Partnerships', *European Journal of Purchasing & Supply Management*, Vol 2, No 4, pp. 169–72.
4. Barry, Anthony (1996), 'Steeling the Show', *Supply Management*, April, pp. 32–3.
5. *Engineer* (1997), British Steel Acts on Supply Chain, 1 May, p. 4.

Summary

Customer service is a multi-faceted concept. It is increasingly important as a means of gaining and maintaining differentiation in the marketplace. Equally, since no two customers are alike it must be recognized that service must be tailored to meet the needs of different customers.

Logistics management can play a key role in enhancing *customer lifetime value* through increasing customer satisfaction and thus customer retention. To achieve this will require the development of a market-driven logistics strategy and the redefinition of service objectives based upon customers' specific requirements. 'Perfect order' achievement should form the basis for the measurement of service performance and the creation of service standards.

References

1. Schonberger, R.J., *Building a Chain of Customers*, The Free Press, 1990.
2. Peters, T.J. and Waterman, R.H., *In Search of Excellence*, Harper and Row, 1982.
3. LaLonde, B.J. and Zinszer, P.H., *Customer Service: Meaning and Measurement*, National Council of Physical Distribution Management, Chicago, 1976.
4. Coca-Cola Retailing Research Council and Andersen Consulting, *The Retail Problem of Out-of-Stock Merchandise*, 1996.
5. Christopher, M., *The Customer Service Planner*, Butterworth Heinemann, 1992.

Measuring logistics costs and performance

This chapter:

Explains the rationale behind Total Cost Analysis, a systematic logistics-oriented cost accounting system and the principal requirements for an effective logistics costing system.

●

Outlines the many ways in which logistics management can impact on overall return on investment and ultimately, shareholder value.

●

Emphasizes the importance of customer profitability analysis based upon an understanding of the 'cost-to-serve'.

●

Introduces the concept of Direct Product Profitability and underlines the need to understand the customers' logistics costs.

●

Highlights the need to identify the cost drivers in the logistics pipeline and to replace traditional forms of cost allocation with more appropriate methods.

After a century or more of reliance upon traditional cost accounting procedures to provide an often unreliable insight into profitability, managers are now starting to question the relevance of these methods.[1] The accounting frameworks still used by the majority of companies today rely upon arbitrary methods for the allocation of shared and indirect costs and hence frequently distort the true profitability of both products and customers. Indeed, as we shall see, these traditional accounting methods are often quite unsuited for analyzing the profitability of customers and markets since they were originally devised to measure product costs.

Because logistics management is a flow-oriented concept with the objective of integrating resources across a pipeline which extends from suppliers to final customers, it is desirable to have a means whereby costs and performance of that pipeline flow can be assessed.

> **Because logistics management is a flow-oriented concept with the objective of integrating resources across a pipeline which extends from suppliers to final customers, it is desirable to have a means whereby costs and performance of that pipeline flow can be assessed.**

Probably one of the main reasons that the adoption of an integrated approach to logistics and distribution management has proved so difficult for many companies is the lack of appropriate cost information. The need to manage the total distribution activity as a complete system, having regard for the effects of decisions taken in one cost area upon other cost areas has implications for the cost accounting systems of the organization. Typically, conventional accounting systems group costs into broad, aggregated categories which do not then allow the more detailed analysis necessary to identify the true costs of servicing customers with particular product mixes. Without this facility to analyze aggregated cost data, it becomes impossible to reveal the potential for cost trade-offs that may exist within the logistics system.

Generally the effects of trade-offs are assessed in two ways: from the point of view of their impact on total costs and their impact on sales revenue. For example, it may be possible to trade-off costs in such a way that total costs increase, yet because of the better service now being offered, sales revenue also increases. If the difference between revenue and costs is greater than before, the trade-off may be regarded as leading to an improvement in cost effectiveness. However, without an adequate logistics-oriented cost accounting system it is extremely difficult to identify the extent to which a particular trade-off is cost-beneficial.

The concept of total cost analysis

Many problems at the operational level in logistics management arise because all the impacts of specific decisions, both direct and indirect, are not taken into account throughout the corporate system. Too often decisions taken in one area can lead to unforeseen results in other areas. Changes in policy on minimum order value, for example, may influence customer ordering patterns and lead to additional costs. Similarly changes in production schedules that aim to improve production efficiency may lead to fluctuations in finished stock availability and thus affect customer service.

The problems associated with identifying the total system impact of distribution policies are immense. By its very nature logistics cuts across traditional company organization functions with cost impacts on most of those functions. Conventional accounting systems do not usually assist in the identification of these company-wide impacts, frequently absorbing logistics-related costs in other cost elements. The cost of processing orders for example is an amalgam of specific costs incurred in different functional areas of the business which generally prove extremely difficult to bring together. Figure 3.1 outlines the various cost elements involved in the complete order processing cycle, each of these elements having a fixed and variable cost component which will lead to a different total cost per order.

Accounting practice for budgeting and standard-setting has tended to result in a compartmentalization of company accounts; thus budgets tend to be set on a functional basis. The trouble is that policy costs do not usually confine themselves within the same watertight boundaries. It is the nature of logistics that, like a stone thrown into a pond, the effects of specific policies spread beyond their immediate area of impact.

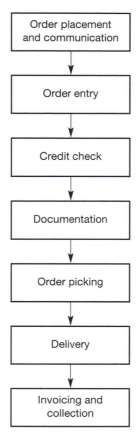

Fig. 3.1 Stages in the order-to-collection cycle

A further feature of logistics decisions which contributes to the complexity of generating appropriate cost information is that they are usually taken against the benchmark of an existing system. The purpose of total cost analysis in this context is to identify the change in costs brought about by these decisions. Cost must therefore be viewed in incremental terms – the change in total costs caused by the change to the system. Thus the addition of an extra warehouse to the distribution network will bring about cost changes in transport, inventory investment and communications. It is the incremental cost difference between the two options which is the relevant accounting information for decision making in this case. Figure 3.2 shows how total logistics costs can be influenced by the addition, or removal, of a depot from the system.

73

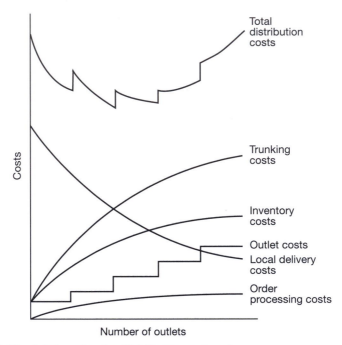

Fig. 3.2 The total costs of a distribution network

Principles of logistics costing

It will be apparent from the previous comments that the problem of developing an appropriate logistics-oriented costing system is primarily one of focus. What is required is the ability to focus upon the output of the distribution system, in essence the provision of customer service, and to identify the unique costs associated with that output. Traditional accounting methods lack this focus, mainly because they were designed with something else in mind.

One of the basic principles of logistics costing, it has been argued, is that the system should mirror the materials flow, i.e. it should be capable of identifying the costs that result from providing customer service in the marketplace. A second principle is that it should be capable of enabling separate cost and revenue analyses to be made by customer type and by market segment or distribution channel. This latter requirement emerges because of the dangers inherent in dealing solely with averages, e.g. the average cost per delivery, since they can often conceal substantial variations either side of the mean.

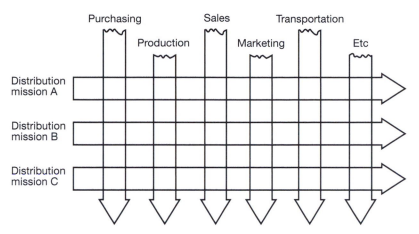

Fig. 3.3 Logistics missions that cut across functional boundaries

To operationalize these principles requires an 'output' orientation to cost-ing. In other words we must first define the desired outputs of the logistics system and then seek to identify the costs associated with providing those outputs. A useful concept here is the idea of 'mission'. In the context of logistics, a mission is a set of customer service goals to be achieved by the system within a specific product/market context. Missions can be defined in terms of the type of market served, by which products and within what constraints of service and cost. A mission by its very nature cuts across traditional company lines. Figure 3.3 illustrates the concept and demon-strates the difference between an 'output' orientation based upon missions and the 'input' orientation based upon functions.

The successful achievement of defined mission goals involves inputs from a large number of functional areas and activity centres within the firm. Thus an effective logistics costing system must seek to determine the total systems cost of meeting desired logistic objectives (the 'output' of the system) and the costs of the various inputs involved in meeting these outputs. Interest has been growing in an approach to this prob-lem, known as 'mission costing'.[2]

Figure 3.4 illustrates how three distribution missions may make a differential impact upon activity centre/functional area costs and, in so doing, provide a logical basis for costing within the company. As a cost or budgeting method, mission costing is the reverse of traditional tech-niques: under this scheme a functional budget is determined now by the demands of the missions it serves. Thus in Figure 3.4 the cost per mis-

	Functional area/ Activity centre 1	Functional area/ Activity centre 2	Functional area/ Activity centre 3	Functional area/ Activity centre 4	Total mission cost
Mission A	100	90	20	80	290
Mission B	50	70	200	20	340
Mission C	70	30	50	70	220
Activity centre inputs	220	190	270	170	850

Fig. 3.4 The programme budget (£'000)

sion is identified horizontally and from this the functional budgets may be determined by summing vertically.

Given that the logic of mission costing is sound, how might it be made to work in practice? The pioneering work of Barrett[3] developed a framework for the application of mission costing. This approach requires firstly that the activity centres associated with a particular distribution mission be identified, e.g. transport, warehousing, inventory, etc, and secondly that the incremental costs for each activity centre incurred as a result of undertaking that mission must be isolated. Incremental costs are used because it is important not to take into account 'sunk' costs or costs which would still be incurred even if the mission were abandoned. We can make use of the idea of 'attributable costs'[4] to operationalize the concept:

Attributable cost is a cost per unit that could be avoided if a product or function were discontinued entirely without changing the supporting organization structure.

In determining the costs of an activity centre, e.g. transport, attributable to a specific mission, the question should be asked: 'What costs would we avoid if this customer/segment/channel were no longer serviced?' These avoidable costs are the true incremental costs of servicing the customer/segment/channel. Often they will be substantially lower than the average cost because so many distribution costs are fixed and/or shared. For example, a vehicle leaves a depot in London to make deliveries in Nottingham and Leeds. If those customers in Nottingham were abandoned, but those in Leeds retained, what would be the difference in the total cost of transport? The answer would be – not very much. However, if the customers in Leeds were dropped, but not those in Nottingham, there would be a greater saving of costs because of the reduction in miles travelled.

This approach becomes particularly powerful when combined with a customer revenue analysis, because even customers with low sales off-take may still be profitable in incremental costs terms if not on an average cost basis. In other words the company would be worse off if those customers were abandoned.

Such insights as this can be gained by extending the mission costing concept to produce profitability analyses for customers, market segments or distribution channels. The term 'customer profitability accounting' describes any attempt to relate the revenue produced by a customer, market segment or distribution channel to the costs of servicing that customer/segment/channel. The principles of customer profitability accounting will be explored in detail later in this chapter.

Logistics and the bottom line

The turbulent business environment of the late 20th century has produced an ever greater awareness amongst managers of the financial dimension of decision making. 'The bottom line' has become the driving force which, perhaps erroneously, determines the direction of the company. In some cases this has led to a limiting, and potentially dangerous, focus on the short term. Hence we find that investment in brands, in R & D and in capacity may well be curtailed if there is no prospect of an immediate pay-back.

Just as powerful an influence on decision making and management horizons is cash flow. Strong positive cash flow has become as much a desired goal of management as profit.

The third financial dimension to decision making is resource utilization and specifically the use of fixed and working capital. The pressure in most organizations is to improve the productivity of capital – 'to make the assets sweat'. In this regard it is usual to utilize the concept of Return on Investment (ROI). Return on investment is the ratio between the net profit and the capital that was employed to produce that profit, thus:

$$ROI = \frac{Profit}{Capital\ employed}$$

This ratio can be further expanded:

$$ROI = \frac{Profit}{Sales} \times \frac{Sales}{Capital\ employed}$$

It will be seen that ROI is the product of two ratios: the first profit/sales, being commonly referred to as the margin and the second, sales/capital employed, termed capital turnover. Thus to gain improvement on ROI one or other, or both, of these ratios must increase. Typically many companies will focus their main attention on the margin in their attempt to drive up ROI, yet it can often be more effective to use the leverage of improved capital turnover to boost ROI. Many successful retailers have long since recognized that very small net margins can lead to excellent ROI if the productivity of capital is high, e.g. limited inventory, high sales per square foot, premises that are leased rather than owned and so on.

Figure 3.5 illustrates the opportunities that exist for boosting ROI through either achieving better margins or higher assets turns or both. Each 'iso-curve' reflects the different ways the same ROI can be achieved through specific margin/asset turn combinations. The challenge to logistics management is to find ways of moving the iso-curve to the right.

The ways in which logistics management can impact on ROI are many and varied. Figure 3.6 highlights the major elements determining ROI and the potential for improvement through more effective logistics management. Let us look at each of these 'boxes' in turn:

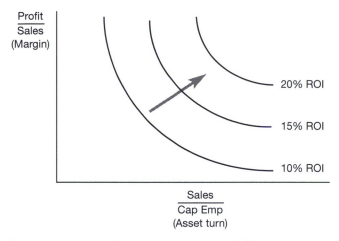

Fig. 3.5 The impact of margin and asset turn on ROI

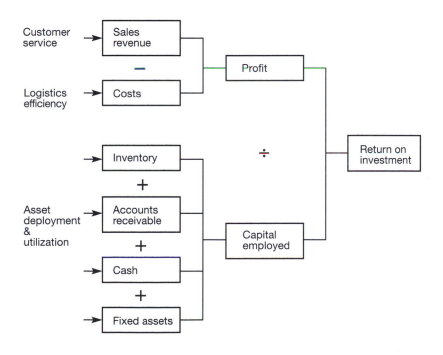

Fig. 3.6 Logistics impact on ROI

Sales revenue

Whilst the direct relationship between service and sales may not be capable of measurement, there is plentiful evidence that superior customer service leads to improved sales. Other things being equal, as we argued in Chapter 2, service can be a powerful source of differentiation in the marketplace.

Costs

Across European and North American industry it has been estimated that distribution costs as a percentage of sales revenue typically are between 5 per cent and 10 per cent.

Whilst over recent years these costs have fallen as a percentage of sales through better control of logistics, they still represent a considerable burden to any company. It must also be recognized that when expressed as a percentage of added value, logistics costs are actually rising for most firms. This is because added value is falling as these companies out-source more and more of their input requirements (e.g. components, packaging, services, etc). There is considerable scope in many companies for the better management of logistics costs and hence for profit leverage. Figure 3.7 highlights the possibility for gearing up profitability when profit margins are low, relative to distribution costs.

In the case shown in Figure 3.7 a 10 per cent reduction in logistics costs becomes, other things being equal, a 20 per cent improvement in profit.

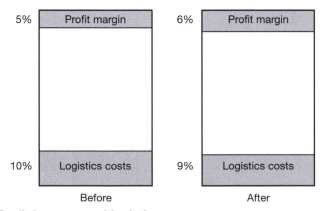

Fig. 3.7 Profit leverage and logistics

A hidden cost of logistics is the interest charged on inventory holding. Because this is rarely separately identified by most management accounting systems, many managers are unaware of what inventory is costing them. Of course it is not just the interest charge or cost of capital that has to be placed against inventory holding. We must also take into account other costs such as obsolescence and deterioration, insurance, stock losses, inventory control costs and so on. It is estimated that in total it costs a minimum of 25 per cent per annum of the book value of inventory just to hold it.

> **Many managers are unaware of what inventory is costing them.**

Asset deployment and utilization

In many countries real interest rates are very high - in other words the nominal interest rate less the rate of inflation. Thus if interest rates are 12 per cent but inflation is 18 per cent then the real interest rate is –6 per cent. If however inflation is only 4 per cent but interest rates are still 12 per cent then the real interest rate is now +8 per cent.

This high real interest rate environment has had a traumatic effect on business and has prompted a search for dramatic improvements in asset productivity. Once again better logistics management has the power to transform performance in this crucial area. Figure 3.8

Balance sheet	Logistics variable
Assets	
Cash	Order cycle time
	Order completion rate
Receivables	Invoice accuracy
Inventories	Inventory policies and service levels
Property, plant and equipment	Distribution facilities
	Transportation equipment
Liabilities	
Current liabilities	Purchasing policies
Dept	Financing options for inventory, plant and equipment
Equity	

Fig. 3.8 Logistics management and balance sheet

summarizes the major elements of the balance sheet and links to each the relevant logistics management component.

By examining each element of the balance sheet in turn it will be seen how logistics variables can influence its final shape.

Cash and receivables

This component of current assets is crucial to the liquidity of the business. In recent years its importance has been recognized as more companies become squeezed for cash. It is not always recognized however that logistics variables have a direct impact on this part of the balance sheet. For example the shorter the order cycle time, from when the customer places the order to when the goods are delivered, the sooner the invoice can be issued. Likewise the order completion rate can affect the cash flow if the invoice is not issued until after the goods are despatched. One of the less obvious logistics variables affecting cash and receivables is invoice accuracy. If the customer finds that his invoice is inaccurate he is unlikely to pay and the payment lead time will be extended until the problem is rectified.

Inventories

Fifty per cent or more of a company's current assets will often be tied up in inventory. Logistics is concerned with all inventory within the business from raw materials, subassembly or bought-in components, through work-in-progress to finished goods. The company's policies on inventory levels and stock locations will clearly influence the size of total inventory. Also influential will be the extent to which inventory levels are monitored and managed, and beyond that the extent to which systems are in operation which minimize the requirements for inventory.

Property, plant and equipment

The logistics system of any business will usually be a heavy user of fixed assets. The plant, depots and warehouses which form the logistics network if valued realistically on a replacement basis will represent a substantial part of total capacity employed (assuming that they are owned rather than rented or leased). Materials handling equipment, vehicles and other equipment involved in storage and transport can also add considerably to the total sum of fixed assets. Many companies fail to recognize the true significance of logistics fixed assets because they are valued for balance sheet purposes at historical cost.

Warehouses, for example, with their associated storage and handling equipment represent a sizeable investment and the question should be asked: 'Is this the most effective way to deploy our assets?'

Current liabilities

The current liabilities of the business are debts which must be paid in cash within a specified period of time. From the logistics point of view the key elements are accounts payable for bought-in materials, components etc. This is an area where a greater integration of purchasing with operations management can yield dividends. The traditional concepts of economic order quantities can often lead to excessive levels of raw materials inventory as those quantities may not reflect actual manufacturing or distribution requirements. The phasing of supplies to match the total logistics requirements of the system can be achieved through the twin techniques of materials requirement planning (MRP) and distribution requirement planning (DRP). If premature commitment of materials can be minimized this should lead to an improved position on current liabilities.

Debt/equity

Whilst the balance between debt and equity has many ramifications for the financial management of the total business it is worth reflecting on the impact of alternative logistics strategies. More companies are leasing plant facilities and equipment and thus converting a fixed asset into a continuing expense. The growing use of 'third-party' suppliers for ware-housing and transport instead of owning and managing these facilities in-house is a parallel development. These changes obviously affect the funding requirements of the business. They may also affect the means whereby that funding is achieved, i.e. through debt rather than equity. The ratio of debt to equity, usually referred to as 'gearing' or 'leverage', will influence the return on equity and will also have implications for cash flow in terms of interest payments and debt repayment.

Logistics and shareholder value

One of the key measures of corporate performance today is share-holder value. In other words what is the company worth? Increasingly senior management within the business are being driven by the goal of enhancing shareholder value. There are a number of complex issues involved in actually calculating shareholder value but at its simplest it is determined by the net present value of future cash flows. These cash flows may themselves be defined as:

Net operating income

less

Taxes

less

Working capital investment

less

Fixed capital investment

=

After tax free cash flow

More recently there has been a further development in that the concept of Economic Value Added (EVA) has become widely used and linked to the creation of shareholder value. The term EVA originated with the consulting firm Stern Stewart[5] although its origins go back to the economist Alfred Marshall who, over 100 years ago, developed the concept of 'economic income'.

Essentially EVA is the difference between operating income after taxes less the true cost of capital employed to generate those profits. Thus:

Economic Value Added (EVA) =
Profit after tax – True cost of capital employed

It will be seen that it is possible for a company to generate a negative EVA. In other words the cost of capital employed is greater than profit after tax. The impact of negative EVA, particularly if sustained over a period of time, is to erode shareholder value. Equally, improvements in EVA will lead to an enhancement of shareholder value. If the net present value of expected future EVAs were to be calculated this would generate a measure of wealth known as Market Value Added (MVA) which is a true measure of what the business is worth to its shareholders. A simple definition of MVA is:

Stock price × issued shares

less

Book value of total capital employed

=

Market value added

and, as we have already noted,

MVA = Net present value of expected future EVA

Clearly, it will be recognized that there are a number of significant connections between logistics performance and shareholder value – not only the impact that logistics service can have upon net operating income (profit) but also the impact on capital efficiency (asset turn). Many companies have come to realize the effect that lengthy pipelines and highly capital intensive logistics

> **Many companies have come to realize the effect that lengthy pipelines and highly capital intensive logistics facilities can have on EVA and hence shareholder value.**

facilities can have on EVA and hence shareholder value. As a result they have focused on finding ways in which pipelines can be shortened and, as a result, working capital requirements reduced. At the same time they have looked again at their fixed capital deployment of distribution facilities and vehicle fleets and in many cases have moved these assets off the balance sheet through the use of third party logistics service providers.

Customer profitability analysis

One of the basic questions which conventional accounting procedures have difficulty answering is: 'How profitable is this customer compared to another?' Usually customer profitability is only calculated at the level of gross profit – in other words the net sales revenue generated by the customer in a period, less the cost of goods sold for the actual product mix purchased. However there are still many other costs to take into account before the real profitability of an individual customer can be exposed. The same is true if we seek to identify the relative profitability of different market segments or distribution channels.

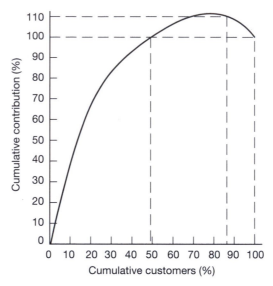

Fig. 3.9 Customer profitability analysis

Source: Hill, G.V., *Logistics – The Battleground of the 1990s*, A.T. Kearney

The significance of these costs that occur as a result of servicing customers can be profound in terms of how logistics strategies should be developed. Firstly, customer profitability analysis will often reveal a proportion of customers who make a negative contribution, as in Figure 3.9. The reason for this is very simply that the costs of servicing a customer can vary considerably – even between two customers who may make equivalent purchases from us. The costs of service begin with the order itself – what time does the salesperson spend with the customer; is there a key account manager whose time is spent wholly or in part working with that customer; what commissions do we pay on those sales?

Then there are the order processing costs which themselves will differ according to the number of lines on the orders and their complexity. Beyond this there will be transport costs, materials handling costs and often inventory and warehousing costs – particularly if the products are held on a dedicated basis for customers, e.g. with own-label products. With many customers it will often be the case that the supplying company is allocating specific funds for customer promotions, advertising support, additional discounts and the like. In the case of promotions (e.g. a special pack for a particular retailer) there will most likely be additional, hidden costs to the supplier. For example the disruption to production schedules and the additional inventory holding cost is rarely accounted for and assigned to customers.

The basic principle of customer profitability analysis is that the supplier should seek to assign all costs that are specific to individual accounts. A useful test to apply when looking at these costs is to ask the question: 'What costs would I avoid if I didn't do business with this customer?'

The benefit of using the principle of 'avoidability' is that many costs of servicing customers are actually shared amongst several or many customers. The warehouse is a good example – unless the supplier could release warehousing space for other purposes then it would be incorrect to allocate a proportion of the total warehousing costs to a particular customer.

A checklist of costs to include when drawing up the 'profit and loss account' for specific customers is given in Table 3.1 and the example of the 'average customer' provided on page 88 clearly shows how important it is to recognize the difference between customer costs.

Table 3.1 The customer profit and loss account

Revenues	● Net Sales Value
Less	
Costs	● Cost of sales (actual product mix)
(attributable costs only)	● Commissions
	● Sales calls
	● Key account management time
	● Trade bonuses and special discount
	● Order processing costs
	● Promotional costs (visible & hidden)
	● Merchandising costs
	● Non-standard packaging/unitization
	● Dedicated inventory holding costs
	● Dedicated warehouse space
	● Materials handling costs
	● Transport costs
	● Documentation/communications costs
	● Returns/refusals
	● Trade credit (actual payment period)

▪ The average customer ▪

'The significance of customer-oriented costs is not their average value, but specifically how they vary by customer, by order size, by type of order and other key factors. Whilst the average cost per customer may be easily calculated, there may be no customer that incurs the average cost to serve. The need is to be aware of the customers at the extremes of the cost range because on the one hand, profits may be eroded by serving them and, on the other, although high profit is being generated, the business is vulnerable to competitive price-cutting. The table below shows an example of the range of values of some customer-oriented costs expressed as a percentage of net sales. This illustrates how misleading the use of averages can be.'

Customer costs as a % of net sales

	Low	Average	High
Order processing	0.2	2.6	7.4
Inventory carrying	1.1	2.6	10.2
Picking and shipping	0.3	0.7	2.5
Interplant freight & handling	0.0	0.7	2.5
Outbound freight	2.8	7.1	14.1
Commissions	2.4	3.1	4.4

Source: Hill, G.V. and Harland, D.V., 'The Customer Profit Centre', *Focus*, Institute of Logistics and Distribution Management, Vol 2, No 2, 1983

Whilst in a business with many thousands of customer accounts it would not be practicable to conduct individual profitability analyses, it would certainly be possible to select representative customers on a sample basis so that a view can be gained of the relative costs associated with different types of account or distribution channels or market segments.

What sort of costs should be taken into account in this type of analysis? Figure 3.10 presents a basic model which seeks to identify only those customer-related costs which are avoidable (i.e. if the customer did not exist, these costs would not be incurred).

The starting point is the gross sales value of the order from which is then subtracted the discounts that are given on that order to the customer. This leaves the net sales value from which must be taken the direct production costs or cost of goods sold. Indirect costs are not allocated unless they are fully attributable to that customer. The same principle applies to

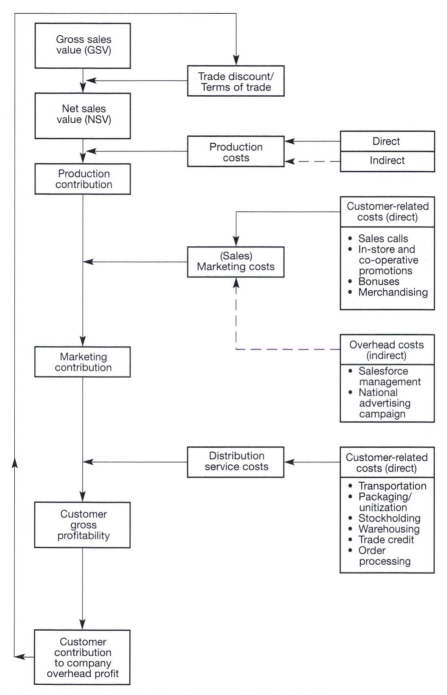

Fig. 3.10 Customer profitability analysis: a basic model

sales and marketing costs as attempts to allocate indirect costs, such as national advertising, can only be done on an arbitrary and usually misleading basis. The attributable distribution costs can then be assigned to give customer gross contribution. Finally any other customer-related costs, such as trade credit, returns etc. are subtracted to give a net contribution to overheads and profit. Often the figure that emerges as the 'bottom line' can be revealing, as shown in Table 3.2.

Table 3.2 Analysis of revenue and cost for a specific customer

	£	£
Gross sales value		100,000
Less discount	10,000	
Net sales value		90,000
Less direct cost of goods sold	20,000	
Gross contribution		70,000
Less sales and marketing costs:		
Sales calls	3,000	
Co-operative promotions	1,000	
Merchandising	3,000	
	7,000	
		63,000
Less distribution costs:		
Order processing	500	
Storage and handling	600	
Inventory financing	700	
Transport	2,000	
Packaging	300	
Refusals	500	
	4,600	
Customer gross contribution		58,400
Less other customer-related costs:		
Credit financing	1,500	
Returns	500	
	2,000	
Customer net contribution		56,400

In this case a gross contribution of £70,000 becomes a net contribution of £56,400 as soon as the costs unique to this customer are taken into account. If the analysis were to be extended by attempting to allocate overheads (a step not to be advised because of the problems usually associated with such allocation) what might at first seem to be a profitable customer could be deemed to be the reverse. However, as long as the net contribution is positive and there is no 'opportunity cost' in servicing that customer, the company would be better off with the business than without it.

The value of this type of exercise can be substantial. The information could be used firstly when the next sales contract is negotiated and, secondly, as the basis for sales and marketing strategy in directing effort away from less profitable types of account towards more profitable business. More importantly it can point the way to alternative strategies for managing customers with high servicing costs. Ideally we require all our customers to be profitable in the medium to long term and where customers currently are profitable we should seek to build and extend that profitability further.

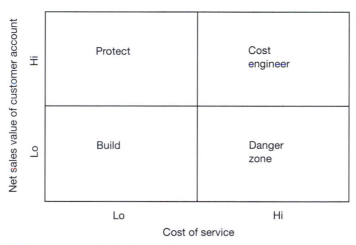

Fig. 3.11 Customer profitability matrix

The customer profitability matrix shown in Figure 3.11 provides some generalized guidance for strategic direction.

Briefly the appropriate strategies for each quadrant of the matrix in Figure 3.11 are:

Build

These customers are relatively cheap to service but their net sales value is low. Can volume be increased without a proportionate increase in the costs of service? Can our sales team be directed to seek to influence these customers' purchases towards a more profitable sales mix?

Danger zone

These customers should be looked at very carefully. Is there any medium- to long-term prospect either of improving net sales value or of reducing the costs of service? Is there a strategic reason for keeping them? Do we need them for their volume even if their profit contribution is low?

Cost engineer

These customers could be more profitable if the costs of servicing them could be reduced. Is there any scope for increasing drop sizes? Can deliveries be consolidated? If new accounts in the same geographic area were developed would it make delivery more economic? Is there a cheaper way of gathering orders from these customers, e.g. telesales?

Protect

The high net sales value customers who are relatively cheap to service are worth their weight in gold. The strategy for these customers should be to seek relationships which make the customer less likely to want to seek alternative suppliers. At the same time we should constantly seek opportunities to develop the volume of business that we do with them whilst keeping strict control of costs.

Ideally the organization should seek to develop an accounting system that would routinely collect and analyse data on customer profitability. Unfortunately most accounting systems are product focused rather than customer focused. Likewise cost reporting is traditionally on a functional basis rather than a transactional basis. So, for example, we know the costs of the transport function as a whole or the costs of making a particular product. What we do not know are the costs of delivering a specific mix of product to a particular customer.

There is a pressing need for companies to move towards a system of accounting for customers and marketing as well as accounting for products. As we have previously observed, it is customers who make profits, not products!

Direct product profitability

An application of logistics cost analysis that has gained widespread acceptance, particularly in the retail industry, is a technique known as direct product profitability – or more simply 'DPP'. In essence it is somewhat analogous to customer profitability analysis in that it attempts to identify all the costs that attach to a product or an order as it moves through the distribution channel.

The idea behind DPP is that in many transactions the customer will incur costs other than the immediate purchase price of the product. Often this is termed the *total cost of ownership*. Sometimes these costs will be hidden and often they can be substantial – certainly big enough to reduce or even eliminate net profit on a particular item.

For the supplier it is important to understand DPP in as much as his ability to be a low cost supplier is clearly influenced by the costs that are incurred as that product moves through his logistics system. Similarly as distributors and retailers are now very much more conscious of an item's DPP it is to the advantage of the supplier equally to understand the cost drivers that impact upon DPP so as to seek to influence it favourably.

Table 3.3 describes the steps to be followed in moving from a crude gross margin measure to a more precise DPP.

Table 3.3 Direct product profit (DPP)

The net profit contribution from the sales of a product after allowances are added and all costs that can be rationally allocated or assigned to an individual product are subtracted = direct product profit.

	Sales
–	Cost of goods sold
=	Gross margin
+	Allowances and discounts
=	Adjusted gross margin
–	Warehouse costs
	Labour (labour model – case, cube, weight)
	Occupancy (space and cube)
	Inventory (average inventory)
–	Transportation costs (cube)
–	Retail costs
	Stocking labour
	Front end labour
	Occupancy
	Inventory
=	Direct product profit

As DPP has been primarily used in the retail industry (although the principle has a much wider application) we explain the concept in the context of retail business.

Direct product profit is the term given to the contribution to profit of an item which is calculated by:

- Adjusting the gross margin for each item to reflect deals, allowances, net forward buy income, prompt payment discounts, etc.
- Identifying and measuring the costs that can be directly attributed to individual products (direct product costs like labour, space, inventory and transport).

Because product characteristics and the associated costs vary so much by item (e.g. cube, weight, case pack count, handling costs, space occupied, turnover) the retailer needs to look at DPP at the item level. Similarly, because shelf space is the limiting factor for the retailer the key measure of performance becomes DPP/square metre. Some examples of how DPP/square metre can differ dramatically from simple gross margin are shown in Table 3.4 for different products moving through a retailer's own distribution system.

Table 3.4 Direct product profit (DPP)

	Gross margin	DPP	Average DPP/Sq metre
	%	%	%
Baby food	11	3.4	0.11
Beans and rice	11	3.9	0.24
Shortening and oil	11	7.3	0.98
Paper products	19	7.2	0.47
Cake mix	19	10.1	0.44
Jelly and jam	22	16.7	1.01
Household cleaners	24	17.3	1.05
Ice cream	23	6.2	0.99
Butter	10	4.6	1.97
Frozen vegetables	34	23.1	2.60
Frozen fruit	24	17.3	3.28
Cigarettes	12	13.2	6.56
Dentrifice	31	18.6	1.42
Facial tissues	15	–	(0.01)

The importance to the supplier of DPP is based on the proposition that a key objective of customer service strategy is 'to reduce the customer's costs of ownership'. In other words the supplier should be looking at his products and asking the question: 'How can I favourably influence the DPP of my customers by changing either the characteristics of the products I sell, or the way I distribute them?' The example on pp. 96 and 97 illustrates some of the possibilities.

From pack design onwards there are a number of elements that the manufacturer or supplier may be able to vary in order to influence DPP/square metre in a positive way, for example, changing the case size, increasing the delivery frequency, direct store deliveries, etc.

Cost drivers and activity-based costing

As we indicated briefly at the start of this chapter there is a growing dissatisfaction with conventional cost accounting, particularly as it relates to logistics management. Essentially these problems can be summarized as follows:

- There is a general ignorance of the true costs of servicing different customer types/channels/market segments.
- Costs are captured at too high a level of aggregation.
- Full cost allocation still reigns supreme.
- Conventional accounting systems are functional in their orientation rather than output oriented.
- Companies understand product costs but not customer costs – yet products don't make profits, customers do.

The common theme that links these points is that we seem to suffer in business from a lack of visibility of costs as they are incurred through the logistics pipeline. Ideally what logistics management requires is a means of capturing costs as products and orders flow towards the customer.

To overcome this problem it is necessary to change radically the basis of cost accounting away from the notion that all expenses must be allocated (often on an arbitrary basis) to individual units (such as products) and instead, to separate the expenses and match them to the activities that consume the resources.[6] The key to activity-based costing (ABC) is to seek out the 'cost drivers' along the logistics pipeline that

■ Direct product profitability and merchandising ■

To date, DPP has been used most in analyzing the performance of individual items (see Matrix opposite).

In the United States, Procter & Gamble have gone so far as to use the 29 cents per case saving, achieved by repackaging its Ivory shampoo, in advertising. The use of a cylindrical plastic bottle, rather than the characteristic curvy shape, resulted not merely in reduced distribution, handling and storage costs, but also in an increase in sales because people perceived the new shape as symbolizing value for money. Similar savings were achieved by Scott by the repackaging of Andrex toilet tissue. 11 per cent more merchandise is now packed per case, and 6 per cent more cases per pallet. Repackaging has also eliminated pallet overhang and resulted in less damage and returns. With a distribution volume in excess of 16 million cases per year the savings are significant.

The trend towards smaller delivery quantities reflects pressure from retailers for improved product profitability. Many manufacturers are receiving requests for mixed pallets to be delivered to central distribution warehouses, and many retailers are now operating break pack facilities which supply individual stores with single units in display packaging only.

The prompt delivery of fashion garments poses a particular challenge for the retail industry. If goods can be delivered ready for display, valuable time can be saved in making them available to customers as well as allowing a reduction in store labour from the removal of the ironing task. Marks & Spencer and many of the high street fashion multiples have shown their commitment to this approach. However, there is a trade-off in the equipment investment and warehousing space required.

A more radical use of DPP is for range rationalization. Woolworths have used the technique extensively in weeding out loss-making lines. Growbags were revealed as a clear loser, and a not entirely flippant suggestion was made that the only way to make them profitable would be to deliver them on fully depreciated tipper trucks running on stolen diesel!

Boots the chemists went further by deleting the whole of its pet food range following an in-depth analysis on its mainframe-based DPP system. This decision is apparently under constant review, particularly since Marks & Spencer moved into the pet food field shortly after Boots' withdrawal from it.

Coca-Cola Schweppes have managed to move the boot onto the other foot by working with a major supermarket multiple on an exercise which reduced their soft drinks range from 41 to 18 products and from 7 to 2 suppliers. Far from causing a loss in volume, this decision improved it, and resulted in a 20 per cent improvement in range profitability – valued at approximately £700,000.

Merchandising matrix

	Lo	Hi
Hi (Unit DPP)	Advertise Upgrade shelf position Stimulate movement Reconsider price	Advertise and promote Display to maximum effect Maintain or increase shelf stock
Lo (Unit DPP)	Reduce shelf allocation Limit variety Reconsider price Discontinue	Review handling method and costs Reconsider price Downgrade shelf position Reduce advertising

Unit volume

Source: Aston, M., 'Method Trade-offs and DPP', *Focus*, Institute of Logistics and Distribution Management, Vol 8, No 8, October 1989

cause costs because they consume resources. Thus for example if we are concerned to assign the costs of order picking to orders then in the past this may have been achieved by calculating an average cost per order. In fact an activity-based approach might suggest that it is the number of lines on an order that consume the order picking resource and hence should instead be seen as the cost driver. Table 3.5 contrasts the ABC approach with the traditional method.

The advantage of using activity-based costing is that it enables each customer's unique characteristics in terms of ordering behaviour and distribution requirements to be separately accounted for. Once the cost attached to each level of activity is identified (e.g. cost per line item picked, cost per delivery, etc) then a clearer picture of the true cost-to-serve will emerge. Whilst ABC is still strictly a cost allocation method it uses a more logical basis for that allocation than traditional methods.

Table 3.5 Activity-based costing vs traditional cost bases

Traditional cost bases	£000's	Activity cost bases	£000's	Cost drivers
Salaries	550	Sales order processing	300	Number of orders
Wages	580	Holding inventory	600	Value of shipment
Depreciation	250	Picking	300	Number of order lines
Rent/electricity/ telephone	700	Packing/assembly of orders	100	Number of order lines
Maintenance	100	Loading	200	Weight
Fuel	200	Transportation	500	Location of customer
		Delivery at customer	200	Number of drops
		Solving problems	380	Number of order lines
	£2,380		£2,580	

Source: Based upon Simmons, G. and Steeple, D., 'Overhead Recovery – It's as Easy as ABC', *Focus*, Institute of Logistics and Distribution Management, Vol 10, No 8, October 1991

There are certain parallels between activity-based costing and the idea of *mission costing* introduced earlier in this chapter. Essentially mission costing seeks to identify the unique costs that are generated as a result of specific logistics/customer service strategies aimed at targeted market segments. The aim is to establish a better matching of the service needs of the various markets that the company addresses with the inevitably limited resources of the company. There is little point in committing incremental costs where the incremental benefits do not justify the expenditure.

There are four stages in the implementation of an effective mission costing process:

1. *Define the customer service segment*
   Use the methodology described in Chapter 2 to identify the different service needs of different customer types. The basic principle is that because not all customers share the same service requirements and characteristics they should be treated differently.

2. *Identify the factors that produce variations in the cost of service*
   This step involves the determination of the service elements which will directly or indirectly impact upon the costs of service, e.g. the product mix, the delivery characteristics such as drop size and frequency or incidence of direct deliveries, merchandising support, special packs and so on.

3. *Identify the specific resources used to support customer segments*
   This is the point at which the principles of activity-based costing and mission costing coincide. The basic tenet of ABC is that the activities that generate cost should be defined and the specific cost drivers involved identified. These may be the number of lines on an order, the people involved, the inventory support or the delivery frequency.

4. *Attribute activity costs by customer type or segment*
   Using the principle of 'avoidability' the incremental costs incurred through the application of a specific resource to meeting service needs are attributed to customers. It must be emphasized that this is not cost allocation but cost attribution. In other words it is because customers use resources that the appropriate share of cost is attributed to them.

Clearly to make this work there is a prerequisite that the cost coding system in the business be restructured. In other words the coding system must be capable of gathering costs as they are incurred by customers from the point of order generation through to final delivery, invoicing and collection.

The basic purpose of logistics cost analysis is to provide managers with reliable information that will enable a better allocation of resources to be achieved. Given that logistics management, as we have observed, ultimately is concerned to meet customer service requirements in the most cost-effective way, then it is essential that those responsible have the most accurate and meaningful data possible.

Summary

Because logistics costs can account for such a large proportion of total costs in the business it is critical that they be carefully managed. However, it is not always the case that the true costs of logistics are fully understood. Traditional approaches to accounting based upon full-cost allocation can be misleading and dangerous. Activity-based costing methods provide some significant advantages in identifying the real costs of serving different types of customers or different channels of distribution.

Logistics management impacts not only upon the profit and loss account of the business but also upon the balance sheet. Logistics is also increasingly being recognized as having a significant impact upon Economic Value Added and hence Shareholder Value. It is likely that in the future, decisions on logistics strategies will be made based upon a thorough understanding of the impact they will have upon the financial performance of the business.

References

1. Johnson, H.T. and Kaplan, R.S., *Relevance lost: The Rise and Fall of Management Accounting*, Harvard Business School Press, 1987.
2. Christopher, M.G., *Total Distribution: A Framework for Analysis, Costing and Control*, Gower Press, 1971.
3. Barrett, T., 'Mission Costing: A New Approach to Logistics Analysis', *International Journal of Physical Distribution and Materials Management*, Vol 12, No 7, 1982.
4. Shillinglow, G., 'The Concept of Attributable Cost', *Journal of Accounting Research*, Vol 1, No 1, Spring 1963.
5. Stewart, G.B., *The Quest for Value*, Harpur Business, 1991 (EVA is a registered trademark of Stern Stewart & Co).
6. Cooper, R. and Kaplan, R.S., 'Profit Priorities from Activity-Based Costing', *Harvard Business Review*, May–June, 1991.

Benchmarking the supply chain

This chapter:

Introduces the concept of competitive bench-marking, outlining its objectives and some of the associated benefits.

●

Explores the concepts of value-adding and non-value adding time and techniques for mapping supply chain processes.

●

Highlights the importance of supplier and distributor benchmarking, benchmarking relationships as well as performance up and down the supply chain.

●

Suggests criteria for setting benchmarking priorities.

●

Identifies logistics performance indicators and out-lines the principles behind the balanced scorecard.

The intense level of competitive activity encountered in most markets has led to a new emphasis on measuring performance not just in absolute terms, but rather in terms relative to the competition, and beyond that to 'best-practice'.

In the past it was usually deemed to be sufficient simply to measure internal performance. In other words the focus was on things such as productivity, utilization, cost per activity and so on. Whilst it is clearly important that such things continue to be measured and controlled it also has to be recognized that such measures only have meaning when they are compared against a relevant 'metric' or benchmark. What should be the metric that is used in assessing logistics and supply chain performance?

There are in fact several dimensions to the measurement problem. The first key point to make is that the ultimate measuring rod is the customer, hence it is customers' perceptions of performance that must be paramount. Secondly it is not sufficient just to compare performance to that of immediate competitors. We must also compare ourselves to the 'best in the class'. Thirdly it is not just outputs that should be measured and compared but also the processes that produce that output. These three ideas lie at the heart of what today is termed competitive benchmarking.

Competitive benchmarking might simply be defined as the continuous measurement of the company's products, services, processes and practices against the standards of best competitors and other companies who are recognized as leaders. The measures that are chosen for the comparison must directly or indirectly impact upon customers' evaluation of the company's performance.

One of the earliest firms to adopt benchmarking was the Xerox Corporation who used it as a major tool in gaining competitive advantage. Xerox first started benchmarking in their manufacturing activity and it was focused on product quality and feature improvements. Following success in the manufacturing area, Xerox top management directed that benchmarking be performed by all cost centres and business units, and by 1981 it was adopted company-wide.

■ Benchmarking ■

Benchmarking world-class performance starts with competitive analysis, but goes far beyond it. While competitive analysis focuses on product comparisons, benchmarking looks beyond products to the operating and management skills that produce the products. Moreover, while competitive analysis is limited to companies that produce more or less similar products or services, benchmarking studies are free to search out the 'best of a breed' of a process or skill, wherever it may be found. And, unlike competitive analysis, which is usually carried out as a staff exercise, benchmarking any process in depth usually requires the active participation of the line personnel who perform that function in their own businesses. Thus benchmarking is more than an analytical process; it can be a tool for the encouragement of change.

Some companies that use benchmarking have found that it has become an all-pervasive element of their management culture. For example, ten years ago, Xerox focused solely on product comparisons – primarily through reverse engineering – to explain Canon's advantage in small copiers. But since then more comprehensive investigations of several leading Japanese manufacturers in a number of industries led to fundamental changes in how Xerox manages suppliers and develops products. These have been the primary sources of Xerox's now well-known competitiveness.

Motorola, which also uses benchmarking effectively, tries to start every new product, every capital programme, and every reform effort with a search for 'best of a breed' in the world at large. 'The further away from our industry we reach for comparisons, the happier we are,' comments a senior Motorola executive. 'We are seeking competitive superiority, after all, not just competitive parity.' Viewed in this way, benchmarking is a skill, an attitude, and a practice that ensures the organization always has its sights set on excellence, not merely on improvement.

Benchmarking can even become a bridge between staff analysis and the design of a line programme for achieving continuous performance improvement. Benchmarking can identify what it is that a company needs to be good at, as well as suggest what needs to be done to the support functions and the cross-integrating mechanisms to close the gap. And, through participation in highly structured field visits, line managers can be brought face-to-face with superior operational practice and satisfy themselves that the benchmarks others achieve are valid and comparable. A properly designed benchmarking exercise thus builds enthusiasm and commitment for change in those line executives who need to be involved for change to take place.

Source: Walleck, A.S. et al., 'Benchmarking World Class Performance', *The McKinsey Quarterly*, No 1, 1991

Initially there was some difficulty in performing benchmarking in departments such as repair, service, maintenance, invoicing and collection and distribution, until it was recognized that their 'product' was, in fact, a process. It was this process which needed to be articulated and compared with that used in other organizations. By looking at competitors' processes step-by-step and operation-by-operation, Xerox were able to identify best methods and practices in use by their competitors.

Initially benchmarking activities were concentrated solely on competitors until it became clear that Xerox's objective in achieving superior performance in each business function was not being obtained by looking only at competitors' practices.

The objective of creating competitive advantage involves outperforming rather than matching the efforts of competitors. This, together with the obvious difficulties in gaining all the information required on competitors and their internal systems and processes, led to a broader perspective on benchmarking being adopted. Thus benchmarking was expanded from a focus solely on competitors to a wider, but selective, focus on the products of top performing companies regardless of their industry sector.

Xerox have successfully used this broader perspective on benchmarking as a major element in increasing both quality and productivity. Collaborative co-operation between firms in non-competing industries offers significant opportunity in this regard. For example, in the Xerox logistics and distribution unit, annual productivity has doubled as a result of benefits obtained from non-competitive collaborative benchmarking.

> Today Xerox is a world role model for quality improvement with some 240 different functional areas of the company routinely involved in benchmarking against comparable areas.

Today Xerox is a world role model for quality improvement with some 240 different functional areas of the company routinely involved in benchmarking against comparable areas. Gains can come from widely different industries. Table 4.1 shows five practices relevant to improving productivity gains in Xerox that were identified from such widely disparate businesses as photographic film manufacturers and drug wholesalers.

Table 4.1 Practices uncovered by Xerox via non-competitive benchmarking

Type of company	Practice
Drug wholesaler	Electronic ordering between store and distribution centre
Appliance manufacturer	Forklift handling of up to six appliances at once
Electrical components manufacturer	Automatic in-line weighing, bar code labelling, and scanning of packages
Photographic film manufacturer	Self-directed warehouse work teams
Catalogue fulfilment service bureau	Recording of item dimensions and weight to permit order-filling quality assurance based on calculated compared with actual weight

Camp[1] has identified a number of benefits a company derives from benchmarking. These include:

- It enables the best practices from any industry to be creatively incorporated into the processes of the benchmarked function.
- It can provide stimulation and motivation to the professionals whose creativity is required to perform and implement benchmark findings.
- Benchmarking breaks down ingrained reluctance of operations to change. It has been found that people are more receptive to new ideas and their creative adoption when those ideas did not necessarily originate in their own industry.
- Benchmarking may also identify a technological breakthrough that would not have been recognized, and thus not applied, in one's own industry for some time to come, such as bar coding, originally adopted and proven in the grocery industry.

What to benchmark?

One useful framework for benchmarking is that devised by a cross-industry association – The Supply Chain Council. Their model, known as SCOR (Supply Chain Operations Reference), is built around four major processes: Plan ● Source ● Make ● Deliver, and covers the key supply chain activities from identifying customer demand through to delivering the product and collecting the cash. The aim of SCOR is to provide a standard way to measure supply chain performance and to use common metrics to benchmark against other organizations. A summary of the SCOR process elements is provided in Table 4.2:

Table 4.2 Supply Chain Council's integrated supply chain metric framework

Metric type	Outcomes	Diagnostics
Customer satisfaction/quality	1. Perfect order fulfillment 2. Customer satisfaction 3. Product quality	9. Delivery to commit date 10. Warranty costs, returns and allowances 11. Customer inquiry response time
Time	4. Order fulfillment lead time	12. Source/Make cycle time 13. Supply chain response time 14. Production plan achievement
Costs	5. Total supply chain costs	15. Value added productivity
Assets	6. Cash-to-cash cycle time 7. Inventory days of supply 8. Asset performance	16. Forecast accuracy 17. Inventory obsolescence 18. Capacity utilization

Benchmarking the logistics process

Many organizations now recognize the need to improve processes if outputs are to be enhanced. In the same way that, some years ago, manufacturing managers found that the key to quality was not to inspect the output but rather to control the process, so too in logistics we are coming to recognize the importance of process improvement and process control. This is the underlying philosophy of logistics process benchmarking.

The key to success in quality improvement is not to rely upon inspection of the output of the process but rather to improve the process itself. Imagine that this process is a 'pipeline' that begins with suppliers, runs through our own business (whether it involves manufacturing or any form of value-adding activity) through intermediaries and on to customers. To ensure that customer satisfaction is achieved at the end of the pipeline requires that everything that happens in the pipeline must be carefully monitored and controlled.

The first step in improving performance in the service pipeline is to understand the structure of the process. Unlike in oil pipelines, the network of materials and information flows, activities and procedures that link suppliers with end users, is complex. A recommended approach to defining the pipeline structure is to flowchart the steps along the chain which begin with a customer's order and ends with delivery. A greatly simplified example is shown in Figure 4.1. The detailed flow chart from which this summary was taken covered a very large sheet of paper!

The next step is to identify the critical points where, if something goes wrong, the entire process will be affected – for instance a stock-out in the warehouse or a failure to meet a production plan. These critical points are where process control must be applied and where benchmarking against the 'best in class' companies – in any industry – can bring significant benefits.

If we think of the chain of events from source of material through to the end user as a series of supplier/customer relationships then it will become clear that what we are advocating is the benchmarking of process and performance at each of the supplier/customer interfaces.

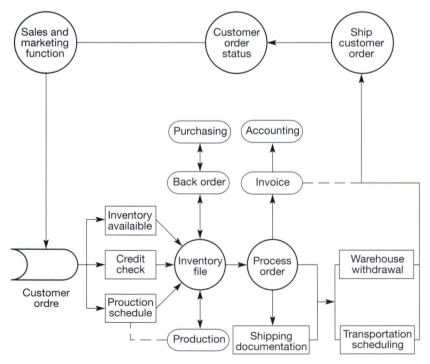

Fig. 4.1 The path of a customer's order

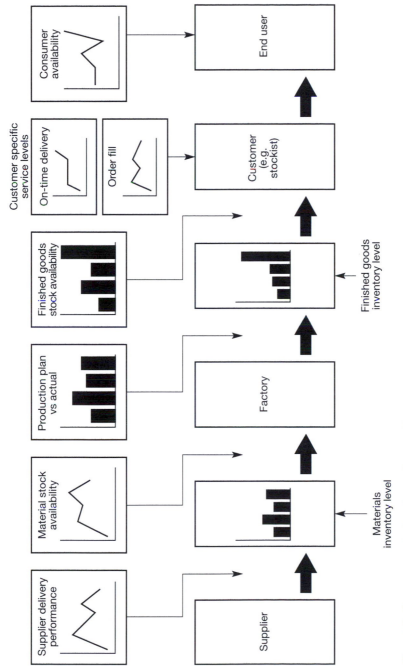

Fig. 4.2 Process control and service quality

Figure 4.2 provides an example of a series of monitors of service level from the source of supply through to the end user which will enable critical activities to be monitored and the processes involved to be continuously appraised.

Mapping supply chain processes

Flowcharting supply chain processes is the first step towards understanding the opportunities that exist for improvements in productivity through reengineering those processes. A critical concept that underpins such reengineering opportunities is the idea of 'value-adding' time versus 'non-value-adding' time.

Very simply, value-adding time is time spent doing something which creates a benefit for which the customer is prepared to pay. Thus we could classify manufacturing as a value-added activity as well as the physical movement of the product and the means of creating the exchange. The old adage 'the right product in the right place at the right time' summarizes the idea of customer value-adding activities. Thus any activity that contributes to the achievement of that goal could be classified as value-adding.

On the other hand, non-value-adding time is time spent on an activity whose elimination would lead to no reduction of benefit to the customer. Some non-value-adding activities are necessary because of the current design of our processes but they still represent a cost and should be minimized.

The difference between value-adding time and non-value-adding time is crucial to an understanding of how logistics processes can be improved. In Chapter 6 we deal specifically with the issue of time reduction in the logistics pipeline and we shall return to the concept of value-adding versus non-value-adding again. However at this point it will be helpful to explore some of the tools that can assist in the identification of value-added versus non-value-added time.

> **The difference between value-adding time and non-value-adding time is crucial to an understanding of how logistics processes can be improved.**

Once processes have been flowcharted the first step is to bring together the managers involved in those processes to debate and agree exactly which elements of the process can truly be described as value-adding. Agreement may not easily be achieved as no one likes to admit that the activity they are responsible for does not actually add any value for customers.

The next step is to do a rough-cut graph highlighting visually how much time is consumed in both non-value-adding and value-adding activities. Figure 4.3 shows a generic example of such a graph.

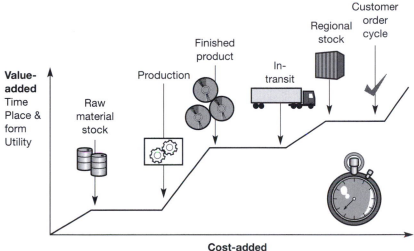

Fig. 4.3 Which activities add cost and which add value?

Figure 4.4 shows an actual analysis where the total process time was 40 weeks and yet value was only being added for 6.2 per cent of that time!

It will be noted from this example that most of the value is added early in the process and hence it is more expensive when held as inventory. Furthermore much of the flexibility is probably lost as the product is configured and/or packaged in specific forms early in that process. Figure 4.5 shows that this product started as a combination of three active ingredients but very rapidly became 25 stock-keeping units because it was packaged in different sizes, formats, etc, and then held in inventory for the rest of the time in the company's pipeline.

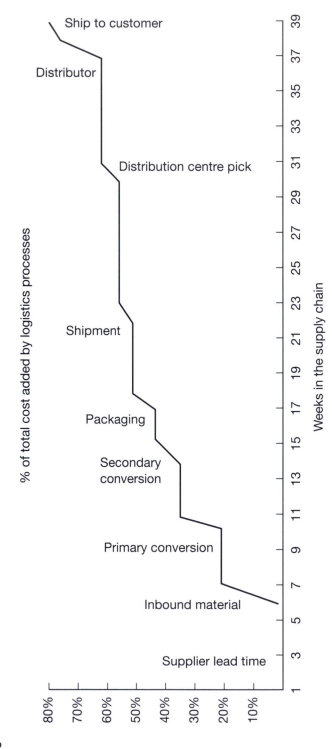

Fig. 4.4 **Value added through time**

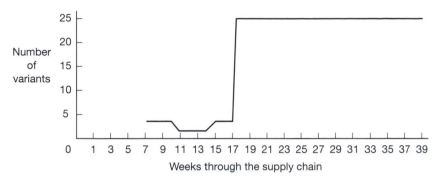

Plot of variety through the supply chain

• Longest period is spent at the maximum variety level
• Greatest flexibility is available when the product is generic

Fig. 4.5 Variety through time

Throughput efficiency in a supply chain can be measured as:

$$\frac{\text{Value-added time}}{\text{End-to-end pipeline time}} \times 100$$

As we have noted this can be as low as 10 per cent, meaning that most time spent in a supply chain is non-value-adding time. To begin to make significant improvements in throughput efficiency first requires a detailed understanding of the processes and activities that together comprise the supply chain. A useful tool here is supply chain mapping.

A supply chain map is essentially a time-based representation of the processes and activities that are involved as the materials or products move through the chain. Simultaneously the map highlights the time that is consumed when those materials or products are simply standing still, i.e. as inventory.

In these maps, it is usual to distinguish between 'horizontal' time and 'vertical' time. Horizontal time is time spent in process. It could be in-transit time, manufacturing or assembly time, time spent in production planning or processing and so on. It may not necessarily be time when customer value is being created but at least something is going on. The other type of time is vertical time, this is time when nothing is happening and hence the material or product is standing still as inventory. No value is being added during vertical time, only cost.

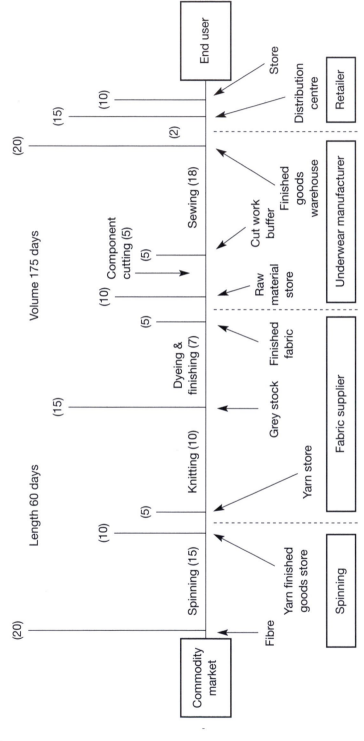

Fig. 4.6 Supply chain mapping – an example

Source: Scott, C. and Westbrook, R. 'New Strategic Tools for Supply Chain Management', *International Journal of Physical Distribution & Logistics Management*, Vol 21, No 1

The labels 'horizontal' and 'vertical' refer to the maps themselves where the two axes reflect process time and time spent as static inventory respectively. Figure 4.6 depicts such a map of the manufacture and distribution of men's underwear.

From this map it can be seen that horizontal time is 60 days. In other words the various processes of gathering materials, spinning, knitting, dyeing, finishing, sewing and so on take 60 days to complete from start to finish. This is important because horizontal time determines the time that it would take for the system to respond to an increase in demand. Hence, if there were to be a sustained increase in demand it would take that long to 'ramp up' output to the new level. Conversely, if there was a downturn in demand then the critical measure is pipeline volume, i.e. the sum of both horizontal and vertical time. In other words it would take 175 days to 'drain' the system of inventory. So in volatile fashion markets, for instance, pipeline volume is a critical determinant of business risk.

Pipeline maps can also provide a useful internal benchmark. Because each day of process time requires a day of inventory to 'cover' that day then, in an ideal world, the only inventory would be that needed to cover the process lead time. So a 60-day total process time would result in 60 days inventory. However, in the case highlighted here there are actually 175 days of inventory in the pipeline. Clearly, unless the individual processes are highly time variable or unless demand is very volatile, there is more inventory than can be justified.

It must be remembered that in multi-product businesses each product will have a different end-to-end pipeline time. Furthermore where products comprise multiple components, packaging materials or sub-assemblies total pipeline time will be determined by the speed of the slowest moving item or element in that product. Hence in procuring materials for and manufacturing a household aerosol air freshener, it was found that the replenishment lead time for one of the fragrances used added weeks to the total pipeline.

Mapping pipelines in this way provides a powerful basis for logistics reengineering projects. Because it makes the total process and its associated inventory transparent, the opportunities for reducing non-value-adding time become apparent. In many cases much of the non-value-adding time in a supply chain is there because it is self-inflicted through the 'rules' that are imposed or that have been inherited. Such rules include: economic batch quantities, economic order quantities, minimum order sizes, fixed inventory review periods, production planning cycles and forecasting review periods.

The importance of strategic lead-time management is that it forces us to challenge every process and every activity in the supply chain and to apply the acid test of 'does this activity add value for a customer or consumer or does it simply add cost?'

Supplier and distributor benchmarking

Because supply chain performance is so obviously bound up in the quality of the relationships that extend upstream to suppliers and downstream to distributors, it is important that they be included in the benchmarking process. Indeed, because for most companies today, 'out-sourcing' has grown to represent 50 per cent or more of all their costs, it is essential that we understand just how efficient and effective those external suppliers are. The same principle applies to distributors or intermediaries who are taking a large proportion of the 'channel margin' – i.e. the difference between the factory gate cost and the final 'street value' of the end customer sale.

In both cases the focus should be upon enhancing both the efficiency and the effectiveness of supply chain relationships with the overall aim in mind of improving the performance of the supply chain as a whole. Thus, in reviewing supplier and distributor performance, the emphasis should be on assessing their contribution to reducing the total delivered cost and increasing end user customer service.

The type of issues that need to be addressed in supplier and distributor benchmarking are such questions as:

- Willingness to work as a partner/co-maker
- Commitment to continuous improvement
- Acceptance of innovation and change
- Focus on throughput time reduction
- Utilization of quality management procedures
- Use regular and formal benchmarking processes themselves
- Flexibility is seen as the prime goal in logistics systems design
- Do their employees share common core values of customer concern?
- Do they actively seek to improve communications with us?
- Does their leadership emphasize the primacy of total quality management?

Figure 4.7 illustrates the key areas for benchmarking in the supply chain. It is important to note that it is not just supplier and distributor performance that should be monitored and compared to best-in-class companies but also how the interfaces are managed. Thus we need to know, for example, how do other organizations manage the transmission of orders to suppliers or how do other companies co-ordinate their production schedules with those of suppliers or customers and so on.

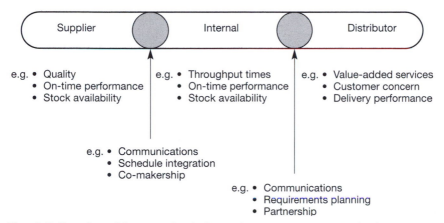

Fig. 4.7 Benchmarking supply chain performance – some typical measures

Many companies are conducting formal appraisals of vendor performance, however the idea of a supplier benchmark is still a relatively new concept. Similarly it is not sufficient just to monitor distributors' performance in absolute terms, it should also be monitored comparatively against other distributors with a reputation for superior performance.

Setting benchmarking priorities

Of all the many things that can be measured and compared to performance achieved by other companies, where should the priority be placed? Walleck *et al.*[2] recommend that the priorities be determined by identifying:

- Which processes and entities in the supply chain are of strategic importance.
- Which processes and entities in the supply chain have a high relative impact on the business.

117

- Where there is a choice between 'make' or 'buy'.
- Where there is internal readiness to change.

See Figure 4.8.

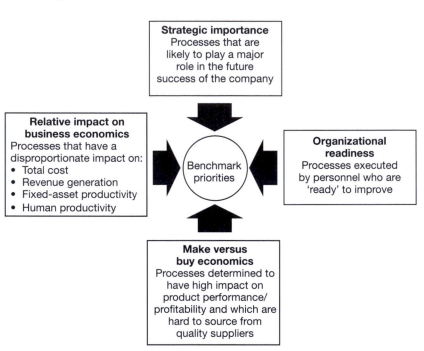

Fig. 4.8 Setting benchmarking priorities
Source: Wallack *et al.*, 'Benchmarking World Class Performance', *The McKinsey Quarterly*, 1991, No 1

The ultimate guide to the selection of benchmark priorities has to be the impact that an activity or function has upon competitive advantage. Using the model presented in Chapter 1, the two dimensions of advantage that are of central concern to any business are relative cost and relative value. Hence the organization's ability to achieve a delivered cost that is superior to its competitors' and a perceived differential advantage through customer service will be instrumental in achieving success in the marketplace. Figure 4.9 highlights the competitive goal.

In a sense, the horizontal axis is a measure of efficiency whilst the vertical axis is a measure of effectiveness. Thus it can be argued that benchmarking priority must be determined by the contributions of an

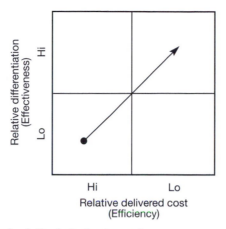

Fig. 4.9 Marketing logistics' strategic goal

activity, process or function to the achievement of these twin goals. In practice, what we find is that many organizations only measure efficiency – and even then, purely from an internal perspective. Such a stance is surely short-sighted since efficiency without effectiveness leads nowhere. For example the company may be able to demonstrate that its warehouses are highly efficient in terms of cost per case handled, utilization of space and so on. However if its competitors have eliminated warehouses and instead deliver direct to customers, thus reducing lead times and inventory costs, then the conclusion may be that its competitors are more effective.

Whilst the benchmarking process only reveals the performance gaps, it does present management with a tangible agenda for action. Successful benchmarking programmes firstly enable logistics strategies to be developed which are firmly based upon customer service requirements, and secondly, ensure that the processes employed are truly leading edge.

The company that commits itself firmly to the benchmarking philosophy is embarking upon a journey that will fundamentally change the way it sees itself. Such companies can never stand still and can never be satisfied with the status quo. For them, the phrase: 'continuous improvement' is not just a cliché, but a way of life. It is also likely that such companies will thrive whilst others who choose not to take this route will ultimately fail. See the BA Case Study overleaf.

Improving supply chain performance at British Airways

British Airways (BA) is the world's largest international passenger airline group, carrying 36.1m passengers per year to 175 destinations aboard its 293 aircraft. For more than a decade the privatized national carrier had sought to establish, then maintain, its position as 'The World's Favourite Airline', through the single-minded pursuit of excellent and innovative customer service. The strategic objective was to build loyalty among regular fliers, particularly business executives, who over a working lifetime might spend up to £1m on air travel. The service-led strategy served BA well and, in May 1997, the airline announced another year of record profits. Far from resting on its laurels, the company's Chief Executive, Robert Ayling, announced his intentions to increase BA's global reach while further boosting profits through a five-year drive to increase passenger revenues, improve asset utilization and reduce operating costs by a total of £1b. Behind the decision is an awareness that, in the past, the overriding desire to deliver superb customer service has not always been tempered by a realistic understanding of the costs involved.

British Airways Catering, part of BA's customer services department, aims to make a significant contribution to the new corporate goals through immediate and longer-term improvements in supply chain management. BA Catering is responsible for delivering 44m meals per year prepared by third-party caterers based at London's Heathrow and Gatwick airports, or through the other 150 smaller third-party run BA supply stations located around the world. The size of its operations is considerable, with the London kitchens alone using some 250 tonnes of chicken, 73 tonnes of eggs, and 38,000 cases of wine and champagne per annum. While BA Catering is not responsible for the supply of perishables into these kitchens, it does manage the 'uplift' of the finished meals and many other 'non-food' items including crockery, glassware, plastics, blankets and non-perishable 'dry foods', plus the catering equipment needed to move and stow the meals on-board. In all, around 40,000 items are pulled through this supply chain every time a Jumbo Jet takes off.

An audit of the supply chain was undertaken by external consultants Logistics Consulting Partners (LCP) which showed that around 1,400 line items were being sourced through over 250 suppliers worldwide. Most were routed through the Heathrow distribution centre, which was found to be holding buffer stocks valued at approximately £15m. Stock holdings were subject to seasonal variations, nevertheless further investigation revealed that sizable buffer stocks (totalling a similar value) were also being maintained throughout the network of smaller supply centres. Items were freely dispatched on a demand-pull basis from the distribution centres to supply bases, but a lack of accountability for stock management within the caterers' contracts led to habitual overstocking, which in turn generated a substantial volume of reverse logistics activity (mostly obsolete items).

The caterers held the buffer stocks to protect themselves from the vagaries of an unreliable replenishment system, which provided infrequent deliveries on long lead times. At the root of the problems were earlier well-meaning cost reduction initiatives which, though achieving their immediate goals, had been implemented without due regard for the wider supply chain effects. For example, to minimize the transportation cost incurred when supplying some overseas stations, BA Catering utilized spare capacity on BA cargo flights – as and when available – at preferred tariffs. This meant that the timing of deliveries was at the convenience of the carrier, not the customer. Likewise, outsourcing of the distribution centre activity allowed aggressively cost-focused operators to reduce their own inventory carrying costs by offloading stock holdings downstream with the catering contractors. To compound the problems further, poor procurement practices upstream of the distribution centres resulted in late and incomplete inbound deliveries of inaccurately labelled and inadequately packed stocks.

New stock management systems were required to effect a step-change in BA Catering's logistics performance, but these would take some time to implement and install. In the meantime a three-point plan was devised to improve operating efficiency in the short term and smooth the way for more radical innovations. The plan aimed to redress BA Catering's cultural imbalance between service and costs, while taking time out of the supply chain and improving the level of co-operation between operating partners.

Lead-time reduction became the starting point. By improving the frequency, accuracy and reliability of deliveries (together with the provision of an emergency quick-response back-up service), the caterers were persuaded to reduce their buffer stock, freeing up costly storage space which could be turned over to revenue generating food preparation activities. Within the first three months, improvements in service levels were accompanied by savings of £1m arising from reduced demand downstream of the distribution centres as excess inventory was used up. Most importantly for the longer term, the measures demonstrated the link between supply chain lead times, accuracy and costs to BA

▶

▶ Catering's own materials management team. It also demonstrated that cost reductions need not be achieved at the expense of service levels, boosting the confidence of the team and preparing them for the implementation of sophisticated new supply chain management systems.

Installation of a raft of new support systems, based around software supplier Industri-Matematik's System ESS, began in 1997. The new systems were a vital link in the BA Catering's wider Supply Chain Project which, in its totality, would deliver savings of around £50m over a five-year period. Moreover, the systems have the potential to add value over and above the incremental increase in efficiency that might be expected from meeting their functional requirements. System ESS has the capabilities to integrate BA Catering's supply chain planning software with BA's yield management and Executive Club databases, allowing the airline to leverage the power of both. By integrating key suppliers into the system, and cross-checking inventory levels against passenger bookings, BA Catering will be able to fine-tune its stock holdings to optimum levels and track stock by destination, flight and, eventually, to individual passengers. As the system is extended to cover all non-food items, it will open up opportunities to redefine customer service by becoming more responsive to the preferences of individual customers. Perhaps ensuring that Executive Club 'Gold Card' members are greeted on board with a glass of their favourite wine or a copy of a particular magazine. Importantly too, the system will enable BA to calculate accurately the real cost of providing this and other services, allowing it to plan wisely and with greater precision how it will manage the direction and demands of future service innovations.

References

Smart, Rosemary (1996), 'Chocs Away', *Logistics Europe*, December, pp. 54–6.
Collinge, Phil and Reynolds, Paul (1997), 'Food for Thought', *Logistics Focus*, November, pp. 2–4, 6–7.
Industri-Matematik (1997), 'British Airways Paves Way for Personalised On-Board Supplies with System ESS', Press Release, 3pp.

Identifying logistics performance indicators

One benefit of a rigorous approach to logistics and supply chain benchmarking is that it soon becomes apparent that there are a number of critical measures of performance that need to be continuously monitored. The idea of 'Key Performance Indicators' (KPIs) is simple. It suggests that whilst there are many measures of performance that can be deployed in an organization, there is a relatively small number of critical dimensions which contribute more than proportionately to success or failure in the marketplace.

Much interest has been shown in recent years in the concept of the 'Balance Scorecard'.[3] The idea behind the balanced scorecard is that there are a number of key performance indicators – most of them probably non-financial measures – that will provide management with a better means of meeting strategic goals than the more traditional financially-oriented measures. These KPIs derive from the strategic goals themselves. Thus the intention is that the balanced scorecard will provide ongoing guidance on those critical areas where action may be needed to ensure the achievement of those goals.

These ideas transfer readily into the management of logistics and supply strategy. If suitable performance measures can be identified that link with the achievement of these strategic goals they can become the basis for a more appropriate scorecard than might traditionally be the case.

A logical four-step process is suggested for constructing such a scorecard:

Step 1: Articulate logistics and supply chain strategy
How do we see our logistics and supply chain strategy contributing to the overall achievement of corporate and marketing goals?

Step 2: What are the measurable outcomes of success?
Typically, these might be summarized as 'Better, Faster, Cheaper'. In other words superior service quality, achieved in shorter time frames at less cost to the supply chain as a whole.

Step 3: What are the processes that impact these outcomes?
In the case of 'Better, Faster, Cheaper' the processes that lead to 'perfect order achievement', shorter pipeline times and reduced cost-to-serve need to be identified.

Step 4: What are the drivers of performance within these processes?
These activities are the basis for the derivation of the key performance indicators. Cause and effect analysis can aid in their identification.

In this framework it is suggested that the three key outcomes of success are: Better, Faster, Cheaper. This triad of inter-connected goals is almost universal in its desirability. These goals are significant because they combine customer-based measures of performance in terms of total quality with internal measures of resource and asset utilization.

Figure 4.10 highlights the customer-facing, process orientation of this concept of performance measurement.

Fig. 4.10 Creating the logistics scorecard

Since 'what gets measured, gets managed' it is inevitable that once measures such as these are put in place, management attention will be directed to these key issues. The role that benchmarking plays is pivotal. In the first place it helps identify what current best practice is and then it focuses on how processes might be reengineered and managed to achieve excellence in these critical competitive arenas.

Summary

Benchmarking logistics processes is a vital first step in any reengineering programme. Understanding the differences between value-adding time and non-value-adding time can help identify opportunities for time compression in the supply chain. Whilst benchmarking often implies comparison outside the business with 'best-in-class' organizations, it can also be a powerful tool for use internally. Of particular value is the technique known as 'supply chain mapping' which can provide an overview of the total pipeline from suppliers through to customers.

Developing a set of relevant and actionable performance measures should be priority for any proposed logistics change programme. Recognizing that 'what gets measured, gets managed', many more companies are now seeking to develop a 'balanced scorecard' which incorporates appropriate indicators of logistics performance.

References

1. Camp, Robert, *Benchmarking: The Search For Industry Best Practices That Lead to Superior Performance*, ASQC Quality Press, 1989.
2. Walleck, A.S. *et al.*, 'Benchmarking World Class Performance', *The McKinsey Quarterly*, No 1, 1991.
3. Kaplan, R.S. and Norton, D.P., *The Balanced Scorecard*, Harvard Business School Press, 1996.

Managing the global pipeline

This chapter:

Discusses the globalization of industry, the emergence of global companies, and the trend towards global production, distribution and marketing strategies.

●

Explores the implications of some of the most significant aspects of globalization in the supply chain: focused factories, centralization of inventories and postponement and localization.

●

Identifies the most pressing challenges for logistics managers arising from the globaliation of supply chains.

●

Considers how managers might structure and manage a global logistics network, balancing the benefits of centralized logistics planning with the need to meet localized customer demands.

●

Raises issues of outsourcing and the co-ordination of network partners and the critical role of logistics information in managing a global logistics pipeline.

'Time has ceased, "space" has vanished. We now live in a global village ...
a simultaneous happening.'

Marshall McLuhan, *The Medium is the Massage*, Bantam Books, USA, 1967

Once, these words might have been considered hyperbole, an exaggeration to underline the point that McLuhan wanted to make about the growing inter-dependence of the world community. However, today we accept such statements as fact and we have come to recognize the necessity of considering markets from a global perspective when formulating production, distribution and marketing strategies.

Global brands and companies now dominate most markets. Over the last two decades there has been a steady trend towards the worldwide marketing of products under a common brand umbrella – whether it be Coca-Cola or Marlborough, IBM or Toyota. At the same time the global company has revised its previously localized focus, manufacturing and marketing its products in individual countries, and now instead will typically source on a worldwide basis for global production.

The logic of the global company is clear: it seeks to grow its business by extending its markets whilst at the same time seeking cost reduction through scale economies in purchasing and production and through focused manufacturing and/or assembly operations.

However, whilst the logic of globalization is strong, we must recognize that it also presents certain challenges. Firstly, world markets are not homogeneous, there is still a requirement for local variation in many product categories. Secondly, unless there is a high level of co-ordination, the complex logistics of managing global supply chains may result in higher costs.

These two challenges are related: on the one hand, how to offer local markets the variety they seek whilst still gaining the advantage of standardized global production and on the other, how to manage the links in the global chain from sources of supply through to end user. There is a danger that some global companies in their search for cost advantage may take too

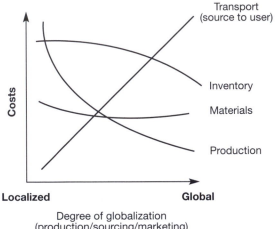

Fig. 5.1 Trade-offs in global logistics

narrow a view of cost and only see the cost reduction that may be achieved by focusing on production. In reality it is a total cost trade-off where the costs of longer supply pipelines may outweigh the production cost saving. Figure 5.1 illustrates some of the potential cost trade-offs to be considered in establishing the extent to which a global strategy for logistics will be cost-justified. Clearly a key component of the decision to go global must be the service needs of the marketplace. There is a danger that companies might run the risk of sacrificing service on the altar of cost reduction through a failure to fully understand the service needs of individual markets.

The trend towards global organization of both manufacturing and marketing is highlighting the critical importance of logistics and supply chain management as the keys to profitability. The complexity of the logistics task appears to be increasing exponentially, influenced by such factors as the increasing range of products, shorter product life cycles, marketplace growth and the number of supply/market channels.

> The trend towards global organization of both manufacturing and marketing is highlighting the critical importance of logistics and supply chain management as the keys to profitability.

There is no doubting that the globalization of industrial activity has become a major issue in business. Articles in the business press, seminars and academic symposia have all focused upon the emerging global trend. The competitive pressures and challenges that have led to this upsurge of interest have been well documented. What are less well understood are the implications of globalization for operations management in general and specifically for logistics management.

At the outset it is important that we define the global business and recognize its distinctiveness from an international or a multinational business. A global business is one which does more than simply export. The global business will typically source its materials and components in more than one country. Similarly it will often have multiple assembly or manufacturing locations geographically dispersed. It will subsequently market its products worldwide. A classic example is the Singer Sewing Machine Company (SSMC). It buys its sewing machine shells from a subcontractor in the United States, the motors from Brazil, the drive shafts from Italy and assembles the finished machine in Taiwan. It then markets the finished machines in most countries of the world.

The trend towards globalization has actually been growing rapidly for some years. What some have called the 'hollow corporation'[1] is in reality part of a worldwide move towards recognizing the interdependence of suppliers, manufacturers and customers in what is truly becoming a 'global village'.

Early commentators like Levitt[2] saw the growth of global brands and talked in terms of the growing convergence of customer preferences that would enable standardized products to be marketed in similar fashion around the world. However, the reality of global marketing is often different, with quite substantial differences in local requirements still very much in evidence. Thus whilst the brand may be global, the product may need certain customization to meet specific country needs, whether it be left or right hand drive cars or different TV transmission standards or local taste.

The trend towards globalization in the supply chain

The growth in world trade has continued to outstrip growth in most countries' Gross National Product throughout the closing years of the 20th century and looks set to continue for the foreseeable future. In part this trend is driven by expanding demand in new markets but also the liberalization of international trade through GATT/WTO accords has had a significant effect.

Once, companies established factories in overseas countries to manufacture products to meet local demand. Now, with the reduction of trade barriers and the development of global transportation infrastructure, fewer factories can produce in larger quantities to meet global, rather than local, demand.

Paradoxically, as the barriers to global movement have come down so have the sources of global competition increased. Newly emerging economies are building their own industries with global capabilities. At the same time, technological change and production efficiencies mean that most companies in most industries are capable of producing in greater quantity at less cost. The result of all of this is that there is now over-capacity in virtually every industry meaning that competitive pressure is greater than ever before.

To remain competitive in this new global environment, companies will have to continually seek ways in which costs can be lowered and service enhanced, meaning that supply chain efficiency and effectiveness will become ever more critical. See the Nike Case Study below.

Nike: the logistics challenge of global business

In little more than the time needed to raise just one generation of rebellious youth, US-based sports company Nike Inc. reinvented the concept of sports shoes. It transformed the cheapest of mass-market footwear into high-tech, high-performance products – imbued with all the cachet of haute couture and carrying price tags to match. Technologically, Nike's products are leading edge, as is its brand-led marketing which successfully used sporting superstar endorsement and advertisements with 'attitude' to establish the brand as an icon of youth subculture. However, as in any global organization, logistics and the management of the supply chain is a crucial strategic issue at Nike.

From its headquarters in Beaverton, Oregon, Nike operates a globe-spanning virtual enterprise. At its core are a set of business processes, designed to combine its state-of-the-art R&D capabilities with a ruthlessly low-cost manufacturing strategy.[1] Nike's 'Air Max Penny' basketball shoe, for example, is designed in Oregon and Tennessee and developed jointly by Asian and US technicians in Oregon, Taiwan and South Korea. The shoes themselves are manufactured in South Korea (men's sizes) and in Indonesia (boys' sizes), from 52 components supplied by companies in Japan, South Korea, Taiwan, Indonesia and the United States. Moreover, the complexity of the product means that each pair of shoes passes through more than 120 pairs of hands during the production process.[2] It also means that there is a danger of extended lead times.

Tying the whole Nike enterprise together are information systems that co-ordinate each step of these far-flung activities, and a logistics infrastructure capable of bringing the components together at precisely the right time, as well as managing the supply of finished goods into the global marketplace. Significantly, both are flexible enough to cope with constant product, materials and process innovation, allowing the company to bring more than 300 new shoe designs to market each year. However, this punishing rate of innovation brings with it high and rising levels of finished inventory if sales forecasts are not achieved.

In the United States and Europe, primary distribution of Nike products is increasingly out-sourced to specialist third parties,[3] who are linked into the company's global sales and customer service support systems. These links allow the contractors to prioritize shipments and manage order fulfilment as cost-effectively as possible, while ensuring that product availability information is readily accessible to all decision makers throughout Nike's virtual enterprise. Importantly too, these organizational capabilities should also hold Nike in good stead should fashionable youth turn away from designer sports shoes, forcing the company to rely more heavily on sales of its widening portfolio of sports equipment, clothing, watches and eyewear. When the supply chains are global and the products are fashion-oriented the management of logistics becomes a key determinant of business success or failure.

References
1. Seth, Andrew (1998), 'Just Doing it', *Marketing Business*, February 1998.
2. Business Wire, 'Nike Equipment Signs up Manlo Logistics to Manage Distribution Centres in North America, Europe', *Business Wire/Reuter Textline*, 5 February 1998.
3. *Far Eastern Economic Review*, 'The Post National Economy: Goodbye Widget, Hello Nike', 29 August 1996, p. 5.

In developing a global logistics strategy a number of issues arise which may require careful consideration. In particular what degree of centralization is appropriate in terms of management, manufacturing and distribution and how can the needs of local markets be met at the same time as the achievement of economies of scale through standardization.

Three of the ways in which businesses have sought to implement their global logistics strategies have been through focused factories, centralized inventories and postponement. These are looked at in more detail below.

1 Focused factories

The idea behind the focused factory is simple: by limiting the range and mix of products manufactured in a single location the company can achieve considerable economies of scale. Typically the nationally oriented business will have 'local-for-local' production, meaning that each country factory will produce the full range of products for sale in that country. On the other hand the global business will treat the world market as one market and will rationalize its production so that the remaining factories produce fewer products in volumes capable of satisfying perhaps the entire market.

One company that has moved in this direction is Mars. Their policy has been to simultaneously rationalize production capacity by seeking to manage demand as a whole on at least a regional level and to concentrate production by category, factory by factory. Hence their M&M's for sale in Moscow are likely to have been produced in the United States. In a similar fashion, Heinz produce tomato ketchup for all of Europe from just three plants and will switch production depending upon how local costs and demand conditions vary against exchange rate fluctuations. A further example is provided by Procter & Gamble who manufacture their successful product 'Pringles' in just two plants to meet worldwide demand.

Such strategies can be expected to become widespread as 'global thinking' becomes dominant.

However a number of crucial logistics trade-offs may be overlooked in what might possibly be a too-hasty search for low cost producer status through greater economies of scale. The most obvious trade-off is the effect on transport costs and delivery lead times. The costs of shipping products, often of relatively low value, across greater distances may erode some or all of the production cost saving. Similarly the longer lead times involved may need to be countered by local stockholding, again possibly offsetting the production cost advantage.

Further problems of focused production may be encountered where the need for local packs exists, e.g. with labelling in different languages or even different brand names and packages for the same product. This problem might be overcome by 'postponing' the final packaging until closer to the point of sale.

Another issue is that created by customers ordering a variety of products from the same company on a single order but which are now produced in a number of focused factories in different locations. The solution here may be some type of transhipment or cross-dock operation where flows of goods from diverse localities and origins are merged for onward delivery to the customer.

Finally what will be the impact on production flexibility of the trend towards focused factories where volume and economies of scale rule the day? Whilst these things are not necessarily mutually incompatible it is possible that organizations that put low cost production at the top of their list of priorities may be at risk in markets where responsiveness and the ability to provide 'variety' are key success factors.

In response to these issues a number of companies are questioning decisions that previously were thought sound. For example one of Europe's leading computer companies, ICL (now owned by Fujitsu), has reviewed its earlier strategy of Far East sourcing of commodity components because it believes that manufacturing cost gains are not sufficient to overcome the high transportation and inventory costs and the longer lead times that this entails.[3] Other high-tech companies are also looking again at their offshore production and sourcing strategies for this same reason. Typically less than 10 per cent of a high-tech company's costs are direct labour. Hence the decision to source offshore, simply to save on labour costs, makes little sense if penalties are incurred elsewhere in the supply chain.

All in all it would appear that the total logistics impact of focused production will be complex and significant. To ensure that decisions are taken which are not sub-optimal it will become even more important to undertake detailed analysis based upon total system modelling and simulation prior to making commitments that may later be regretted.

▪ Centralized logistics at Lever Europe ▪

Lever, part of the global corporation Unilever, manufacture and market a wide range of soaps, detergents and cleaners. As part of a drive to implement a European strategy for manufacturing and the supply chain they created a centralized manufacturing and supply chain management structure – Lever Europe. A key part of this strategy involved a rationalization of their production facilities from a total of 16 across Western Europe to 11. The remaining facilities became 'focused factories', each one concentrating on certain product families. So, for example, most bar soaps for Europe are now made at Port Sunlight in England; Mannheim in Germany makes all the Dove soap products, not just for Europe but for much of the rest of the world; France focuses on machine dishwasher products and so on.

Because national markets are now supplied from many different European sources they have retained distribution facilities in each country to act as a local consolidation centre for final delivery to customers.

Whilst some significant production cost savings have been achieved, a certain amount of flexibility has been lost. There is still a high level of variation in requirement by individual market. Many countries sell the same product but under different brand names, the languages are different hence the need for local packs, and sometimes the formulations also differ.

A further concern is that as retailers become more demanding in the delivery service they require and as the trend towards Efficient Consumer Response (ECR) and just-in-time deliveries grows, the loss of flexibility becomes a problem. Even though manufacturing economies of scale are welcome, it has to be recognized that the achievement of these cost benefits may be more than offset by the loss of flexibility and responsiveness in the supply chain as a whole.

---

2 Centralization of inventories

In the same way that the advent of globalization has encouraged companies to rationalize production into fewer locations so too has it led to a trend towards the centralization of inventories. Making use of the well-known statistical fact that consolidating inventory into fewer locations can substantially reduce total inventory requirement, organizations have been steadily closing national warehouses and amalgamating them into regional distribution centres (RDCs) serving a much wider geographical area.

For example, Philips has reduced its consumer electronics products warehouses in Western Europe from 22 to just four. Likewise Apple

Computers replaced their 13 national warehouses with two European RDCs. Similar examples can be found in just about every industry.

Whilst the logic of centralization is sound, it is becoming increasingly recognized that there may be even greater gains to be had by not physically centralizing the inventory but rather by locating it strategically near the customer or the point of production but managing and controlling it centrally. This is the idea of 'virtual' or 'electronic' inventory. The idea is that by the use of information the organization can achieve the same stock reduction that it would achieve through centralization whilst retaining a greater flexibility by localizing inventory. At the same time the penalties of centralizing physical stock holdings are reduced, i.e. double handling, higher transport charges and possibly longer total pipelines.

One of the arguments for centralized inventory is that advantage can be taken of the 'square root rule'.[4] Whilst an approximation, this rule of thumb provides an indication of the opportunity for inventory reduction that is possible through holding inventory in fewer locations. The rule states that the reduction in total system inventory that can be expected is proportional to the square root of the number of stock locations before and after rationalization. Thus if previously there were 25 stock locations and now there are only four then the overall reduction in inventory would be in the ratio of $\sqrt{25}$ to $\sqrt{4}$ or 5:2, i.e. a 60% reduction.

Many organizations are now recognizing the advantage of managing worldwide inventories on a centralized basis. To do so successfully however requires an information system that can provide complete visibility of demand from one end of the pipeline to another in as close to real time as possible. Equally such centralized systems will typically lead to higher transport costs in that products inevitably have to move greater distances and often high cost air express will be necessary to ensure short lead times for delivery to customer.

Xerox in its management of its European spares business has demonstrated how great benefits can be derived by centralizing the control of inventory and by using information systems and, in so doing, enabling a much higher service to its engineers to be provided but with only half the total inventory! SKF is another company that for 15 years or more has been driving down its European inventory of bearings whilst still improving service to its customers. Again, the means to this remarkable achievement has been through a centralized information system.

3 Postponement and localization

Although the trend to global brands and products continues, it should be recognized that there are still significant local differences in customer and consumer requirements. Even within a relatively compact market like Western Europe there are major differences in consumer tastes and, of course, languages. Hence there are a large number of markets where standard, global products would not be successful. Take for example the differences in preference for domestic appliances such as refrigerators and washing machines. Northern Europeans prefer larger refrigerators because they shop once a week rather than daily, whilst Southern Europeans, shopping more frequently, prefer smaller ones. Similarly, Britons consume more frozen foods than most other European countries and thus require more freezer space.

> Although the trend to global brands and products continues, it should be recognized that there are still significant local differences in customer and consumer requirements.

In the case of washing machines, there are differences in preference for top-loading versus front-loading machines – in the United Kingdom almost all the machines purchased are front loaders whilst in France the reverse is true.

How is it possible to reconcile the need to meet local requirements whilst seeking to organize logistics on a global basis? Ideally organizations would like to achieve the benefits of standardization in terms of cost reduction whilst maximizing their marketing success through localization.

One strategy that is increasingly being adopted is the idea of *postponement*. Postponement, or delayed configuration, is based on the principle of seeking to design products using common platforms, components or modules but where the final assembly or customization does not take place until the final market destination and/or customer requirement is known.

The advantages of the strategy of postponement are several. Firstly inventory can be held at a generic level so that there will be fewer stock-keeping variants and hence less inventory in total. Secondly, because the inventory is generic, its flexibility is greater, meaning that the same components, modules or platforms can be embodied in a variety of end products. Thirdly, forecasting is easier at the generic level than at the level of the finished item. This last point is particularly relevant in global markets where local forecasts will be less accurate

136

than a forecast for worldwide volume. Furthermore the ability to customize products locally means that a higher level of variety may be offered at lower total cost – this is the principle of 'mass-customization'.

To take full advantage of the possibilities offered by postponement often requires a 'design for localization' philosophy. Products and processes must be designed and engineered in such a way that semi-finished products can be assembled, configured and finished to provide the highest level of variety to customers based upon the smallest number of standard modules or components. In many cases the final finishing will take place in the local market, perhaps at a distribution centre and, increasingly, the physical activity out-sourced to a third party logistics service provider.

The challenge of global logistics

Clearly managing a global network of materials and information flows is not only more complex than managing a purely national logistics system, but it also involves some specific, additional considerations.

Four factors can be identified which are critically important to global supply chains as against those with smaller horizons. These factors exist in the planning of all supply chains but are relatively more dominant in terms of mix and extent in a global context; they create the need for different solutions. The factors are as follows.

Extended lead times of supply

The consolidation of global production into a single or a limited number of manufacturing sites creates contention in terms of the demands of the various markets, possibly requiring local product variations. Manufacturing management have tended to impose long lead times under the misguided assumption that long lead times provide a buffer against the competing demands of different customers. Leading edge practice shows that the imposition of long manufacturing lead times is a largely artificial constraint. In many cases it should be possible to make to order on very short timescales for specific customers in contrast to supplying from inventory.

It is also normally essential for the global chain to hold a level of intermediate inventory between manufacturing and the customer to buffer against extended transit times. However, if the size of the buffer reflects inflexibility in manufacturing or poor materials management procedures, then the need for facilities and stock holding in specific markets may well be suspect.

Extended and unreliable transit times

In Europe we have become accustomed to lengthy transit times for shipments from and to the Far East, Australia and the United States. Sea freight from Japan has a transit time to Rotterdam of about five weeks. In contrast the total elapsed time from despatch to receipt of air freight is about five days. The use of sea freight can represent considerable investment in inventory on the high seas; it also seriously constrains the application of the basic logistics principle of postponement: i.e. delay shipping decisions until the last possible moment.

Increasingly it is the case that as true supply chain costs become more clearly understood the use of air freight is growing. Such are the penalties of high inventories and inflexible response to marketplace needs that the trade-off will increasingly swing towards shorter transit times and hence swifter transit modes.

Shipping, consolidation and customs clearance all contribute to delays and variability in the lead time of global supply chains. This is well documented[5] and is highlighted in Figure 5.2. Experience confirms this as a major issue for most companies operating globally. It has the consequence that local managers tend to compensate for this unreliability by over-ordering, double buffering, and applying competitive pressure on manufacturing and the central allocation organization.

	Depart Far East	Arrive N'lands	Arrive de-groupage centre	Arrive central w/house	Booking in system	∑ of all segments
Maximum	6	1	5	3	7	22
Average	4.5	1	2.3	1.4	2.4	11.6
Minimum	3	1	1	0	1	6
Variation						16

Fig. 5.2 Pipeline lead times (calendar days)

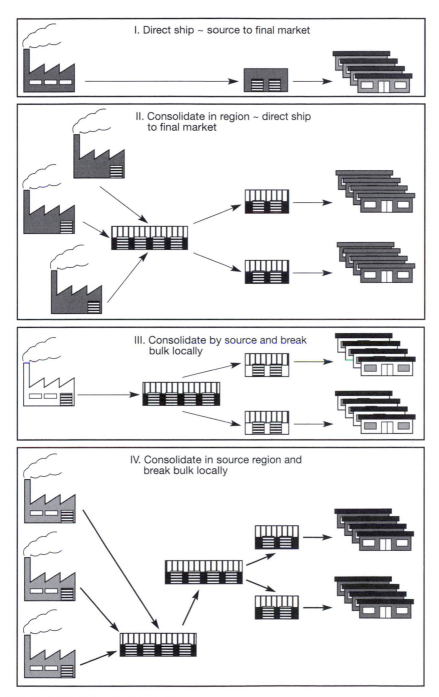

Fig. 5.3 Global shipping options

Multiple consolidation and break bulk options

The options for the management of international freight are several and the trade-offs will be complex and may vary for different product/ market channels. Figure 5.3 shows the European options for shipment from the Far East from multiple source points for different products. They can be summarized under four main headings:

- Direct ship from each source to final market in full containers.
- Consolidate in the supply region for final market in full containers.
- Consolidate from each source for each theatre of operation with break bulk/intermediate inventory in the theatre for specific markets.
- Consolidate in the supply region and also break bulk in the theatre of operations.

Obviously the inventory holding, warehousing, customer service and freight costs balance will be different for each of these and will be determined by the characteristics of the product and the profile of demand.

Multiple freight mode and cost options

The mix of freight methods which may be practical in the context of the required lead time must be overlaid on the point above. Shipping companies offer mixed sea/air services, different container sizes, scheduled and unscheduled services. As previously observed the extended lead times involved in long sea passages are forcing companies to use air freight to an extent which appears costly but which, in the context of inventory holding costs, potential lost revenue and market flexibility, may be a worthwhile expense.

Negotiating through the maze of freight options is a highly specialized skill; as is persuading a company to spend apparently more on one mode versus another. An increasingly attractive option is the use of 'door-to-door' transport providers, or the so-called 'integrators' of which DHL is probably the current market leader, with companies like Federal Express, TNT and UPS also very active. The benefits that door-to-door can provide are typically in the form of shorter and more reliable transit times, swifter and less complex procedures for customs clearance and, usually, a worldwide tracking and tracing system.

In the context of global logistics the transportation management function needs to broaden to include responsibility for pipeline management and, in particular, end-to-end lead times. In the past it was often the case that the lead times for international logistics flows were poorly managed. Partly this was due to a fragmentation of control, so that many key decisions would be taken independently, by 'export departments', 'shipping departments' and external agencies such as freight forwarders. The emergence of international logistics service companies, such as Ocean or P&O Global Logistics is a response to the need for a totally co-ordinated and fully integrated approach to pipeline management.

A further problem with the conventionally organized international business is that if transport decisions are taken purely on the basis of costs – as they frequently are – then this will tend to lead to sub-optimal decisions in many cases. One such example is an international electronics company that sought to reduce its air freight costs on components moving from the Far East into Europe. It consolidated container loads in Singapore to achieve lower transportation costs per unit, but in doing so it produced considerably greater variability in lead times since the time taken to fill a consolidated container and then to procure space on a cargo flight varied considerably. The alternative solution was to use a 'door-to-door' integrated logistics solution through a company such as DHL or Federal Express. Whilst the per unit transport costs were obviously higher, the total logistics costs were lower (because of the reduced requirement for inventory at either end of the pipeline and because of the greatly reduced end-to-end lead time). At the same time variability in the lead time of supply was dramatically reduced.

Organizing for global logistics

As companies have extended their supply chains internationally they have been forced to confront the issue of how to structure their global logistics organization. In their different ways these companies have moved towards the same conclusion: effectiveness in global logistics can only be achieved through a greater element of centralization. This in many respects runs counter to much of the conventional wisdom which tends to argue that decision-making responsibility should be devolved and decentralized at least to the strategic business unit level. This philosophy has manifested itself in many companies in the form of strong local management, often with autonomous decision making at the country level. Good though this may be for encouraging local initiatives, it tends to be dysfunctional when integrated global strategies are required.

Clearly there will still be many areas where local decision making will be preferable, for example sales strategy and, possibly, promotional and marketing communications strategy. Likewise the implementation of global strategy can still be adjusted to take account of national differences and requirements.

How then can the appropriate balance of global versus local decision making be achieved in formulating and implementing logistics strategy?

Because specific market environments and industry characteristics will differ from company to company it is dangerous to offer all-embracing solutions. However a number of general principles are beginning to emerge:

- The strategic structuring and overall control of logistics flows must be centralized to achieve worldwide optimization of costs.
- The control and management of customer service must be localized against the requirements of specific markets to ensure competitive advantage is gained and maintained.
- As the trend towards out-sourcing everything except core competencies increases then so does the need for global co-ordination.
- A global logistics information system is the pre-requisite for enabling the achievement of local service needs whilst seeking global cost optimization.

1 Structure and control

If the potential trade-offs in rationalizing sourcing, production and distribution across national boundaries are to be achieved then it is essential that a central decision-making structure for logistics is established. Many companies that are active on an international basis find that they are constrained in their search for global optimization by strongly entrenched local systems and structures. Only through centralized planning and co-ordination of logistics can the organization hope to achieve the twin goals of cost minimization and service maximization.

> If the potential trade-offs in rationalizing sourcing, production and distribution across national boundaries are to be achieved then it is essential that a central decision-making structure for logistics is established.

For example location decisions are a basic determinant of profitability in international logistics. The decision on where to manufacture, to assemble, to store, to transship and to consolidate can make the difference between profit and loss. Because of international differences in basic factor costs and because of exchange rate movements, location decisions are fundamental. Also these decisions tend to involve investment in fixed assets in the form of facilities and equipment. Decisions taken today can therefore have a continuing impact over time on the company's financial and competitive position.

As the trend towards global manufacturing continues, organizations will increasingly need to look at location decisions through total cost analysis. The requirement there is for improved access to activity-related costs such as manufacturing, transportation and handling. Accurate information on inventory holding costs and the cost/benefit of postponement also becomes a key variable in location decisions.

The opportunities for reducing costs and improving throughput efficiency by a reappraisal of the global logistics network, and in particular manufacturing and inventory locations, can be substantial. By their very nature, decisions on location in a global network can only be taken centrally.

2 Customer service management

Because local markets have their own specific characteristics and needs there is considerable advantage to be achieved by shaping marketing strategies locally – albeit within overall global guidelines. This is particularly true of customer service management where the opportunities for tailoring service against individual customer requirements are great. The management of customer service involves the monitoring of service needs as well as performance and extends to the management of the entire order fulfilment process – from order through delivery. Whilst order fulfilment systems are increasingly global and centrally managed there will always remain the need to have strong local customer service management.

3 Out-sourcing and partnerships

As we have previously noted, one of the greatest changes in the global business today is the trend towards out-sourcing. Not just out-sourcing the procurement of materials and components but also out-sourcing of services that traditionally have been provided in-house. The logic of this trend is that the organization will increasingly focus on those activities in the value chain where it has a distinctive advantage – the core competencies of the business – and everything else it will out-source. This movement has been particularly evident in logistics where the provision of transport, warehousing and inventory control is increasingly subcontracted to specialists or logistics partners.

To manage and control this network of partners and suppliers requires a blend of both central and local involvement. The argument once again is that the strategic decisions need to be taken centrally with the monitoring and control of supplier performance and day-to-day liaison with logistics partners being best managed at a local level.

4 Logistics information

The management of global logistics is in reality the management of information flows. The information system is the mechanism whereby the complex flows of materials, parts, subassemblies and finished products can be co-ordinated to achieve cost-effective service. Any organization with aspirations to global leadership is dependent upon the visibility it can gain of materials flows, inventories and demand throughout the pipeline. Without the ability to see down the pipeline into end user markets, to read actual demand and subsequently to manage replenishment in virtual real-time the system is doomed to depend upon inventory. To 'substitute information for inventory' has become something of a cliché but it should be a prime objective nevertheless. Time lapses in information flows are directly translated into inventory. The great advances that are being made in introducing 'quick response' logistics systems are all based upon information flow from the point of actual demand directly into the supplier's logistics and replenishment systems. On a global scale we typically find that the presence of intervening inventories between the plant and the

144

marketplace obscure the view of real demand. Hence the need for information systems which can read demand at every level in the pipeline and provide the driving power for a centrally controlled logistics system.

The future

The implementation of global pipeline control is highly dependent upon the ability of the organization to find the correct balance between central control and local management. It is unwise to be too prescriptive but the experience that global organizations are gaining every day suggests that certain tasks and functions lend themselves to central control and others to local management. Table 5.1 summarizes some of the possibilities.

Table 5.1 Global co-ordination and local management

Global	Local
● Network structuring for production and transportation optimization	● Customer service management
● Information systems development and control	● Gathering market intelligence
● Inventory positioning	● Warehouse management and local delivery
● Sourcing decisions	● Customer profitability analyses
● International transport mode and sourcing decisions	● Liaison with local sales and marketing management
● Trade-off analyses and supply chain cost control	● Human resource management

Much has been learned in the last ten years or so about the opportunities for cost and service enhancement through better management of logistics at a national level. Now organizations are faced with applying those lessons on a much broader stage. As international competition becomes more intense and as national barriers to trade gradually reduce, the era of the global business has arrived. Increasingly the difference between success and failure in the global marketplace will be determined not by the sophistication of product technology or even of marketing communications, but rather by the way in which we manage and control the global logistics pipeline.

Summary

For the last decade or so the continued trend towards the globalization of business has been evident. Markets have become global in the sense that the same brands and products are increasingly offered for sale around the world. Equally apparent has been the move towards global sourcing and manufacturing as companies concentrate their operations so that often just one or two factories serve the whole world.

Paradoxically the trend to globalization has increased the complexity of logistics. Often pipelines are longer with greater reliance on out-sourced supply chain partners. Furthermore local differences in requirements still exist so the the needs of local markets must be balanced against the economic advantages of standardized products. Thus the challenge to global logistics management is to structure a supply chain that is agile and flexible enough to cope with differences in customer requirements and yet can enable the benefits of focused manufacturing to be realized.

References

1. The Hollow Corporation, *Business Week*, 3 March 1986.
2. Levitt, T., 'The Globalization of Markets', *Harvard Business Review*, Vol 61, May–June 1983.
3. Roberts, J., 'Formulating and Implementing a Global Logistics Strategy', *International Journal of Logistics Management*, Vol 1, No 2, 1990.
4. Sussams, J.E., 'Buffer Stocks and the Square Root Law', *Focus*, Institute of Logistics, U.K., Vol 5, No 5, 1986.
5. Ploos van Amstel, M.J., 'Managing the Pipeline Effectively', *Journal of Business Logistics*, Vol 11, No 1, 1990.

Strategic lead-time management

This chapter:

Explores the 'cost-of-time' and the drivers of time-based competition: shortening product life cycles, customers' desire for reduced inventories and the dangers of being forecast dependent in an increasingly volatile marketplace.

●

Examines the concept of lead time, the order-to-delivery cycle, its components and the need to consider the wider context of the order-to-cash cycle.

●

Looks at how the reduction of lead times can impact on the goals of logistics pipeline management.

●

Outlines some of the ways in which inadequate system design can lengthen lead times and engineer costs rather than value into the logistics process.

●

Introduces the concept of the lead-time gap, offering a number of suggestions for lead times.

'Time is money' is perhaps an over-worked cliché in common parlance, but in logistics management it goes to the heart of the matter. Not only does time represent cost to the logistics manager but extended lead times also imply a customer service penalty. As far as cost is concerned there is a direct relationship between the length of the logistics pipeline and the inventory that is locked up in it; every day that the product is in the pipeline it incurs an inventory holding cost. Secondly, long lead times mean a slower response to customer requirements, and, given the increased importance of delivery speed in today's internationally competitive environment, this combination of high costs and lack of responsiveness provides a recipe for decline and decay.

Time-based competition

Customers in all markets, industrial or consumer, are increasingly time-sensitive. In other words they value time and this is reflected in their purchasing behaviour. Thus, for example, in industrial markets buyers tend to source from suppliers with the shortest lead times who can meet their quality specification. In consumer markets customers make their choice from amongst the brands available at the time; hence if the preferred brand is out of stock it is quite likely that a substitute brand will be purchased instead.

> **Customers in all markets, industrial or consumer, are increasingly time-sensitive.**

In the past it was often the case that price was paramount as an influence on the purchase decision. Now, whilst price is still important, a major determinant of choice of supplier or brand is the 'cost of time'. The cost of time is simply the additional costs that a customer must bear whilst waiting for delivery or whilst seeking out alternatives.

To the supplier who fails to recognize the importance of time as a competitive variable or whose systems cannot meet the needs of fast-changing markets, the cost can be considerable. In 1994 Compaq Computers, the world's leading manufacturer of personal computers (PCs), estimated that it had lost between $500m and $1bn in sales that year because of stock-outs on its laptop and desktop computers.[1]

Conversely, throughout the 1990s the Laura Ashley retail chain suffered severe financial pressure as a result of supply chain failures where paradoxically the company often had too much inventory at the wrong locations and times leading to significant mark-downs in price.

It is not just in high technology and fashion markets where the importance of timing is paramount. Amongst the many pressures leading to the growth of time-sensitive markets are:

1. Shortening life cycles
2. Customers' drive for reduced inventories
3. Volatile markets making reliance on forecasts dangerous

1 Shortening life cycles

The concept of the product life cycle is well established. It suggests that for many products there is a recognizable pattern of sales from launch through to final decline (see Figure 6.1).

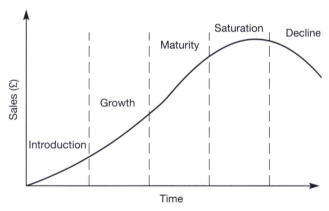

Fig. 6.1 The product life cycle

A feature of the last few decades has been the shortening of these life cycles. Take as an example the case of the typewriter. The early mechanical typewriter had a life cycle of about 30 years – meaning that an individual model would be little changed during that period. These mechanical typewriters were replaced by the electro-mechanical typewriter which had a life cycle of approximately 10 years. The electro-mechanical typewriter gave way to the electronic typewriter with a four-year life cycle. Now word-processors have taken over with a life cycle of one year or less!

In situations like this the time available to develop new products, to launch them and to meet marketplace demand is clearly greatly reduced. Hence the ability to 'fast track' product development, manufacturing and logistics becomes a key element of competitive strategy. Figure 6.2 shows the effect of being late into the market and slow to meet demand.

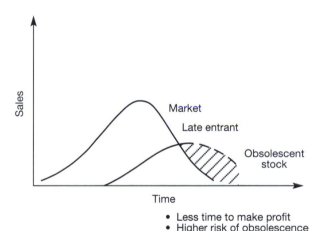

Fig. 6.2 Shorter life cycles make timing crucial

However it is not just time-to-market that is important. Once a product is on the market the ability to respond quickly to demand is equally important. Here the lead time to resupply a market determines the organization's ability to exploit demand during the life cycle. In Chapter 7 we discuss the mechanisms of 'quick response' logistics in detail, but it will be apparent that those companies that can achieve reductions in the order-to-delivery cycle will have a strong advantage over their slower competitors.

2 Customers' drive for reduced inventories

One of the most pronounced phenomena of recent years has been the almost universal move by companies to reduce their inventories.

Whether the inventory is in the form of raw materials, components, work-in-progress or finished products, the pressure has been to release the capital locked up in stock and hence simultaneously to reduce the holding cost of that stock. The same companies that have reduced their inventories in this way have also recognized the advantage that they gain in terms of improved flexibility and responsiveness to their customers.

The knock-on effect of this development upstream to suppliers has been considerable. It is now imperative that suppliers can provide a just-in-time delivery service. Timeliness of delivery – meaning delivery of the complete order at the time required by the customer – becomes the number one order-winning criterion.

Many companies still think that the only way to service customers who require just-in-time deliveries is for them, the supplier, to carry the inventory instead of the customer. Whilst the requirements of such customers could always be met by the supplier carrying inventory close to the customer(s), this is simply shifting the cost burden from one part of the supply chain to another – indeed the cost may even be higher. Instead what is needed is for the supplier to substitute responsiveness for inventory whenever possible.

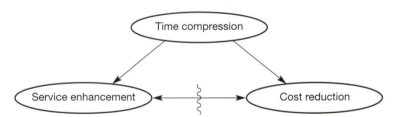

Fig. 6.3 Breaking free of the classic service/cost trade-off

Responsiveness essentially is achieved through time compression in the supply chain. Not only can customers be serviced more rapidly but the degree of flexibility offered can be greater and, furthermore, the cost should be less because the pipeline is shorter. Figure 6.3 suggests that time compression can enable companies to break free of the classic trade-off between service and cost. Instead of having to choose between either higher service levels or lower costs it is possible to have the best of both worlds.

■ 'Time as a source of differentiation' ■

Reinhold Messner, the Italian climber, is one of the great sports heroes of Europe. His claim to fame is not so much that he has climbed all 14 of the world's highest peaks, although no one else has ever accomplished that feat. Messner's primary achievement is that he introduced a totally new way of climbing – the direct alpine approach – which uses little equipment and no oxygen support to reach the top.

Conventional mountaineering strategy is based on massive amounts of support, including extra oxygen, thought essential for climbs over 25,000 feet. Men such as Sir Edmund Hillary and Chris Bonington relied on hundreds of guides who carried food, oxygen and other supplies; an American expedition to climb Everest in 1963 included 900 porters laboriously trudging up the mountain with 300 tonnes of equipment.

Messner argues that under this strategy, the slowest man sets the pace. His goal is speed of execution. Although assisted by guides up the base of the mountain, Messner usually makes the final assault by himself, or with one other person, in a single day. He scaled the north face of Everest solo, without oxygen.

The similarities between mountain climbing strategy before Messner and corporate strategy today are becoming increasingly evident. Most companies' strategies are burdened with undue complexity and an excess of outmoded gear. They are bogged down in principles that produce look-alike responses to competition.

Source: Bleeke, A. Joel, 'Peak Strategies', *McKinsey Quarterly*, Spring 1989

---

3 Volatile markets make reliance on forecasts dangerous

A continuing problem for most organizations is the inaccuracy of forecasts. It seems that no matter how sophisticated the forecasting techniques employed, the volatility of markets ensures that the forecast will be wrong! Whilst many forecasting errors are the result of inappropriate forecasting methodology the root cause of these problems is that forecast error increases as lead time increases.

The evidence from most markets is that demand volatility is tending to increase, often due to competitive activity, sometimes due to unexpected responses to promotions or price changes and as a result of intermediaries' re-ordering policies. In situations such as these there are very few forecasting methods that will be able to predict short-term changes in demand with any accuracy.

All forecasts are prone to error and the further ahead the forecast horizon is the greater the error. Figure 6.4 shows how forecast error increases more than proportionately over time.

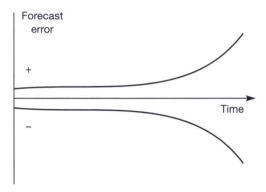

Fig. 6.4 Forecast error and planning horizons

The conventional response to such a problem has been to increase the safety stock to provide protection against such forecast errors. However it is surely preferable to reduce lead times in order to reduce forecast error and hence reduce the need for inventory. If shorter lead times are the route to more effective competitiveness how might lead-time reduction be achieved?

■ Breaking the planning loop ■

Companies are systems; time connects all the parts. The most powerful competitors understand this axiom and are breaking the debilitating loop that strangles much of traditional manufacturing planning.

Traditional manufacturing requires long lead times to resolve conflicts between various jobs or activities that require the same resources. The long lead times, in turn, require sales forecasts to guide planning. But sales forecasts are inevitably wrong; by definition they are guesses, however informed. Naturally, as lead times lengthen, the accuracy of sales forecasts declines. With more forecasting errors inventories balloon and the need for safety stocks at all levels increases. Errors in forecasting also mean more unscheduled jobs that have to be expedited, thereby crowding out scheduled jobs. The need for longer lead times grows even greater and the planning loop expands even more, driving up costs, increasing delays, and creating system inefficiencies.

Managers who find themselves trapped in the planning loop often respond by asking for better forecasts and longer lead times. In other words, they treat the symptoms and worsen the problem. The only way to break the planning loop is to reduce the consumption of time throughout the system; that will, in turn, cut the need for lead time, for estimates, for safety stocks, and all the rest. After all, if a company could ever drive its lead time all the way to zero, it would have to forecast only the next day's sales. While that idea, of course, is unrealistic, successful time-based competitors in Japan and in the West have kept their lead times from growing and some have even reduced them, thereby diminishing the planning loop's damaging effects.

One approach to time-based competition in a fashion market is illustrated by the Zara Case Study.

ZARA: Time-based competition in a fashion market

Zara is one of Spain's most successful and dynamic apparel companies, producing fashionable clothing to appeal to an international target market of 18–35 year-olds. In the twenty or so years since the company was founded it has established sizeable production facilities in Spain, purchasing operations in Southeast Asia and the Caribbean, a finance holding company in the Netherlands and around 200 company-owned retail outlets in Europe and the Americas.

Zara's international market positioning places it in direct competition with some of the most skilled operators in the business, including Italian fashion giant Benetton and US-based The Gap and The Limited. Its rapid growth and ongoing success in such a fiercely competitive environment is in fact a testament to its ability to implement its own operating strategy – based on the dual objectives of working without stocks and responding quickly to market needs[1] – as well as, or even more effectively than, its internationally acclaimed rivals. The pursuit of these dual objectives has led Zara to develop one of the most effective quick-response systems in its industry.

▶

155

▶ The whole process of supplying goods to the stores begins with the cross-functional teams – comprising fashion, commercial and retail specialists – working within Zara's Design Department at the company's headquarters in La Coruña. The designs reflect the latest in international fashion trends, with inspiration gleaned through visits to fashion shows, competitors' stores, university campuses, pubs, cafes and clubs, plus any other venues or events deemed to be relevant to the lifestyles of the target customers. The team's understanding of directional fashion trends is further guided by regular inflows of EPOS data and other information from all of the companies' stores and sites around the world.

Fashion specialists within the Design Department are responsible for the initial designs, fabric selection and choice of prints and colours. It is then up to the team's commercial management specialists to ascertain the likely commercial viability of the items proposed. If the design is accepted, the commercial specialists proceed to negotiate with suppliers, agree purchase prices, analyze costs and margins, and fix a standard cross-currency price position for the garment. The size of the production run – i.e. the number of garments required – and launch dates (the latter vary between countries in accordance with custom and climate) are also determined at this point.

Raw materials are procured through the company's buying offices in the United Kingdom, China and the Netherlands, with most of the materials themselves coming in from Mauritius, New Zealand, Australia, Morocco, China, India, Turkey, Korea, Italy and Germany. This global sourcing policy using a broad supplier base provides the widest possible selection of fashion fabrics, while reducing the risk of dependence on any source or supplier. Approximately 40 per cent of garments – those with the broadest and least transient appeal – are imported as finished goods from low-cost manufacturing centres in the Far East. The rest are produced by quick-response in Spain, using Zara's own highly automated factories and a network of smaller contractors.

Zara's manufacturing systems are similar in many ways to those developed and employed so successfully by Benetton in Northern Italy, but refined using ideas developed in conjunction with Toyota. Only those operations which enhance cost-efficiency through economies of scale are conducted in-house (such as dyeing, cutting, labelling and packaging). All other manufacturing activities, including the labour-intensive finishing stages, are completed by networks of more than 300 small subcontractors, each specializing in one particular part of the production process or garment type. These subcontractors work exclusively for Zara's parent, Inditex SA. In return they receive the necessary technological, financial and logistical support required to achieve stringent time and quality targets. Inventory costs are kept to a minimum because Zara pays only for the completed garments. The system is flexible enough to cope with sudden changes in demand, though production is always kept at a level slightly below expected sales, to keep stock moving. Zara has opted for undersupply, viewing it as a lesser evil than holding slow-moving or obsolete stock.

Finished goods are forwarded to the company's huge distribution centre in La Coruña, where they are labelled, price-tagged (all items carry international price-tags showing the price in all relevant currencies) and packed. From there they travel by third-party contractors by road and/or air to their penultimate destinations. The shops themselves receive deliveries of new stock on a twice weekly basis, according to shop-by-shop stock allocations calculated by the Design Department. The whole production cycle takes only two weeks. In an industry where lead times of many months are still the norm, Zara has reduced its lead-time gap for more than half of the garments it sells to a level unmatched by any of its European or North American competitors.

Reference

1. Bonache, Jaime and Cervino, Julio (1997), 'Global Integration Without Expatriates', *Human Resource Management Journal*, Vol 7, No 3, pp. 89–100.

The concept of lead time

From the customer's viewpoint there is only one lead time: the elapsed time from order to delivery. Clearly this is a crucial competitive variable as more and more markets become increasingly time competitive. Nevertheless it represents only a partial view of lead time. Just as important, from the supplier's perspective, is the time it takes to convert an order into cash and, indeed, the total time that working capital is committed from when materials are first procured through to when the customer's payment is received.

Let us examine each of these lead time concepts in turn.

1 The order-to-delivery cycle

From a marketing point of view the time taken from receipt of a customer's order through to delivery (sometimes referred to as order cycle time (OCT)) is critical. In today's just-in-time environment short lead times are a major source of competitive advantage. Equally important however is the reliability or consistency of that lead time. It can actually be argued that reliability of delivery is more important than the length of the order cycle – at least up to a point – because the impact of a failure to deliver on time is more severe than the need to order further in advance. However, because, as we have seen, long lead times require longer-term forecasts, the pressure from the customer will continue to be for deliveries to be made in ever-shorter time-frames.

What are the components of order cycle time? Figure 6.5 highlights the major elements.

Customer places order	Order entry	Order processing	Order assembly	Transport	Order received

Fig. 6.5 The order cycle

Each of these steps in the chain will consume time. Because of bottlenecks, inefficient processes, and fluctuations in the volume of orders handled there will often be considerable variation in the time taken for these various activities to be completed. The overall effect can lead to a substantial reduction in the reliability of delivery. Figure 6.6 shows the cumulative effect of variations in an order cycle which results in a range of possible cycle times from five days to 25 days.

In those situations where orders are not met from stock but may have to be manufactured, assembled or sourced from external vendors, then clearly lead times will be even further extended with the possibility of still greater variations in total order-to-delivery time. Figure 6.7 highlights the key activities in such extended lead times.

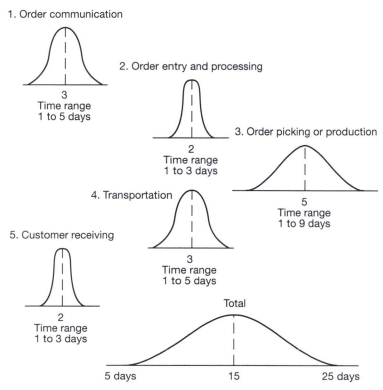

1. Order communication

2. Order entry and processing

3. Order picking or production

4. Transportation

5. Customer receiving

Fig. 6.6 Total order cycle with variability
Source: Stock, J.R. and Lambert, D.M., *Strategic Logistics Management*, 2nd Edition, Irwin 1987

2 The cash-to-cash cycle

As we have already observed, a basic concern of any organization is: How long does it take to convert an order into cash? In reality the issue is not just how long it takes to process orders, raise invoices and receive payment, but also how long is the pipeline from the sourcing of raw material through to the finished product because throughout the pipeline, resources are being consumed and working capital needs to be financed.

From the moment when decisions are taken on the sourcing and procurement of materials and components, through the manufacturing and assembly process to final distribution and after-market support, time is being consumed. That time is represented by the number of days of inventory in the pipeline, whether as raw materials, work-in-progress, goods in transit, or time taken to process orders, issue replenishment orders, as well as time spent in manufacturing, time in queues or bottle-

159

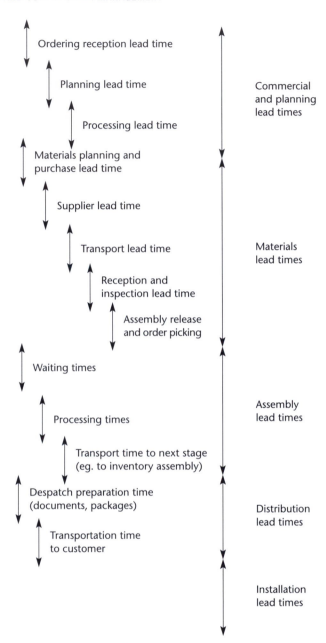

Fig. 6.7 Lead-time components

necks and so on. The control of this total pipeline is the true scope of logistics lead-time management. Figure 6.8 illustrates the way in which cumulative lead time builds up from procurement through to payment.

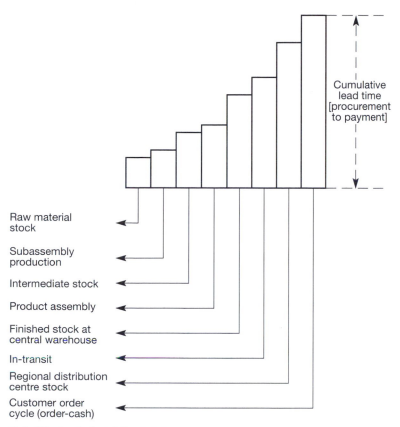

Raw material stock

Subassembly production

Intermediate stock

Product assembly

Finished stock at central warehouse

In-transit

Regional distribution centre stock

Customer order cycle (order-cash)

Fig. 6.8 Strategic lead-time management

As we shall see later in this chapter, the longer the pipeline from source of materials to the final user the less responsive to changes in demand the system will be. It is also the case that longer pipelines obscure the 'visibility' of end demand so that it is difficult to link manufacturing and procurement decisions to marketplace requirements. Thus we find an inevitable build-up of inventory as a buffer at each step along the supply chain. An approximate rule of thumb suggests that the amount of safety stock in a pipeline varies with the square root of the pipeline length.

> The longer the pipeline from source of materials to the final user the less responsive to changes in demand the system will be.

Overcoming these problems and ensuring timely response to volatile demand requires a new and fundamentally different approach to the management of lead times.[2]

Logistics pipeline management

The key to the successful control of logistics lead times is pipeline management. Pipeline management is the process whereby manufacturing and procurement lead times are linked to the needs of the marketplace. At the same time, pipeline management seeks to meet the competitive challenge of increasing the speed of response to those market needs.

The goals of logistics pipeline management are:

- Lower costs
- Higher quality
- More flexibility
- Faster response times

The achievement of these goals is dependent upon managing the supply chain as an entity and seeking to reduce the pipeline length and/or to speed up the flow through that pipeline. In examining the efficiency of supply chains it is often found that many of the activities that take place add more cost than value. For example, moving a pallet into a warehouse, repositioning it, storing it and then moving it out, in all likelihood has added no value but has added considerably to the total cost. As previously defined in Chapter 4, value-adding activities are those activities that make the product more 'saleable'. Whilst it is inevitable that all activities add cost, it is also the case that only a minority of activities in the logistics pipeline add value. Conversely, a non-value-adding activity is one that can be eliminated with no deterioration of utility to the customer, e.g. performance, functionality, quality and perceived value. In looking at its total order cycle from order to delivery, one firm found that only 10 per cent of the time was spent in value-adding activities – the other 90 per cent actually only added cost. Figure 6.9 shows how cost-adding activities can easily outstrip value-adding activities.

The challenge to pipeline management is to find ways in which the ratio of value-added to cost-added time in the pipeline can be improved. Figure 6.10 graphically shows the goal of strategic lead-time management: to compress the chain in terms of time consumption so that cost-added time is reduced.

Pipeline management is concerned to remove the blockages and the fractures that occur in the pipeline and which lead to inventory build-ups and lengthened response times. The sources of these blockages and

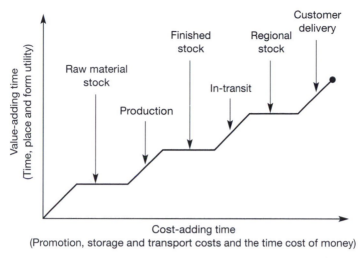

Fig. 6.9 Cost-added versus value-added time

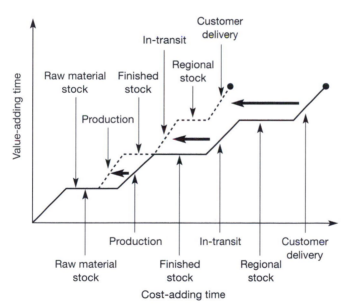

Fig. 6.10 Reducing non-value-adding time improves service and reduces cost

fractures are such things as extended set-up and change-over times, bottlenecks, excessive inventory, sequential order processing and inadequate pipeline visibility.

To achieve improvement in the logistics process requires a focus upon the lead time as a whole, rather than the individual components

163

of that lead time. In particular the interfaces between the components must be examined in detail. These interfaces provide fertile ground for logistics 'value engineering'.

Logistics value engineering

Many businesses have invested heavily in automation in the factory with the aim of reducing throughput times. In some cases processes that used to take days to complete now only take hours and activities that took hours now only take minutes. However it is paradoxical that many of those same businesses that have spent millions of pounds on automation to speed up the time it takes to manufacture a product are then content to let it sit in a distribution centre or warehouse for weeks waiting to be sold! The requirement is to look across the different stages in the supply chain to see how time as a whole can be reduced through reengineering the way the chain is structured.

One of the basic fallacies of management is that long lead times provide security and cover against uncertainty. In fact the reverse is true! Imagine a Utopian situation where a company had reduced its procurement, manufacturing and delivery lead time to zero. In other words as soon as a customer ordered an item – any item – that product was made and delivered instantaneously. In such a situation there would be no need for a forecast and no need for inventory and at the same time a greater variety could be offered to the customer!

Whilst clearly zero lead times are hardly likely to exist in the real world, the target for any organization should be to reduce lead times, at every stage in the logistics pipeline, as close to zero as possible. In so many cases it is possible to find considerable opportunity for total lead-time reduction, often through some very simple changes in procedure. Three examples are given to underline this point.

Example 1: Planning cycle/manufacturing lead time

A fashion retailer that also designs and arranges the manufacture of its garments is accustomed to working on two seasonal cycles per year. Indeed, this is the basis on which most fashion businesses operate with spring/summer and autumn/winter collections.

Its method of operation is to design and specify one season in advance. So for example it would be committing to its autumn sales programme with its suppliers in February or March. This lead time is necessary in order to show the garments and gain their acceptance from the franchisees, as well as 'book' the capacity with its suppliers. When the goods are ready for distribution to the outlets, the unit of dispatch tends to be either threes or sixes by size within a style. The selection of the size of the distribution quantity is made at clerical level without reference to the outlet's capability to sell the garments allocated or the probability of having to distribute a second tranche later in the season. During the selling season, the company is generally unable to respond to styles which have sold especially well by securing more supplies since the workshops are already committed to next season's production. The company is also unable to move garments between outlets to respond to variations in both style and size across the country. The consequence of this method of operation has been that average stock holding is in excess of four months and 60 per cent of all products are sold at a discount in the 'end of season sales'.

The cost of inventory financing and lost profit due to markdown represents nearly 30 per cent of actual turnover and is almost equivalent to the entire annual manufacturing budget. Even a modest improvement in the company's lead-time efficiency would double profits. It is not sufficient to fall back on the excuse that the industry practice cannot be changed: Benetton, the Italian fashion company, have shortened their total cycle to as little as four weeks by the use of integrated lead-time arrangements from the point of demand to the factory.

Example 2: Forecasting and ordering of supplies

A computer company is sourcing its production on a worldwide basis to sell in individual national markets. Factories/suppliers require a six-month 'build plan' to enable components to be sourced and to plan factory loadings. National sales and marketing operations are required to forecast requirements in line with this lead time. Because of the rapidly changing marketplace the individual countries regularly suffer from the twin difficulties of excessive slow moving stock and an inability to service customers with the items they really want. Forecasting accuracy can be less than 50 per cent at the marketing company level and there are constant disputes with factories and suppliers over supply accuracy due to the frequency with which requirements are changed.

The consequence of the situation has been inventories 40 per cent above those which are really necessary, together with an increased risk of technical obsolescence and inventory write-off. There is also a significant level of lost sales due to the inability to supply. The opportunity cost for the current operation was as much as 5 per cent on gross margin.

The lead time to make any substantial changes to the supply programme is four months or more, and with such low forecast accuracy the benefits of changes to requirements are somewhat doubtful.

Furthermore, experience has taught management to hold higher levels of safety stock in terms of weeks of cover in order to meet customer service goals. Time is locked solidly into this operation and is attracting major costs, i.e:

Lead time of supply	4 months +
Safety stock	1 month +
Forecast review	2 months +

Example 3: Warehouse picking and distribution

A company distributing parts to field service engineers established a 'hot order' channel to allow the engineers to request urgent shipment of parts for machines on repair. The service concept was simple: order and pick today, dispatch tonight, receive and fit tomorrow. Management was delighted that the concept received strong acceptance and the proportion of items dispatched by this method increased rapidly to 60 per cent. Subsequent survey work showed that 70 per cent of all parts dispatched by this method remained unfitted seven days after receipt. The company was effectively wasting premium dispatch costs in excess of £100,000 per year through its poor management of lead times, e.g. lead time to complete repair – up to two weeks but assumed as 24 hours universally; lead time to deliver parts – 24 hours. It was also found that non-urgent dispatches handled on a 24-hour basis occasionally affected customers who really required prompt service by putting parts temporarily out of stock.

These are just isolated examples of lead times which are embedded in company systems. In all cases, the opportunity for reducing cost and improving customer service through better management of lead times is substantial.

These examples confirm the point that every lead-time component of a company's system must be challenged both individually and for its effect on the total business to ensure that the firm is securing the maximum value from its assets and the optimum customer service performance.

All of this seems obvious; so why have companies not picked up these ideas more quickly? The reasons seem to be fourfold:

- Few managers retain a grasp of process from one end of the pipeline to the other. As a result the way things get done can reflect convenience for the doers, a desire to protect functional boundaries and a lack of understanding of the consequences, both upstream and downstream of individual processes.

- Initiatives for change are largely functional and seldom reflect the total cost of the system. So, for example, manufacturing based on JIT may simply push inventory back on to the suppliers or into finished goods warehouses. On occasions this can actually increase total cost and reduce flexibility.

- Lead times are 'protected' by their custodians as a means of providing 'breathing space' and as a way of providing some hidden flexibility to respond. Individual functional lead times inevitably contain some slack and where these become embodied in a company's processing systems then they are institutionalized.

- Systems hold lead times as parameters which are taken for granted. Few executives will dare to challenge the basic principles of the computer systems in the business, far less the accuracy with which they complete the task. As a result, systems regularly operate on outdated or inappropriate lead-time constraints which have not been reviewed for years.

The lead-time gap

Most organizations face a fundamental problem: the time it takes to procure, make and deliver the finished product to a customer is longer than the time the customer is prepared to wait for it.

This is the basis of the lead-time gap. Figure 6.11 highlights the problem.

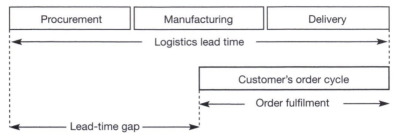

Fig. 6.11 The lead-time gap

The customer's order cycle refers to the length of time that the customer is prepared to wait, from when the order is placed through to when the goods are received. This is the maximum period available for order fulfilment. In some cases this may be measured in months but in others it is measured in hours.

Clearly the competitive conditions of the market as well as the nature of the product will influence the customer's willingness to wait. Thus a customer may be willing to wait a few weeks for delivery of a car with particular options but only a day for a new set of tyres.

> **The competitive conditions of the market as well as the nature of the product will influence the customer's willingness to wait.**

In the conventional organization the only way the gap between the logistics lead time (i.e. the time taken to complete the process from goods inwards to delivered product) and the customer's order cycle (i.e. the period they are prepared to wait for delivery) is by carrying inventory. This normally implies a forecast. Hence the way most companies address this problem is by seeking to forecast the market's requirements and then to build inventory ahead of demand. Unfortunately all our experience suggests that no matter how sophisticated the forecast, its accuracy is always less than perfect. It has been suggested that all mistakes in forecasting end up as an inventory problem – whether too much or too little!

Whilst improving forecast accuracy will always be a desirable goal it may be that the answer to the problem lies not in investing ever greater sums of money and energy in improving forecasting techniques, but rather in reducing the lead-time gap.

The company that achieves a perfect match between the logistics lead time and the customer's required order cycle has no need of forecasts and no need for inventory.

The challenge for logistics management is to search for the means whereby the gap between the two lead times can be reduced if not closed (see Figure 6.12).

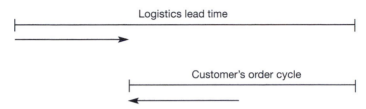

Fig. 6.12 Closing the lead-time gap

Reducing the gap can be achieved by shortening the logistics lead time (end-to-end pipeline time) whilst simultaneously trying to move the customer's order cycle closer by gaining earlier warning of requirements through improved visibility of demand.

Reducing logistics lead time

Because companies have typically not managed well the total flow of material and information that links the source of supply with the ultimate customer, what we find is that there is an incredibly rich opportunity for improving the efficiency of that process.

In those companies that do not recognize the importance of managing the supply chain as an integrated system it is usually the case that considerable periods of time are consumed at the interfaces between adjacent stages in the total process and in inefficiently performed procedures.

Because no one department or individual manager has complete visibility of the total logistics process, it is often the case that major opportunities for time reduction across the pipeline as a whole are not recognized. One electronics company in Europe did not realize for many years that, although it had reduced its throughput time in the factory from days down to hours, finished inventory was still sitting in the warehouse for three weeks! The reason was that finished inventory was the responsibility of the distribution function which was outside of the concern of the production management.

169

Even within functional areas there are usually substantial opportunities for time compression. Whilst traditional work study and organization and methods (O&M) techniques have tended to be neglected, there is a great need for business fundamentally to reappraise and reengineer the basic processes within their systems. The priority today has to be to question why we do things the way we do.

■ Why did we design inefficient processes? ■

In a way, we didn't. Many of our procedures were not designed at all; they just happened. The company founder one day recognized that he didn't have time to handle a chore, so he delegated it to Smith. Smith improvised. Time passed, the business grew and Smith hired his entire clan to help him cope with the work volume. They all improvised. Each day brought new challenges and special cases and the staff adjusted its work accordingly. The hodge-podge of special cases and quick fixes was passed from one generation of workers to the next.

We have institutionalized the *ad hoc* and enshrined the temporary. Why do we send foreign accounts to the corner desk? Because 20 years ago, Mary spoke French and Mary had the corner desk. Today Mary is long gone, and we no longer do business in France, but we still send foreign accounts to the corner desk. Why does an electronics company spend $10m a year to manage a field inventory worth $20m? Once upon a time the inventory was worth $200m and managing it cost $5m. Since then warehousing costs have escalated, components have become less expensive, and better forecasting techniques have minimized units in inventory. But the inventory procedures, alas, are the same as always.

Of the business processes that were designed, most took their present forms in the 1950s. The goal then was to check over-ambitious growth – much as the typewriter keyboard was designed to slow typists who would otherwise jam the keys. It is no accident that organizations stifle innovation and creativity. That's what they were designed to do.

Nearly all of our processes originated before the advent of modern computer and communications technology. They are replete with mechanisms designed to compensate for 'information poverty'. Although we are now information affluent, we still use those mechanisms which are now deeply embedded in automated systems.

It is not just the reduction in paperwork (and hence the opportunity for error) that is important but rather the reduction in time that it takes to issue and transmit the documentation. The basic principle to be noted is that every hour of time is directly reflected in the quantity of   inventory in the pipeline and thus the time it takes to respond to marketplace requirements.

A simple analogy is with an oil pipeline. Imagine a pipeline from a refinery to a port that is 500 kilometres long. In normal conditions there will be 500 kilometres equivalent of oil in the pipeline. If there is a change in requirement at the end of the pipeline (say for a different grade of oil) then 500 kilometres of the original grade has to be pumped through before the changed grade reaches the point of demand.

In the case of the logistics pipeline time is often consumed not just in slow-moving processes but also in unnecessary stock holding – whether it be raw materials, work-in-progress, waiting at a bottleneck or finished inventory.

All the logistics processes can be viewed as a network of inter-linked activities that can only be optimized as a whole by focusing on total throughput time. Any attempt to manage by optimizing individual elements or activities in the process will lead to a less-than-optimal result overall. A significant contribution to the way we view logistics processes has been made by Goldratt[3] who has developed the theory of constraints which is more usually known as Optimized Production Technology (OPT).

The essence of OPT is that all activities in a logistics chain can be categorized as either 'bottlenecks' or 'non-bottlenecks'. A bottleneck is the slowest activity in a chain and whilst it may often be a machine, it could also be a part of the information flow such as order processing. The throughput time of the entire system is determined by bottleneck activities. It follows therefore that to speed up total system throughput time it is important to focus on the bottlenecks, to add capacity where possible and to reduce set-ups and set-up times if applicable.

Equally important however is the realization that non-bottlenecks should not be treated in the same way. It is unnecessary to improve throughput at non-bottlenecks as this will only lead to the build-up of unwanted inventory at the bottleneck. Thus the output of non-bottlenecks that feed bottlenecks must be governed by the requirements of the bottlenecks they serve.

These ideas have profound implications for the reengineering of logistics systems where the objective is to improve throughput time overall, whilst simultaneously reducing total inventory in the system. The aim is to manage the bottlenecks for throughput efficiency which implies larger batch quantities and fewer set-ups at those crucial points, whereas non-bottlenecks should minimize batch quantities even though more set-ups will be involved. This has the effect of speeding up the flow of work-in-progress and these 'transfer batches' merge into larger 'process batches' at the bottlenecks, enabling a faster flow through the bottleneck. It follows that idle time at a non-bottleneck need not be a concern, indeed it should be welcomed if the effect is to reduce the amount of work-in-progress waiting at a bottleneck.

Further opportunities for pipeline time reduction can normally be found at the interface with suppliers' logistics systems. Lengthy, paper-based re-ordering systems add to total lead time significantly. Even more of an issue is the fact that customers rarely share their usage data with their suppliers and hence the supplier is forced to forecast requirements and carry inventory - thus exacerbating the problem. Many organizations are facing replenishment lead times of months when, if properly managed, those lead times could be reduced to weeks or even days.

Improving visibility of demand

The idea that it could be possible to 'extend' the customer's order cycle may at first sight seem implausible. Certainly it is unrealistic to expect that customers could be persuaded to wait longer for delivery of their order – if anything, as we have seen – the pressure is on to reduce order cycle times.

No, what is meant by extending the customer's order cycle is that we should seek to obtain significantly earlier warnings of the customer's requirements. What we frequently find is that first of all the *demand penetration point* is too far down the pipeline and that secondly, real demand is hidden from view and all we tend to see are orders. Both these points need further explanation; firstly the concept of the demand penetration point.

The simplest definition of the demand penetration point is that it occurs at that point in the logistics chain where real demand meets the plan. Upstream from this point everything is driven by a forecast and/or a plan.

Downstream we can respond to customer demand. Clearly in an ideal world we would like everything to be demand-driven so that nothing is purchased, manufactured or shipped unless there is a known requirement.

A key concern of logistics management should be to seek to identify ways in which the demand penetration point can be pushed as far as possible upstream. This might be achieved by the use of information so that manufacturing and purchasing get to hear of what is happening in the marketplace faster than they currently do. The means of achieving this will be discussed in Chapter 7. The other route to achieving an upstream shift of the order penetration point is by postponing the final commitment of the product to its final form. For example, paint manufacturers can now offer customers an infinite variety of colours of paint by combining a limited number of base colours at the point of sale. Rather than holding a wide range of finished products as inventory against a forecast, they only need to hold a limited number of items and hence both greatly reduce inventory holding costs whilst increasing the service and choice to the customer. Figure 6.13 illustrates a range of possible demand penetration points in different industrial and market contexts.

Perhaps the greatest opportunity for extending the customer's order cycle is by gaining earlier notice of their requirements. In so many cases the supplying company receives no indication of the customer's actual usage until an order arrives. For example the customer may be using 10 items a day but because he orders only intermittently the supplier sometimes receives an order for 100, sometimes for 150 and sometimes for 200. If the supplier could receive 'feed-forward' on what was being consumed he would anticipate the customer's requirement and better schedule his own logistics activities.

In a sense the information we receive, if we only have the order to rely on, is like the tip of an iceberg. Only a small proportion of the total iceberg is visible above the surface. Likewise the order cycle time (i.e. the required response time from order to delivery) may only be the visible tip of the 'information iceberg' (see Figure 6.14).

The area below the surface of the iceberg represents the ongoing consumption, demand or usage of the product which is hidden from the view of the supplier. It is only when an order is issued that demand becomes transparent.

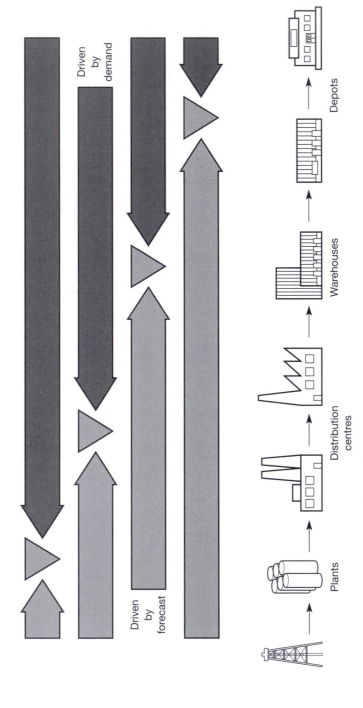

Fig. 6.13 Demand penetration points and strategic inventory

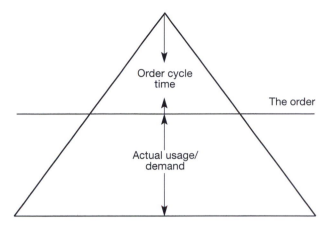

Fig. 6.14 The information iceberg

There are now signs that buyers and suppliers are recognizing the opportunities for mutual advantage if information on requirements can be shared on a continuing basis. If the supplier can see right to the end of the pipeline then the logistics system can become much more responsive to actual demand. Thus, whilst the customer will still require ever swifter delivery, if an ongoing

> There are now signs that buyers and suppliers are recognizing the opportunities for mutual advantage if information on requirements can be shared on a continuing basis.

feed-forward of information on demand or usage can be established there is a greater chance that the service to the customer will be enhanced and the supplier's costs reduced.

This twin-pronged approach of simultaneously seeking to reduce the logistics lead time whilst extending the customer's order cycle may never completely close the lead time gap. However, the experience of a growing number of companies is that substantial improvements can be made both in responsiveness and in the early capture of information on demand – the end result of which is better customer service at lower cost.

Summary

In a world of shortening product life-cycles, volatile demand and constant competitive pressure the ability to move quickly is critical. It is not just a question of speeding up the time is takes to get new products to market but rather the time it takes to replenish existing demand. Markets today are often 'time-sensitive' as well as 'price-sensitive' thus the search is for logistics solutions that are more responsive but low-cost.

Time compression in the pipeline has the potential both to speed up response times and to reduce supply chain cost. The key to achieving these dual goals is through focusing on the reduction of non-value adding time – and particularly time spent as inventory. Whereas in the past logistics systems were very dependent upon a forecast, with all the problems that entailed, now the focal point has become lead-time reduction.

References

1. *Fortune Magazine*, 28 November 1994.
2. Christopher, M. and Braithwaite, A., 'Managing Strategic Lead Times', *Logistics Information Management*, December 1989.
3. Goldratt, E.M., *Theory of Constraints*, North River Press, 1990.

Just-in-time and 'quick response' logistics

This chapter:

Compares the philosophy of Japanese-style Just-in-Time (JIT) logistics and its practices to the statistically-based reasoning behind conventional Western methods of inventory management.

●

Considers the logistics implications of JIT and how developments in information technology have been harnessed to leverage its power, leading to the emergence of Quick Response (QR) logistics.

●

Introduces Vendor Managed Inventory (VMI) and its more co-operatively managed derivative Co-Managed Inventory (CMI) as the basis for demand management and replenishment systems.

●

Outlines the 'Forrester Effect' and 'Acceleration Effects' as key concepts from the field of industrial dynamics, explaining the significance of each for the management of logistics systems.

●

Presents production strategies for Quick Response, emphasizing the need for firms to develop flexible manufacturing systems with the capabilities for mass-customization.

There have been many new ideas and concepts in business management over the last thirty or so years, some of which have endured and others discarded. However, perhaps one of the most significant principles to become widely adopted and practised is that of just-in-time. Just-in-time, or JIT, is a philosophy as much as it is a technique. It is based upon the simple idea that wherever possible no activity should take place in a system until there is a need for it.

Thus no products should be made, no components ordered, until there is a downstream requirement. Essentially JIT is a 'pull' concept where demand at the end of the pipeline pulls products towards the market and behind those products the flow of components is also determined by that same demand. This contrasts with the traditional 'push' system where products are manufactured or assembled in batches in anticipation of demand and are positioned in the supply chain as 'buffers' between the various functions and entities (see Figure 7.1).

The conventional approach to meeting customer requirements is based upon some form of statistical inventory control which typically might rely upon reordering when inventory levels fall to a certain pre-determined point – the so-called reorder point (ROP).

Under this approach a reorder point or reorder level is pre-determined based upon the expected length of the replenishment lead time (see Figure 7.2). The amount to be ordered may be based upon the economic order quantity (EOQ) formulation which balances the cost of holding inventory against the costs of placing replenishment orders.

Alternative methods include the regular review of stock levels with fixed intervals between orders when the amount to be ordered is determined with reference to a pre-determined replenishment level, as in Figure 7.3.

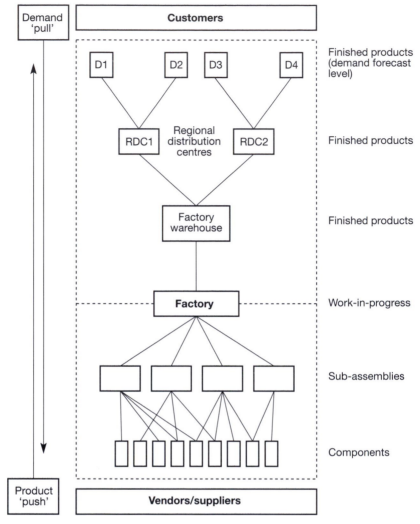

Fig. 7.1 'Push' versus 'pull' in the logistics chain

There are numerous variations on these themes and the techniques have been well documented and practised for many years. However they all tend to share one weakness, that is they frequently lead to stock levels being higher or lower than necessary, particularly in those cases where the rate of demand may change or occurs in discrete 'lumps'. This latter situation frequently occurs when demand for an item is 'dependent' upon demand for another item, e.g. demand for a TV component is dependent upon the demand for TV sets; or where

180

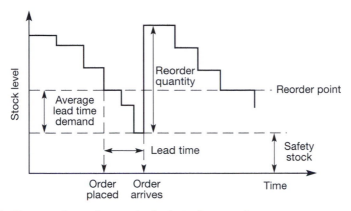

Fig. 7.2 The reorder point method of stock control

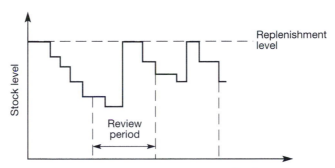

Fig. 7.3 A replenishment system based upon periodic review

demand is 'derived', e.g. the demand for TV sets at the factory is determined by demand from the retailer which is derived from ultimate
demand in the marketplace.

The implications of dependent demand are illustrated in the example
given in Figure 7.4 which shows how a regular off-take at the retail
level can be converted into a much more 'lumpy' demand situation at
the plant by the use of reorder points.

A similar situation can occur in a multi-echelon distribution system
where the combined demand from each level is aggregated at the next
level in the system. Figure 7.5 demonstrates such an occurrence.

The common feature of these examples is that demand at each level
in the logistics system is dependent upon the demand at the next
level in the system. Demand is termed 'dependent' when it is directly

1. Regional distribution centre (RDC) inventory:
   many small independent demands from customers

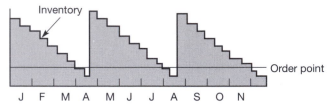

2. Central warehouse inventory:
   few large demands dependent on RDC demand

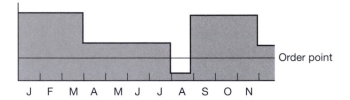

3. Plant inventory:
   irregular demand dependent on warehouse demand

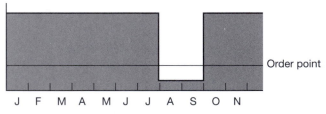

Fig. 7.4 Order point and dependent demand

related to, or derives from, the demand for another inventory item or product. Conversely, the demand for a given item is termed 'independent' when such demand is unrelated to demand for other items – when it is not a function of demand for other items. This distinction is crucial because whilst independent demand may be forecast using traditional methods, dependent demand must be calculated, based upon the demand at the next level in the logistics chain.

> **Whilst independent demand may be forecast using traditional methods, dependent demand must be calculated, based upon the demand at the next level in the logistics chain.**

Using the example in Figure 7.5 it would clearly be inappropriate to attempt to forecast demand at the plant using data based upon the

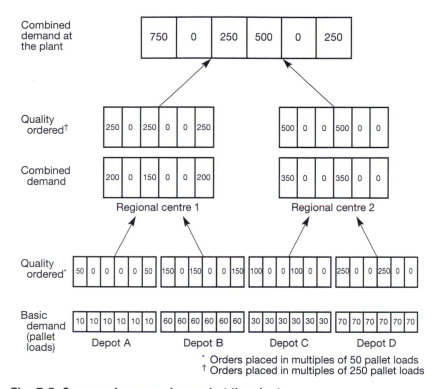

Fig. 7.5 Causes of uneven demand at the plant

pattern of combined demand from the regional centres. Rather it has to be calculated from the identified requirements at each of the preceding levels. It is only at the point of final demand, in this case at the depots, where forecasts can sensibly be made – in fact in most cases demand at the depot would itself be dependent upon retailers' or other intermediaries' demand, but since this is obviously outside the supplier's direct control it is necessary to produce a forecasted estimate of demand.

The classic economic order quantity (EOQ) model has tended to channel our thinking towards the idea that there is some 'optimum' amount to order (and hence to hold in stock). The EOQ model arrives at this optimum by balancing the holding cost of inventory against the cost of issuing replenishment orders and/or the costs of production set-ups (see Figure 7.6).

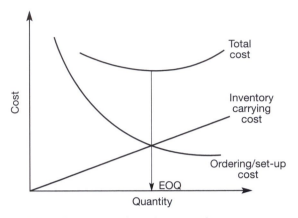

Fig. 7.6 Determining the economic order quantity

The EOQ can be easily determined by the formula:

$$EOQ = \sqrt{\frac{2AS}{i}}$$

A = Annual usage
S = Ordering cost/set-up cost
i = Inventory carrying cost

So, for example, if we use 1,000 units of product X a year, each costing £40 and each order/set-up costs £100 and the carrying cost of inventory is 25 per cent then:

$$EOQ = \sqrt{\frac{2 \times 1000 \times 100}{40 \times 0.25}} = 141$$

The problem is that this reorder quantity means that we will be carrying more inventory than is actually required per day over the complete order cycle (except on the last day). For example if the EOQ were 100 units and daily usage was 10 units then on the first day of the cycle we will be overstocked by 90 units, on the second day by 80 units, and so on.

To compound the problem we have additional inventory in the form of 'safety' stock which is carried in order to provide a safeguard against demand during the replenishment lead time being greater than expected and/or variation in the lead time itself.

The result is that we end up with a lot of unproductive inventory which represents a continuing drain on working capital.

The Japanese philosophy

It has often been said that the scarcity of space in industrialized Japan has made the nation conscious of the need to make the most productive use of all physical resources, including inventory – whether this is true is of academic interest only – what is the case is that it is the widely held view in Japan that inventory is waste.

An analogy that is frequently drawn in Japan is that an organization's investment in inventory is like a large, deep lake (see Figure 7.7). Well below the surface of this lake are numerous jagged rocks, but because of the depth of the water, the captain of the ship need have no fear of striking one of them.

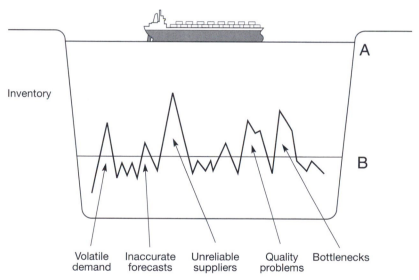

Fig. 7.7 Inventory hides the problems

The comparison with business is simple: the depth of the water in the lake represents inventory and the rocks represent problems. These problems might include such things as inaccurate forecasts, unreliable suppliers, quality problems, bottlenecks, industrial relations

185

problems and so on. The Japanese philosophy is that inventory merely hides the problems. Their view is that the level of water in the lake should be reduced (say to level 'B' in Figure 7.7). Now the captain of the ship is forced to confront the problems – they cannot be avoided. In the same way if inventory is reduced then management must grasp the various nettles of forecast inaccuracy, unreliable suppliers, and so on.

The Japanese developed the so-called Kanban concept as a way of lowering the water in the lake. Kanban originated in assembly-type operations but the principles can be extended across the supply chain and to all types of operations. The name Kanban comes from the Japanese for a type of card that was used in early systems to signal to the upstream supply point that a certain quantity of material could be released.

Kanban is a 'pull' system which is driven by the demand at the lowest point in the chain. In a production operation the aim would be to produce only that quantity needed for immediate demand. When parts are needed on the assembly line they are fed from the next stage up the chain in just the quantity needed at the time they are needed. Likewise this movement now triggers demand at the next workstation in the chain and so on.

By progressively reducing the Kanban quantity (i.e. the amount demanded from the supplying workstation) bottlenecks will become apparent. Management will then focus attention on the bottleneck to remove it by the most cost-effective means possible. Again the Kanban quantity will be reduced until a further bottleneck is revealed. Hence the Kanban philosophy essentially seeks to achieve a balanced supply chain with minimal inventory at every stage and where the process and transit quantities of materials and stock are reduced to the lowest possible amount. The ultimate aim, say the Japanese, should be the 'economic batch quantity of 1'!

In fact this logic does not necessarily conflict with the traditional view of how the economic batch (or order) quantity is determined. All that is different is that the Japanese are seeking to minimize the batch quantity by shifting the curve that represents the cost of ordering or the cost of set-ups to the left (see Figure 7.8). In other words, they focus on finding ways to reduce set-up costs and ordering costs.

186

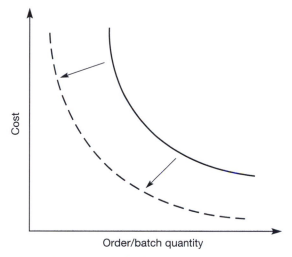

Fig. 7.8 Reducing set-up costs/ordering costs

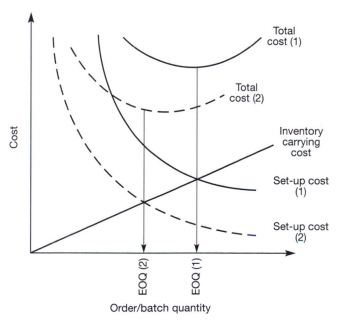

Fig. 7.9 Reducing the economic batch/order quantity

The effect of moving the curve to the left on the economic batch/order quantity is seen in Figure 7.9.

Implications for logistics

In the same way that the conventional wisdom in production and manufacturing was to maximize batch quantities, similar thinking could be found in the rest of the supply chain. Thus we used to seek to ship by the container or truck load, customers were discouraged from ordering in smaller quantities by price penalties, and delivery schedules were typically based on optimizing the efficiency of routes and the consolidation of deliveries. Clearly such an approach runs counter to the requirements of a JIT supply chain. Under the JIT philosophy the requirement is for small shipments to be made more frequently and to meet the precise time requirements of the customer.

The challenge to logistics management is to find ways in which these changed requirements can be achieved without an uneconomic escalation of costs. There may have to be trade-offs but the goal must be to improve total supply chain cost-effectiveness.

Already a significant number of organizations have responded to this challenge in a variety of ways. The basic principle of JIT logistics is to ensure that all elements of the chain are synchronized and that there must be early identification of shipping and replenishment requirements and, most importantly of all, there must be the highest level of planning discipline. With regard to this latter, the onus on the customer is to commit to a pre-determined schedule so as to 'freeze' that schedule. In other words once the requirements have been communicated to the upstream supplier within the agreed lead time, then those requirements cannot be changed.

A further implication of JIT logistics is that if excessive inventory holding by the supplier is to be avoided, then the management of inbound materials flow becomes a crucial issue. In particular the search for consolidation opportunities has to be a priority. Thus for example, rather than one supplier making a series of JIT deliveries in small quantities to a customer, the orders from a number of suppliers are combined into a single delivery. It is perhaps not surprising that the emergence of JIT as a management philosophy has coincided with the growth of third-party distribution and logistics companies specializing in providing an inbound consolidation service.

■ The effect of JIT on a company's culture ■

Issue	Conventional wisdom	JIT strategic thinking
Quality vs cost	Least cost with 'acceptable quality'	Top, consistent quality 'zero defects'
Inventories	Large inventories from: – Quantity purchase discounts – Manufacturing economies of scale – Safety stock protection	Low inventories with reliable 'continuous' flow delivery
Flexibility	Long 'minimum' lead times; minimal flexibility	Short lead times; customer-service driven, much flexibility
Transportation	Least cost within 'acceptable service levels'	Totally reliable service levels
Vendor/carrier	Tough 'adversarial' negotiations	Joint venture 'partnerships'
Number of suppliers/carriers	Many; avoid sole source – no leverage and dependency exposure	Few; long-term open relationship
Vendor/carrier communications	Minimal; many secrets; tightly controlled	Open; sharing of information; joint problem solving; multiple relationships
General	Business is cost driven	Business is customer service driven

Source: George A. Isaac III, *Creating a Competitive Advantage Through Implementing Just-in-Time Logistics Strategies*, Touche Ross, Chicago, U.S.A.

These third-party services can manage the pick-up of materials and components from suppliers on a 'milk round' basis, using a central 'hub' or transshipment centre for re-sorting and consolidating for inbound delivery. They may also perform certain value-adding activities such as quality control, kitting, sequencing or final finishing.

A good example of such a third-party service is that provided in the United Kingdom by TNT on behalf of the Rover Group car company. Here both suppliers and TNT deliver consolidated quantities to a specially designed transshipment centre owned and operated by TNT near to Rover's factory. Components and subassemblies are then sequenced for delivery to the point of use on the assembly line in the required quantities at the required time. This enables the smooth flow of in-bound material with no congestion of delivery vehicles at the plant.

In complex assembly operations such as motor manufacture the prior sequencing of parts and components prior to assembly is a crucial activity (see the example below of seat delivery to Nissan's assembly line in north-east England).

■ Synchronized delivery – how Nissan Motors UK receives vehicle seats ■

Elapsed Hours

0 – Painted body passes to trim line in Nissan
  – Precise vehicle specifications of next 12 vehicles transmitted by computer from Nissan to seat suppliers
  – Supplier transfers information to picking lists
  – Seat covers selected from range

1 – Covers prepared for assembly (in reverse order)
  – Seat assembly from synchronized manufacture of subassemblies (frames, foams, finishers, plastic parts)

2 – Quality audit and load
  – Delivery of seats to stock-holding point by special purpose vehicle
  – Stock to lineside

3 – Rear seats fitted followed by front seats (waiting stillages returned to empty wagon)
  – Delivery frequency now every 15–20 minutes

A further requirement for effective JIT logistics is the closest possible linkage between the customer and the supplier at least in terms of sharing information and co-ordinating plans. The relationship between Volkswagen and its component suppliers (see opposite) is one such example.

It should be emphasized that JIT solutions may not always be appropriate or justified. It is not so much a question of the volume of the requirement which justifies JIT – indeed on high volume and hence usually predictable demand items it will usually be most cost-effective to work on the basis of classic economic batch quantities – the variables which really affect the viability of JIT logistics are the variety of options within a category (e.g. different styles, shapes and colour of bumpers in the Volkswagen example) and the value of the items.

■ Bumpers just-in-time ■

At the end of 1988 Volkswagen began operating two new assembly lines for the Passat model at its Emden factory.

Peguform, a specialist in injection moulding of large components, was selected to supply the Passat bumpers, ready for assembly according to just-in-time principles.

At Peguform's new plant in Oldenburg, 50 km away from Emden, VW's 'estimated assembly schedule' is received six months in advance of actual assembly and is constantly updated, allowing for moulding and painting adequate batch sizes of bumpers which are held in an intermediate store containing 84 variants.

Six hours before actual assembly in Emden the final assembly schedule is provided to Peguform. Every 39 seconds a set of bumpers is transferred out of the intermediate store in the correct sequence to coincide with final assembly six hours later at Volkswagen.

The sets are transported via chain conveyor to two bumper assembly lines, where they are fitted with steel inlays, fog lamps, caravan hooks, mounting aids and other appliances.

More than 300 variants are possible.

Each bumper assembly line produces a bumper set every 78 seconds. Bumpers are placed on to special pallets, which are loaded on to trucks. Whenever an interchangeable container is fully loaded, it is moved to the VW Emden plant. Loading in Oldenburg and unloading in Emden are organized so that the final assembly sequence is not interrupted.

Between the unloading in Emden and the assembly point, a one hour buffer is employed.

Source: Miebach Logistics Systems Ltd

Typically the greater the demand for variety and the higher the value, the more that JIT and, in particular, synchronized delivery, becomes preferable (see Figure 7.10).

To summarize, the pre-requisites for successful JIT logistics are:

- A disciplined approach to planning and scheduling of inbound requirements.
- A high degree of communication and planning linkage between supply chain partners.
- More often than not the use of 'third parties' or logistics partners to manage the inbound consolidation and sequencing of deliveries.

- The design of vehicles and physical facilities to make small shipment quantities easy to load and unload rapidly.
- The value and variety of the materials required tend to be higher than average.

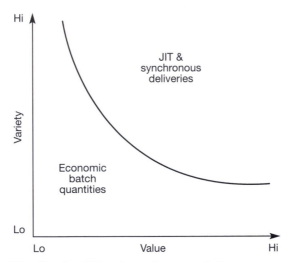

Fig. 7.10 Justification for JIT and synchronous delivery

'Quick response' logistics

An outgrowth of the JIT philosophy has emerged in recent years under the banner of 'quick response logistics'. The basic idea behind quick response (QR) is that in order to reap the advantages of time-based competition it is necessary to develop systems that are responsive and fast. Hence QR is the umbrella term for the information systems and the JIT logistics systems that combine to provide 'the right product in the right place at the right time'.

> The basic idea behind quick response (QR) is that in order to reap the advantages of time-based competition it is necessary to develop systems that are responsive and fast.

What has made QR possible is the development of information technology and in particular the rise of electronic data interchange (EDI), bar coding, the use of electronic point of sale (EPOS) systems and laser scanners.

Essentially the logic behind QR is that demand is captured in as close to real-time as possible and as close to the final consumer as possible.

The logistics response is then made directly as a result of that information. An example of such an approach is provided in the United States by Procter and Gamble who receive sales data directly from the checkout counters of North America's largest retailer, Wal-Mart. Making use of this information P & G can plan production and schedule delivery to Wal-Mart on a replenishment basis. The result is that Wal-Mart carries less inventory yet has fewer stock-outs and P & G benefit because they get better economies in production and logistics as a result of the early warning and – most importantly – they have greatly increased their sales to Wal-Mart. Whilst the investment in the information system is considerable, so too is the payback. Early experience with QR suggests that paybacks of less than two years can be expected.

QR is obviously a classic case of the substitution of information for inventory. Figure 7.11 indicates the relative advantage of QR when higher service levels are demanded. Whilst QR may have a high fixed cost the incremental costs of service improvements are relatively low.

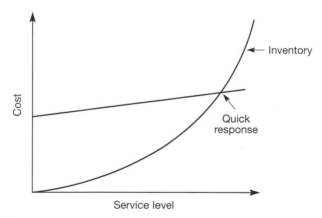

Fig. 7.11 Quick response system versus traditional inventory-based system

A further feature in favour of QR systems is that by speeding up processing time in the system, cumulative lead times are reduced. This can then result in lower inventory (see Figure 7.12) and thus further reduce response times. In effect a 'virtuous circle'!

Quick response systems have begun to emerge in the fashion and apparel industry where the costs of traditional inventory-based systems based upon buyers' prior purchase decisions (in effect a 'push' system) can be considerable. In the United States one estimate[1] of the costs to

193

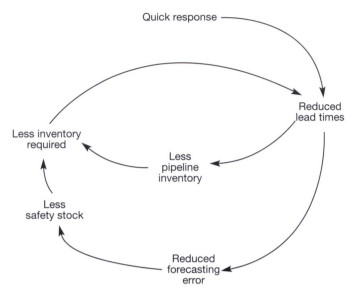

Fig. 7.12 Quick response system can trigger a 'virtuous circle' in logistics

the US textile and apparel industry of conventional logistics systems is given as $25bn. This comprises the following elements:

Forced markdowns	$14.08 bn
Stock-outs	$6.08 bn
Inventory carrying costs	$5.08 bn
Total:	**$25.24 bn**

There could be massive advantages to be gained by all parties in the supply chain if the concept of QR was adopted throughout the chain. Thus in the case of fashion garments the aim should be to link retail sales with the apparel manufacturers, who in turn are linked to the textile producers who themselves are linked to the suppliers of fibres. One such reported case is the linkage through shared information of the US textile company Milliken with the Seminole Manufacturing Company (a manufacturer of men's slacks), and the retailer Wal-Mart. Information on end user demand was captured at the point of sale and rapidly fed back up the supply chain enabling dramatic reductions in lead times to be achieved and hence substantial reductions in inventory.

Another case from the United States is provided by the chain of retail fashion stores, 'The Limited'. Each of the several thousand stores in the chain tracks consumer preferences daily using their point-of-sale data.

194

Based upon this, orders are sent by satellite links to the suppliers around the world. Using Hong Kong as a consolidation centre, goods are flown back to the United States on board a chartered Boeing 747 which makes four journeys a week to The Limited's distribution centre in Columbus, Ohio. At the distribution centre the goods are price-marked and re-sorted for immediate onward shipment by truck and plane to the retail stores. The whole cycle from reorder to in-store display can be achieved in six weeks. Conventional systems take more like six months.

Vendor managed inventory

Traditionally, customers place orders on their suppliers. Whilst the logic of this might seem obvious, the inherent inefficiencies are significant. Firstly, the supplier has no advance warning of requirements – they are forced to make forecasts and, as a result, carry unnecessary safety stocks. Secondly, the supplier is often faced with unexpected short-term demands for products which leads to frequent changes to their production and distribution schedules and thus additional cost. The paradoxical end result is that customer service suffers because of the inevitably higher level of stock-outs.

There is now emerging an alternative way of managing demand. In this revised model the customer no longer places orders but instead shares information with the vendor. This information relates to the actual usage or sales of their product, their current on-hand inventory and details of any additional marketing activity such as promotions.

On the basis of this information, the supplier takes responsibility for replenishment of the customer's inventory. No orders are received, but instead an indication is given by the customer of the upper and lower limits of stock that they wish to keep on hand.

It is the responsibility of the supplier to maintain the customer's inventory within the specified stock bands.

The benefit to the customer is that inventory levels can be significantly reduced whilst the risk of stock-outs diminishes. Furthermore it is often the case that the customer does not pay for the inventory until after it has been sold or used – so there is a considerable cash flow benefit. The advantage to the supplier is that because they have direct access to information on real demand, usually transmitted through

Electronic Data Interchange (EDI), they can much better plan and schedule production and distribution – thus improving capacity utilization – and at the same time the requirement for safety stock is considerably reduced.

This system of demand management and replenishment is known as Vendor Managed Inventory (VMI) although, because such arrangements are usually based upon close co-operation between the customer and the supplier, the term Co-Managed Inventory (CMI) is probably more appropriate. See the Whitbread Beer Company Case Study below.

Implementing Co-Managed Inventory (CMI) at the Whitbread Beer Company

The Whitbread Beer Company is the brewing division of Whitbread Plc, the brewing, leisure and drinks retailing group. The group is one of the UK's leading brewers, with an extensive portfolio of pubs, restaurant chains and hotels. It is also the largest owner of high-street off-licences in the country. Its brewing interests were formally separated from the group's extensive on-trade retailing interests in response to the Monopolies and Mergers Commission's 1992 'Beer Orders'. Nevertheless, the Beer Company continues to manage the supply of its own beers and a range of third-party produced drinks to the group's on-trade and off-trade retail networks, as well as to other third-party retailers – mainly the large grocery multiples.

The changing demands of the marketplace have meant that The Whitbread Beer Company, like most of its competitors, has diversified its product portfolio, but the proliferation of new brands has created complications for the manufacturing side of the brewing business, which is geared to large batch runs. Pressure to optimize production could lead to high stocks of finished product, which become difficult to manage when dispersed through an extensive distribution system. This in turn could threaten product quality, resulting in problems with shelf life, particularly for the low-volume premium brands.

Whitbread had been gradually reorganizing and rationalizing its drinks logistics structure since the early 1990s, to develop a more efficient and flexible network.[1] Wherever possible Whitbread's own product inventory was consolidated and moved back upstream within the network. Meanwhile, just-in-time deliveries were introduced from the group's own manufacturing sites to its 3850 pubs and inns, and to its 1524 high-street off-licences.[2] In 1995, falling beer prices in the off-trade led Whitbread to investigate the possibility of further reducing stock holdings within its own distribution network by moving major third-party suppliers of drinks for resale onto Co-Managed Inventory (CMI) agreements. It was believed that the introduction of CMI could ease the stress on Whitbread's own business, while improving stock availability and effecting a step-change in lead-time and order cycle reduction.

As a first step overtures were made to Whitbread's largest volume off-trade supplier, US-based Anheuser Busch. Anheuser is the Goliath of the international brewing industry, controlling a massive 45 per cent of its domestic market. It is widely recognized as having the lowest inventories of any major US brewer and prides itself on the freshness of its products.[3] Whitbread is Anheuser's largest customer in the United Kingdom, with four of its products accounting for 9 per cent of Whitbread's off-trade sales, so there were critical mass benefits for both sides. Anheuser's expertise and the fact that its trade with Whitbread was relatively predictable, involving high volumes and low SKUs, made the US brewer an ideal pilot partner. The two companies adopted an EDI facilitated partnership approach for the project, with GE Information Services as its network supplier.

Under the pilot programme Whitbread provided Anheuser with a 13-week rolling forecast, along with daily updates of Anheuser's stock holdings at each of Whitbread's distribution centres. These told Anheuser what Whitbread was planning to sell and let the supplier know what had actually been sold on a day-by-day basis. Anheuser was then allowed to determine what to ship in terms of mix and quantity, provided that stocks stayed within pre-determined stock bands (usually 2–4 days) and in line with an agreed overall product mix. This flexibility allowed the supplier to manage its production and transport planning to best effect. Whitbread required 24 hours' notice ahead of delivery as a safeguard, but were pleased to discover that on no occasion throughout the first year of CMI trading was it necessary to amend a supplier-raised order.

The pilot reduced Whitbread's stock of Anheuser products from 8 to 4 days (a saving of £300k), while service levels rose from 98.6 per cent to 99.3 per cent. The fact that Whitbread produces a number of substitute products gave Anheuser a strong incentive not to allow stock-outs to occur. Some inventory was displaced to the supplier, but inventory levels

▶

▶ within the system as a whole were reduced. Anheuser benefited from access to better forecasting and sales information, and better utilization of assets. As a CMI supplier it received preferential treatment in the allocation of prime-time overnight delivery slots and was allowed to deliver mixed consignments in full truck-loads. The regularity and volume of the shipments – three per day to each of Whitbread's five distribution centres – meant that further transport efficiencies could be realized by back-loading vehicles. The Anheuser pilot was fully live by March 1996.

In July 1996 Whitbread held a supplier conference for the top seven of its 72 suppliers, to share the knowledge gained from the CMI pilot and discuss the extension of the programme. These top 10 per cent of suppliers account for around 50 per cent of Whitbread's inventory costs, 60 per cent of sales by volume, 55 per cent of invoice volume and 80 per cent of invoice value (there are just over 500 product lines between the entire supplier base). Whitbread estimated that rolling the CMI programme out to include the other six top suppliers would achieve a one-off stock reduction of £1.4m. Moreover, lower inventories meant smaller depots and fewer distribution centres, resulting in substantial savings in the longer term.

By late 1996, two of Whitbread's other leading suppliers, soft drinks manufacturer Britvic and rival brewers Guinness, were well on the way to joining Anheuser with full CMI between themselves and Whitbread. Bass is also among Whitbread's group of seven largest suppliers and interestingly its own brewing, pub and leisure interests means that it is at once a supplier, competitor and customer of the Whitbread group. Nevertheless Bass is also working towards full CMI supplier status with Whitbread. The remaining core suppliers were expected to be fully involved by June 1998. Aligning its core suppliers of drinks for resale was Whitbread's top priority, but the company is also investigating the possibility of extending the CMI programme to include suppliers of raw materials, bumping the number of CMI suppliers up eventually to around a dozen. In the meatime, in the interests of efficiency, EDI links were extended to a further 32 suppliers during 1997.

References

1. Cunningham, F. (1997), 'Roll Out the Barrel', *Logistics Europe*, April, pp. 10–17.
2. Callingham, M. (1997), 'Integration of Whitbread's Marketing Databases', Presentation to the Marketing Process Benchmarking Network, Cranfield School of Management, 24 April.
3. *Business Wire* (1997), 'Anheuser-Busch announces record sales, earnings and beer volume for full year 1996', *Business Wire: Reuter Textline*, 5 February (Q2:190).

Logistics information systems

Increasingly, it seems that successful companies have one thing in common – their use of information and information technology (IT) to achieve quick response. Information systems are re-shaping the organization and also the nature of the linkages between organizations. Information has always been central to the efficient management of logistics but now, enabled by technology, it is providing the driving force for competitive logistics strategy.

We are now starting to see the emergence of integrated logistics systems that link the operations of the business, such as production and distribution, with the supplier's operations on the one hand and the customer on the other. These systems are often referred to generically as Enterprise Planning Systems or Enterprise Resource Planning (ERP). Already it is the case that companies can literally link the replenishment of product in the marketplace with their upstream operations and those of their suppliers through the use of shared information. The use of these systems has the potential to convert supply chains into demand chains in the sense that the system can now respond to known demand rather than having to anticipate that demand through a forecast.

A classic case in point is provided by the information system that drives the replenishment process for the clothing and apparel sold by BhS through their UK stores. Daily information from the point of sale enables head office to determine replenishment requirements. This information is transmitted direct to the suppliers who package individual store requirements into bar-coded parcels. These parcels are then collected by a logistics service provider and are then taken to a transshipment centre operated by the logistics service provider where they are sorted for store delivery. In effect, a just-in-time delivery is achieved which enables minimum stock to be carried in the stores and yet transport costs are contained through the principles of consolidation (see Figures 7.13 and 7.14).

In other cases organizations are finding that through information they can manage dispersed inventories as if they were a single inventory. The benefits of this can be considerable. If inventory management is centralized and decisions on replenishment and order quantities are taken on the basis that it is a single stock, then only one safety stock instead of many is required. The stock itself can be carried anywhere in

199

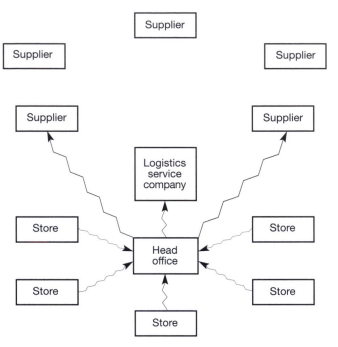

Fig. 7.13 Daily sales data drives the replenishment order system

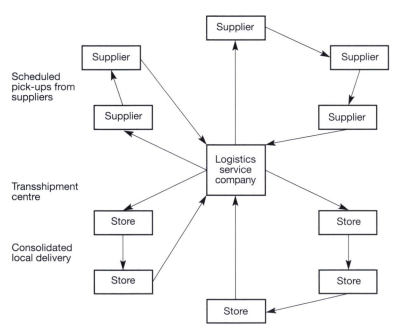

Fig. 7.14 Acting on this information a consolidated pick-up and store delivery sequence is activated

the system, either near the point of production or the point of consumption. This is the concept of 'virtual' inventory management or electronic inventory, as it is sometimes known.

SKF, the Swedish bearing company, has established a European-wide network it calls its global forecasting and supply system (GFSS). GFSS is a demand management system that captures demand as customers across Europe place orders with their local SKF sales office or through electronic data interchange (EDI). In real-time the computer-based system identifies where items required are currently held in stock, or, if they are not available, when they are next scheduled for production at one of SKF's five major European production sites. At the same time the customer's order is accepted by GFSS and a confirmation of the delivery date can be issued, since the information system also concurrently schedules transport!

This type of system is now becoming commonplace as open system architecture enables computer-to-computer linkage to be achieved more easily. Digital Equipment Corporation has developed a general purpose integrated logistics information system which enables organizations to manage demand from one end of the pipeline to another.[2] Figure 7.15 summarizes the architecture of the system.

Logistics information systems should not be thought of purely as a vehicle for achieving integration in the supply chain – crucial though that is. The internal management of the business can be greatly facilitated through the ability to plan, co-ordinate and control all the activities relating to order fulfilment. Figure 7.16 represents the basic functions of a logistics information system and shows how, from a common data base, it is possible to provide information to better manage each of the vital elements in the logistics process.

Logistics systems dynamics

One of the major advantages of moving to QR and JIT-type logistics strategies is that by reducing lot quantities and increasing the rate of throughput in the logistics system, modulations in the level of activity in the pipeline can be reduced.

Logistics systems are prone to what has been called the 'Forrester Effect', after Jay Forrester, who developed a set of techniques known as Industrial Dynamics.[3] Forrester defined industrial dynamics as:

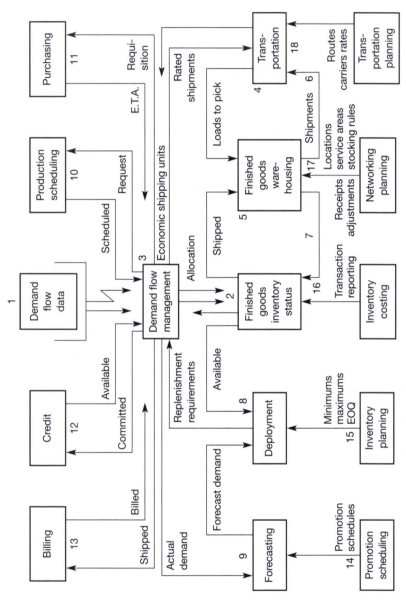

Fig. 7.15 An integrated logistics information system

Source: Digital Equipment Corporation

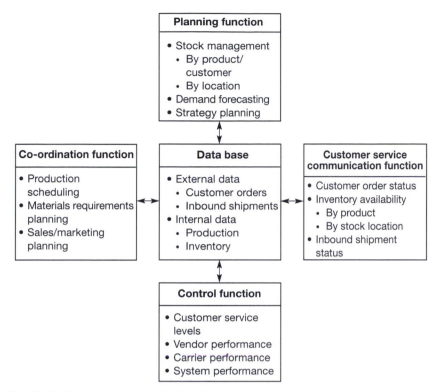

Fig. 7.16 Functions of a logistics information system

'The study of the information feedback characteristics of industrial activity to show how organizational structure, amplification (in policies) and time delays (in decisions and returns) interact to influence the success of the enterprise. It treats the interactions between the flows of information, money, orders, materials, personnel, and capital equipment in a company, an industry or a national economy.'

'Industrial dynamics provides a single framework for integrating the functional areas of management – marketing, production, accounting, research and development and capital investment.'

Using a specially-developed computer simulation language, DYNAMO, Forrester built a model of a production/distribution system involving three levels in the distribution channel: a retailer's inventory, a distributor's inventory and a factory inventory. Each level was inter-connected through information flows and flows of goods. The model used real-world relationships and data and included parameters such as order transmission times, order processing times, factory lead times and shipment delivery times. Management could then examine the effects on the total system of, say, a change in retail sales or the impact of changing production levels or any other policy change or combination of changes.

What becomes apparent from this modelling of complex systems is that small disturbances in one part of the system can very quickly become magnified as the effect spreads through the pipeline.

Many consumer product companies that are heavy spenders on trade promotions (e.g. additional discounts, incentives, etc.) do not realize what the true costs of such activities are. In the first instance there is the loss of profit through the discount itself, and then there is the hidden cost of the disturbance to the logistics system. Considering firstly the loss of profit. When a discount is offered for a limited period then that discount obviously will apply to all sales – not just any

> **Many consumer product companies that are heavy spenders on trade promotions do not realize what the true costs of such activities are.**

incremental sales. So if sales during the promotional period are, say, 1100 cases but without the promotion they would have been 1000, then whilst the incremental revenue comes only from the additional 100 cases, the discount applies to all 1100. Additionally the retailer may decide to take advantage of the discount and 'forward order'; in other words buy ahead of requirement to sell at a later time at the regular price. One study[4] found that for these reasons only 16 per cent of promotions were profitable, the rest only 'bought sales' at a loss. Table 7.1 highlights the problem.

The second impact of promotional activity on profit is the potential it provides for triggering the 'acceleration effect' and hence creating a Forrester-type surge throughout the logistics pipeline. This is because in most logistics systems there will be 'leads and lags', in other words the response to an input or a change in the system may be delayed. For example the presence of a warehouse or a stock-holding intermediary in the distribution channel can cause a substantial distortion in demand at the factory. This is due to the 'acceleration effect' which can cause self-generated fluctuations in the operating characteristics of a system.

Table 7.1 The unprofitable economics of trade promotions

	Cases	Gross dollars
Baseline*		
(Sales that would have occurred during the four-week promotion period even without the promotion)	400	4,000
Incremental sales to customer†		
Due to one week of feature	100	1,000
Due to 50 per cent of stores with three weeks of display and price reduction	250	2,500
Due to 50 per cent of stores with four weeks of price reduction only	80	800
Total	430	4,300
Ten weeks of forward buying by retailers†	1,000	10,000
Total sales during promotion	1,830	18,300
Cost of promotion		
($18,300 x 15% discount)		2,745
Cost per incremental dollar of sales		
(Promotion cases divided by total incremental sales)		.64
Promotion efficiency		
(Incremental cases sold to consumer divided by total cases sold)		23.5%

*Assume weekly base sales of 100 cases and a list price of $10 per case.
†Based on analysis of single-source data and retailer promotion purchases.

Despite the ideal conditions of this hypothetical example, the promotion ends up costing the manufacturer 64 cents for each incremental dollar it generates. Unless the product's gross margin is greater than 64 per cent, the promotion will lose money.

Taking the example of a manufacturing company that sells its output to a wholesaler, who then sells it to retailers, it is possible to illustrate the effect of accelerated disturbances. The company has a service policy which requires it to keep the equivalent of eight weeks' stock as a buffer; the wholesaler keeps 12 weeks' stock and the retailer three weeks' stock. For some reason, say a promotion, final consumer demand increases in the month by 10 per cent over the previous month. If the retailer wishes to maintain his previous service level he will increase his order to the wholesaler not by 10 per cent but by 11 per cent (i.e. 10 + 10 (3/52)) in order to maintain three weeks' safety stock. The wholesaler is now faced with an increase in demand of 11 per cent which, if he readjusts his stock levels, will result in an increase in his monthly order to the manufacturer of 13 per cent (i.e. 11 + 11 (12/52)). Similarly, the manufacturer producing for stock and wishing to maintain eight weeks' safety stock increases production by 15 per cent (i.e. 13 + 13 (8/52)). Thus an initial increase in consumer demand of 10 per cent has resulted in an eventual increase in production of 15 per cent. If final demand were to fall back in the next period the same process in reverse would be experienced.

It is not unusual for companies undertaking frequent promotional activity to experience considerable upswings and downswings in factory shipments on a continuing basis. Figure 7.17 illustrates the lagged and magnified effect of such promotional activity upon the factory. It can be imagined that such unpredictable changes in production requirement add considerably to the unit costs of production.

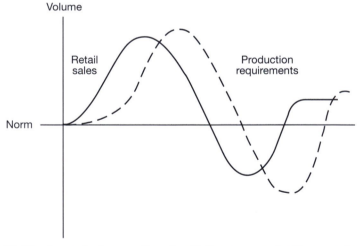

Fig. 7.17 The impact of promotional activity upon production requirements

In the grocery industry, where much of this promotional activity is found, there is a growing recognition of the need to achieve a closer linkage between the ordering policies of the retail trade and the manufacturing schedules of the supplier. In the United States it was estimated that the time from the end of the production line to purchase by the consumer in a retail store was 84 days for a typical dry grocery product (see Figures 7.18 and 7.19).

This means that the 'tidal wave' effect of changes in demand can be considerably magnified as they pass through all the intermediate stock-holding and reorder points. One of the benefits of a quick response system is that by linking the retail checkout desk to the point of production through electronic data transfer, the surge effect can be dramatically reduced. This fact alone could more than justify the initial investment in linked buyer/supplier logistics information systems.

Production strategies for quick response

As the demand by all partners in the supply chain for a quick response increases, the more will be the pressure placed upon manufacturing to meet the customer's needs for variety in shorter and shorter time-frames.

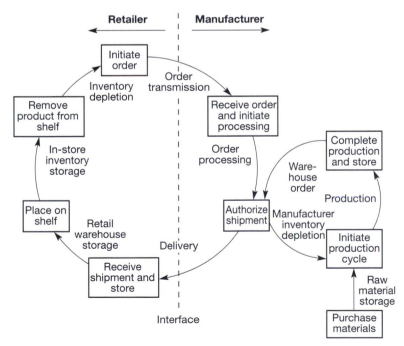

Fig. 7.18 Grocery industry delivery system order cycle
Source: Grocery Manufacturers Association of America

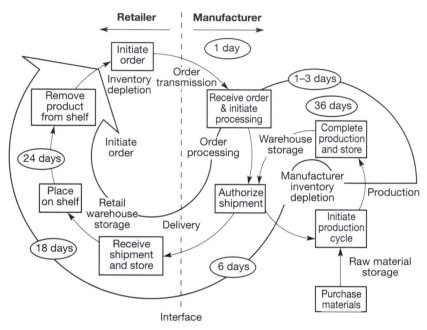

Fig. 7.19 Grocery industry product flow
Source: Grocery Manufacturers Association of America

The answer has to lie in flexibility. As we have already observed, if it were possible to reduce manufacturing and logistics lead times to zero then total flexibility could be achieved. In other words the organization could respond to any request that was technologically feasible in any quantity. Whilst zero lead times are obviously not achievable, the new focus on flexible manufacturing systems (FMS) has highlighted the possibility of substantial progress in this direction.

The key to flexibility in manufacturing is not just new technology, e.g. robotics, although this can contribute dramatically to its achievement. The main barrier to flexibility is the time taken to change; to change from one level of volume to another and to change from making one variant to another. Typically we call this 'set-up time'. It will be apparent that if set-up times can be driven as close as possible to zero then flexible response to customer requirements presents no problem.

The Japanese, not surprisingly, have led the way in developing techniques for set-up time reduction. 'Single minute exchange of die', or SMED, is the goal in many Japanese plants. In other words constant attention by management and the workforce is focused upon the ways

208

in which set-up times can be reduced. Sometimes it will involve new technology, but more often than not it is achieved through taking a totally different look at the process itself. In many cases set-up times have been reduced from hours down to seconds, simply by questioning conventional wisdom.

What in effect we are seeing is a fundamental shift away from the economies of scale, which is volume-based and hence implies long production runs with few change-overs, to the economies of scope which is based upon producing small quantities of a wider range, hence requiring more change-overs.

It has been suggested that under the economies of scope model:

'... a single plant can produce a variety of output at the same cost as (if not lower than) a separate plant, dedicated to producing only one type of product at a given level. In other words an economic order quantity (EOQ) of one unit, and specific production designs, engender no additional costs. Economies of scope change the materials-driven, batch-system technology into a multi-functional, flow system configuration.'[5]

The marketing advantages that such flexibility brings with it are considerable. It means that in effect the company can cater for the precise needs of multiple customers and instead of the old Henry Ford Model 'T' motto – 'Any colour you like, as long as it's black' – we can offer even higher levels of customization. In today's marketplace where customers seek individuality and where segments or 'niches' are getting ever smaller, a major source of competitive advantage can be gained by linking production flexibility to customers' needs for variety.

A classic example is provided by Benetton, the Italian fashion goods manufacturer and distributor, who have created a worldwide business based upon responsiveness to fashion changes – with a particular emphasis upon colour. By developing an innovative process whereby entire knitted garments can be dyed in small batches, they reduced the need to carry inventory of multiple colours and because of the small batch sizes for dyeing they greatly enhanced their flexibility. Benetton's speed of response is also assisted by the investment that they have made in high speed distribution systems which are themselves aided by rapid feedback of sales information from the marketplace.

Many companies are now seeking to construct supply chains to enable them to support a marketing strategy of mass customization. The idea behind this is that today's customers in many markets are increasingly demanding tailored solutions for their specific requirements. The challenge is to find ways of achieving this marketing goal without increasing finished goods inventory and without incurring the higher costs of production normally associated with make-to-order.

> Today's customers in many markets are increasingly demanding tailored solutions for their specific requirements.

Often this can be achieved by postponing the final configuration or assembly of the product until the actual customer requirement is known – a strategy pursued by Dell and Hewlett Packard for example.

In other cases high technology in the form of computer aided design/computer aided manufacturing (CAD/CAM) can provide the means for this mass customization. One interesting example of how technology can assist the tailoring of products to individual customer requirements is provided by Custom Foot,[6] a small shoe company in the United States. Their stores carry no inventory, only examples of styles, leather-types, colours, etc. Customers can make their choice from amongst the available options and then their feet are precisely measured by means of an advanced scanner which enables a precise fit to be achieved. An electronic order is then dispatched to their Italian suppliers and the finished product is delivered to customers in the United States within three weeks. All this is achieved at a price that is highly competitive.

In Japan, Toyota have used the principles of flexible manufacturing and logistics to provide higher levels of responsiveness to customer needs, albeit with a reduced level of options (see Figure 7.20).

A feature of the Toyota production system is the concept of a 'full daily mix schedule'. This means that the aim is to make at least some of every variant every day. Ideally every factory ought to aim to make every product every day (assuming that there is a demand). The aim is to achieve a 'level schedule' with an optimum mix of variants so that demand can be met from the minimum of stock.

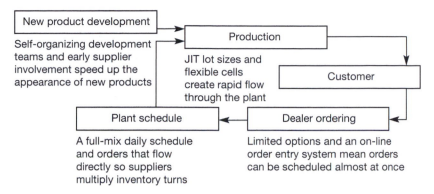

Fig. 7.20 Toyota performs critical operations faster

In Western Europe also, many car manufacturers are now moving towards a 'make-to-order' strategy rather than 'make-to-forecast'. However, at a company like Rover the philosophy is not to achieve this by reducing customer choice through limiting the number of options available – which is the Toyota strategy – but rather by managing the pipeline better. Thus, for example they have centralized the control of finished inventory of vehicles, rather than have the dealers carry stock. Secondly, they take advantage of the 80/20 rule which tells them that 80 per cent of the total demand will be for just 20 per cent of the variants. These are the models and options that are made to forecast whereas the other 20 per cent of demand is only made against firm orders but is given priority in the production schedule.

There is now much evidence to suggest that quick response logistics linked to just-in-time manufacturing and delivery is providing those companies who adopt it with a substantial competitive edge. As we have seen, markets in all sectors, industrial, consumer and service, are becoming much more sensitive to time. Hence the importance of creating the 'responsive organization' where, through a linkage of information and flexibility of operations, the company can achieve what was previously thought to be impossible: rapid response to customers' individual requirements.

211

Summary

One of the greatest influences for transformation within the supply chain has come from the so-called just-in-time revolution. Originating in manufacturing the JIT philosophy has now extended across the supply chain. The principle is simple: no products should be made or shipped until there is a demand for them. The aim is to move from the traditional 'push' type system based on forecasts and batches to a 'pull' type system where real demand triggers a response of just the required quantity.

'Quick Response' is the broad term used to characterize logistics strategies which aim to meet the precise customer requirement in short time-frames with minimal inventory. Essentially these strategies are based upon the idea of 'substituting information for inventory'. In this case the critical information relates to actual market demand and the challenge is to create the means for accurately capturing that demand and to transmit it back up the supply chain as quickly as possible.

References

1. Frazier, R.M. 'Quick Response in Soft Lines', *Discount Merchandiser,* January 1986.
2. Sherman, R.J., 'Improving Customer Service Through Integrated Logistics', *Council of Logistics Management Annual Conference Proceedings*, 1991.
3. Forrester, J., *Industrial Dynamics*, MIT Press, 1961.
4. Abraham, M.M. and Lodish, L.M., 'Getting the Most Out of Advertising and Promotion', *Harvard Business Review,* May–June 1990.
5. Lei, D. and Goldhar, J.D., 'Computer-Integrated Manufacturing (CIM): Redefining the Manufacturing Firm into a Global Service Business', *International Journal of Operations and Production Management,* Vol 11, No 10, 1991.
6. *Fortune*, 10 November 1997.

8

Managing the
supply chain

This chapter:

Considers some of the organizational impediments to the implementation of logistics strategies, highlighting the costs to the organization of functionally-focused management systems.

●

Identifies logistics as a planning and co-ordination activity, a force for organizational change, and one of several core processes within a horizontally organized market-facing business.

●

Stresses the need to extend logistics integration upstream to suppliers and downstream to distributors and customers, outlining a series of measures which facilitate the development of integrated end-to-end supply chain processes.

●

Highlights the trends towards network competition and the development of mutually beneficial collective strategies between co-operating players within a supply chain.

●

Introduces Efficient Consumer Response (ECR) – an industry-wide initiative to lift the competitiveness of the grocery sector – as one of several contemporary examples of how organizations are looking to create customer value through co-operative supply chain strategies.

The transition to the 21st century seems to have been accompanied by ever-higher levels of turbulence in the business environment. Companies that were market leaders a decade ago have in many cases encountered severe reversals of fortune. Mergers and takeovers have changed the shape of many markets and the advent of European and global competition have changed for all time the rules of the game. On top of all this, as we have noted, has been a growing demand from the marketplace for ever-higher levels of service and quality. These pressures have combined to produce a new imperative for the organization: the need to be responsive.

The responsive organization not only seeks to put the customer at the centre of the business, but it designs all its systems and procedures with the prime objective of improving the speed of response and the reliability of that response. Traditional organizations have grown heavy with layer upon layer of management and bureaucracy. Such companies have little chance of remaining competitive in the new marketplace. Neither is it sufficient to rely upon restructuring the organization through removing layers of management, i.e. 'flattening' the organizational chart – as many companies are now seeking to do – if such 'de-layering' is not accompanied by equivalent change to the networks and systems that deliver service to the customer.

> **Traditional organizations have grown heavy with layer upon layer of management and bureaucracy.**

Creating the logistics vision

Making service happen is the ultimate challenge. Whilst it is by no means easy to develop strategies for service that will lead to improved competitive performance, the hardest task is to put that strategy into action. How do we develop an organization that is capable of delivering high quality service on a consistent, ongoing basis?

These days most companies are familiar with the idea of 'mission statements' as an articulation of the vision of the business. The mission statement seeks to define the purpose of the business, its boundaries and its aspirations. It is now by no means uncommon for organizations to have such statements for the business as a whole and for key constituent components. What some companies have found is that there can be significant benefits to defining the logistics vision of the firm.

The purpose of the logistics vision statement is to give a clear indication of the basis whereby the business intends to build a position of advantage through closer customer relationships. Such statements are never easy to construct. There is always the danger that they will descend into vague 'motherhood' statements that give everyone a warm feeling but provide no guidelines for action.

Ideally the logistics vision should be built around the simple issue of 'How do we intend to use logistics and supply chain management to create value for our customers?' To operationalize this idea will necessitate a detailed understanding of how customer value is (or could be) created and delivered in the markets in which the business competes. Value chain analysis will be a fundamental element in this investigation as will the definition of the core competencies and capabilities of the organization. Asking the questions 'What activities do we excel in?' and 'What is it that differentiates us from our competitors' is the starting point for creating the logistics vision statement.

Earlier it was suggested that the three words 'Better, Faster, Cheaper' summarized the ways in which logistics management can provide value for customers. The criterion for a good logistics vision statement is that it should provide the road map for how these three goals are to be achieved.

The problems with conventional organizations

Amongst experienced observers and commentators of the logistics management process there is general agreement that the major barrier to the implementation of the logistics concept is organizational. In other words, a major impediment to change in this crucial managerial area is the entrenched and rigid organizational structure that most established companies are burdened with.

There is a great danger that those companies that do not recognize the need for organizational change, or that lack the will to make it happen, will never achieve the improvements in competitive advantage that integrated logistics management can bring. The argument advanced here is that the demands of the marketplace for enhanced service provision combined with dramatically heightened competition call for a paradigm shift in the way in which we think about our organizations.

The concept of integrated logistics management, whereby flows of information and material between source and user are co-ordinated and managed as a system is now widely understood, if not widely implemented. The logic of linking each step of the process as materials and products move closer to the customer is based upon the principles of optimization. In other words the goal is to maximize customer service whilst simultaneously minimizing costs and reducing assets locked up in the logistics pipeline.

However, in the conventional organization, this poses an immediate problem. Most companies are organized on a functional basis. In other words they have sought a division of responsibility by functions, so we might find a purchasing function, a production function, a sales function and so on. Typically the organization chart would look like that in Figure 8.1.

Each of the 'vertical' functions in the conventional organization is normally headed up by senior managers who come to regard their functional area as their 'territory'. Indeed in many companies these functional heads are 'barons' who wield considerable power and who jealously guard those territories from what they perceive as unwarranted incursions from other functional barons.

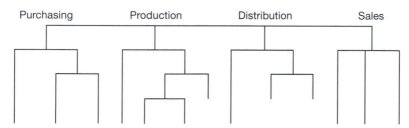

Fig. 8.1 The functional organization

217

Further reinforcing the functional or vertical orientation in the conventional organization is the budgeting system. Typically, each function will be driven by a budget that seeks to control the resources consumed by those functions. It is almost as if the company is working on the assumption that the prime purpose of any enterprise is to control the consumption of resources. In fact, the leading-edge companies have long since realized that the sole purpose of the business is to create profitable outputs and that outputs, not inputs, should form the basis both for the way we organize as well as for the way we plan and control.

We will look in detail later at the alternative models for organization and for planning and control, but first let us highlight some of the real problems that the conventional organization creates that hamper the successful implementation of integrated logistics management.

Inventory builds up at functional boundaries

If individual functions are encouraged to 'optimize' their own costs – because of the budgeting system – then this will often be at the expense of substantially increased inventory across the system as a whole. What happens if, say, production seeks to minimize the unit costs of production by maintaining long production runs with large batch quantities, is the creation of more inventory than is normally required for immediate requirements. Likewise if purchasing management seeks low material costs through bulk purchases then again the inventory of raw materials ahead of production will often be excessive. Similar buffers of inventory will exist right across the supply chain at boundaries within organizations and, indeed, at boundaries between organizations.

Not only is this increased inventory a financial burden and a further strain on working capital, it also obscures our 'visibility' of final demand. Thus upstream activities may not have any clear view of what the real demand is downstream, as all they see is a reorder-point-generated order hitting them at short notice (or more often than not, no notice at all). Figure 8.2 illustrates this point.

Pipeline costs are not transparent

Closely related to the preceding issue is the problem of cost 'transparency'. What this means is that costs relating to the flows of material across functional areas are not easy to measure. Hence the real costs to serve different customers with different product mixes are rarely revealed.

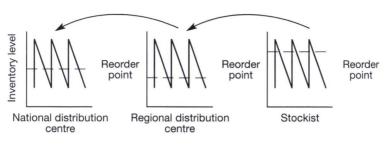

Fig. 8.2 Inventory hides demand

Once again the problem is that the conventional organization will normally only identify costs on a functional basis, and even then at a fairly high level of aggregation. Hence we may well know our transport costs in total but not necessarily how they vary by customer category or by delivery characteristics, e.g. central delivery to a regional distribution centre or local delivery to a supermarket. Where attempts to estimate the costs of outputs are made they usually require, out of necessity, crude allocation procedures. As we noted in Chapter 3, there has recently emerged a lot of interest in 'throughput accounting' and 'activity-based costing', both of which are attempts to pin down costs as they occur and hence to make the total pipeline costs easier to identify. The problem need not exist, it is only a problem because the costing systems we have are designed to monitor functional or input costs rather than flow or output costs. Figure 8.3 makes this point.

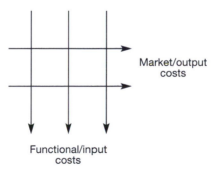

Fig. 8.3 Alternative cost concepts

Functional boundaries impede process management

The process of satisfying customer demand begins with inbound supply and continues through manufacturing or assembly operations and onwards by way of distribution to the customer. Logically the ideal way to manage this process is as a complete system, not by fragmenting it into watertight sections. Yet that is more or less what happens in the conventional business as we have seen. Not only is this inefficient, it actually leads to a loss of effectiveness in competitive terms.

Many of the causes of variation in the order-to-delivery cycle, for example, stem from the variability that inevitably arises in the inefficient processes that have to be created to manage the interfaces between functions. The time taken to process orders for instance is often extended purely because of the paperwork, checking and re-checking, that conventional systems generate. Because organizations grow organically they tend to add to existing processes in a patchwork manner rather than taking a 'clean piece of paper' approach. As a result the systems in use tend to owe more to history than to any concept of holistic management. This phenomenon is further compounded by the inability of managers to detach themselves from their familiar surroundings and to see the 'big picture'. Instead there is a natural tendency to focus on piecemeal improvements within their own narrow functional area.

To achieve a smooth-flowing logistics pipeline requires an orientation that facilitates end-to-end process management. The principle can be compared to the management of an industrial process, say an oil refinery, where to ensure the achievement of optimum efficiency the entire process is managed and controlled as a system, not as a series of adjacent, independent activities.

> To achieve a smooth-flowing logistics pipeline requires an orientation that facilitates end-to-end process management.

The cost to an organization, and indeed to the economy as a whole, of these fragmented processes can only be guessed at, but it must be huge.

Conventional organizations present many faces to the customer

Perhaps the most damning criticism of the traditional organization is that it does not present a 'single face' to the customer. Rather than the customer having to do business with just one organization, in effect they deal with many.

This criticism goes beyond the obvious problems that arise when a customer, seeking, say, information on an order, is passed from one section of the company to another – although that is a common enough occurrence. The real problem is that no one person or department is empowered to manage a customer from enquiry, through to order delivery, in other words to service the customer.

Consider for a moment how the conventional organization processes orders. Typically there will be a sequence of activities beginning with order entry. The point of entry may be within the sales or commercial function but then it goes to credit control, from where it may pass to production planning or, in a make-to-stock environment, to the warehouse. Once the order has been manufactured or assembled it will become the responsibility of distribution and transport planning. At the same time there is a separate process involving the generation of documents such as bills of lading, delivery notes, invoices and so on. The problem is that these activities are sequential, performed in series rather than in parallel. Each function performs its task and then passes the order on to the next function, at each step it is as if the order is 'thrown over the wall'. Figure 8.4 depicts this classic process.

Developing the logistics organization

Some commentators have suggested that the solution to the problems outlined above lies in creating a higher level of authority in the form of a logistics function that links together the purchasing, production and distribution tasks. Appealing as this may appear at first sight, it will

Traditional sequential order processing system

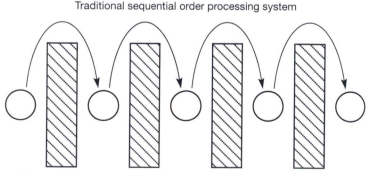

Fig. 8.4 Managing the order

not solve the underlying conflicts that the traditional organization creates. It merely adds another layer of management. At a time when the trend is towards 'flattening' organizations, this solution is unlikely to gain ground.

Instead radical solutions must be sought which may require a restructuring of the conventional 'vertical' organization and lead to the creation of a 'horizontal' or market-facing business. Figures 8.5 and 8.6 contrast the 'vertical' with the 'horizontal' organization.

The horizontal organization has a number of distinguishing characteristics. It is:

- Organized around processes, not tasks
- Flat and de-layered
- Built upon multi-functional teams
- Guided by performance metrics that are market-based

It is the focus on processes rather than functions that is the key to the horizontal organization. The basic precept of process management is that it is through processes that customer value is created. Hence the logic of seeking to manage processes on an integrated basis.

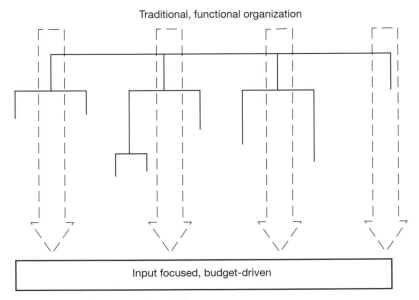

Fig. 8.5 Vertical organizational focus

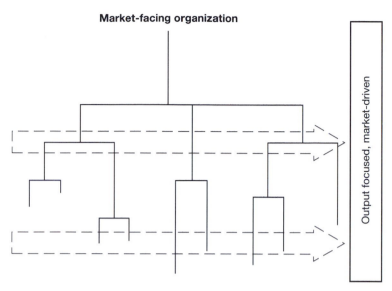

Fig. 8.6 Horizontal organizational focus

In most organizations there will only be a limited number of core processes and the following are likely to be central to most businesses:

- Brand development (including new product development)
- Consumer development (primarily focused on building loyalty with end users)
- Customer management (creating relationships with intermediaries)
- Supplier development (strengthening upstream and alliance relationships)
- Supply chain management (the cash-to-cash process)

Typically companies that focus upon process management have recognized that they are best managed by cross-functional teams. These teams will comprise specialists drawn from the functional areas (which now become 'centres of excellence') and will be led by 'integrators' whose job it is to focus the process team around the achievement of market-based goals. In such organizations a different type of skills profile is clearly required for managers at all levels. Equally the reward systems need to change as the horizontal organization by definition is flatter and hence the traditional upward promotion opportunities are fewer.

Making the change from the 'vertical' to the 'horizontal' poses many challenges and yet it is critical to the implementation of a market-driven logistics strategy.

The achievement of this transformation might begin with the recognition that logistics is essentially a planning orientation, in other words the logistics management process entails the linking of production plans with materials requirements plans in one direction and distribution requirements plans in the other. The aim of any organization should be to ensure that production produces only what the marketplace requires whilst purchasing supplies production with what it needs to meet its immediate requirements. How can this fairly obvious idea be converted into reality?

■ Developing process management skills at Unipart ■

Unipart Group of Companies (UGC) was formed in 1987, when the group's Chief Executive John Neill led a buy-out of a disparate collection of functional parts of the failing nationalized Rover Group. Within the privatized UGC the autonomous functional groups – automotive parts manufacturing, warehousing and distribution, sales, marketing, information systems and communications – became divisions of UGC.[1] Most prominent was the large and successful automotive parts manufacturing division, Unipart Industries, which had found itself in the happy position of being able to acquire leading-edge lean manufacturing and process management know-how from two of its Japanese customers, Honda and Toyota.

UGC's divisions, though operating as independent business units were to some extent interdependent, and the company's senior management were quick to recognize that the less efficient and agile parts of the business would, in time, impede the development of the others. To lift the competitiveness of the whole enterprise, each division was charged with identifying best practice in its field, tailoring it to Unipart's needs and then – as a centre of excellence within the business – passing this learning on to other departments. Unipart's now famous training establishment, the 'Unipart University', was devised as a means of transcending divisional barriers and speeding the dissemination of know-how throughout the business. In practice this meant that all employees, from shop floor to directors, became involved in continuous learning programmes and team-based problem-solving exercises. Unipart was in fact amongst the first

---

British companies to introduce truly cross-functional team working. The move highlighted the need for employees to acquire a working knowledge of each others' roles and to extend their own skills beyond those required to perform their functional tasks. The Unipart University is therefore equipped to help and encourage all employees to acquire voluntarily a much wider range of skills and qualifications, offering everything from remedial adult literacy programmes to the chance to study for an MBA.[2]

The development of process management skills throughout the business has been amongst the most significant breakthroughs in organizational learning at UGC. Unipart Industries had been working to strengthen its relationships with key suppliers since 1985, through a mutually agreed continuous improvement process known as 'Tend-to-Zero'. Tend-to-Zero provides a framework for identifying the ten most critical factors in the business relationship – quality, cost, delivery times, product range, environmental issues, etc. – and assessing the shortcomings of each on a scale of zero to ten. A score of ten means that something is unacceptable, so both sides work together towards a world-class zero, with scores continually reassessed as the relationship and business performance improves.

The transfer of this process expertise from Unipart Industries to the former warehouse and distribution division, Unipart Demand Chain Management (DCM), became an early priority within the group. The aim was to get DCM to co-operate more closely with Unipart Industries and its major suppliers, so that together they could work more effectively to fill orders on time. DCM went on to place an increasing focus on teaching employees how to improve both internal and supplier processes to eliminate waste from the supply chain.[3] The expertise has placed DCM in a position to explore significant new business opportunities including, in 1995, an agreement with Hewlett Packard to distribute computer parts for 'next day' and 'following day' delivery services in the United Kingdom. The contract was a milestone for DCM, firstly because Hewlett Packard was sufficiently impressed with its capabilities to entrust DMC with responsibility for a full spectrum of logistics services, and secondly, because of the learning opportunities arising from working alongside a world-class partner within an entirely new business setting.

References

1. Womack, James P. and Jones, Daniel T. (1994), 'From Lean Production to the Lean Enterprise', *Harvard Business Review*, March–April, pp. 93–102.
2. Bassett, Philip (1997), *The Times*, 28 May.
3. Unipart Group of Companies (1995), *Annual Review*, pp. 9, 21.

The key lies in the recognition that the order and its associated information flows should be at the heart of the business. It may be a truism but the only rationale for any commercial organization is to generate orders and to fulfil those orders. Everything the company does should be directly linked to facilitating this process and the process must itself be reflected in the organizational design and in its planning and control systems.

All of this leads to the conclusion that the order fulfilment process should be designed as an integrated activity of the company with the conventional functions of the business supporting that process. To assist this transition the development of a customer order management system is a vital prerequisite.

A customer order management system is a planning framework that links the information system with the physical flow of materials required to fulfil demand. To achieve this requires the central management of forecasts, requirements plans, material and production control and purchasing.

Figure 8.7 outlines the key tasks and responsibilities of the order management system.

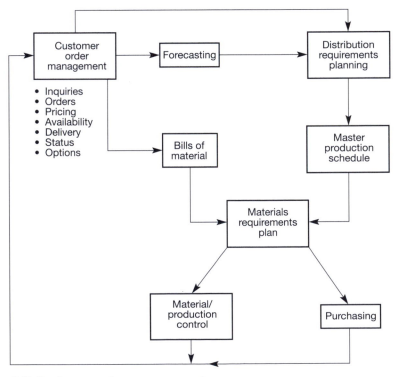

Fig. 8.7 Customer order management

At the heart of the customer order management system is a requirements plan which is market-driven. The inputs to this plan include data and information relating to inquiries and orders, price changes, promotional activity and product availability. This information provides the basis for the forecast which then drives the requirements plan. Alongside this is a process for the fulfilment of current orders. They are not separated but closely integrated through the information system.

Two practical steps for improving customer order management processes are suggested below:

1 Eliminate the 'non-value-added' activities

In reviewing the existing order processing system each element and each link in the chain should be critically examined to identify the value that it creates and the cost that it adds. 'Value' in this context refers to customer value, meaning a benefit that will contribute to the total utility of the product or offer in the eyes of the customer – and hence their willingness to pay.

It has already been noted that in many service processes it is the case that a large proportion of the time spent is non-value-added time. For example, delays in paperwork, time that is 'consumed' whilst a product sits as inventory in a warehouse, time spent on checking and re-checking and so forth. The target should be to eliminate or reduce all non-value-added activities.

The order processing system is a fabulous hunting ground in which to seek out and remove non-value-adding activities. So often we find that no one has ever questioned the way in which paperwork is managed, or the sequence in which activities take place or indeed why those activities take place at all! Where possible the goal should be to look for opportunities to combine steps in the processes, to integrate separate groups of people performing adjacent tasks and to simplify processes by reducing paperwork and reports. It should always be remembered that a major part of the time consumed in meeting customer requirements is actually redundant and its elimination will improve the consistency and reliability of the delivered service, thus enhancing its 'value' in the eyes of the customer.

2 Order fulfilment groups

Given that from a systems viewpoint the process of managing orders can be refined along the lines described above, what scope exists for improving the 'process architecture'?

Several companies have experimented with the idea of a cross-functional, cross-departmental team to take responsibility for the management of orders. This team may be termed the order fulfilment group. The idea behind such a group is that rather than having an organizational structure for order management where every activity is separated with responsibility for each activity fragmented around the organization, instead these activities should be grouped together both organizationally and physically. In other words instead of seeing each step in the process as a discrete activity we cluster them together and bring the people involved together as well – ideally in a single open-plan office. Thus the order fulfilment group might comprise commercial or sales office people, credit control and accounts, production scheduler and transport scheduler – indeed anyone involved in the crucial business processes of *converting an order into cash*.

It is likely that in a large business serving many different customers a number of these teams may be required. Indeed for the biggest, most important accounts it is probable that a single dedicated team will be required to manage the relationship.

The effect that such groups can have is often dramatic. Because all the key people in the order fulfilment process are brought together and linked around a common entity – the order – they are better able to sort out problems and eliminate bottlenecks. Order cycle times can be dramatically reduced as teamwork prevails over inter-departmental rivalry. New ways of dealing with problems emerge, more non-value-added activities are eliminated and customer service problems – when they arise – can quickly be resolved, since all the key people are in close connection with each other.

Schonberger[1] gives a number of examples of how the concept of a manufacturing 'cell' – where linked actions are performed in parallel by multi-functional teams – can work just as effectively in order processing. One of the cases he quotes, Ahlstrom, a Finnish company, has reduced lead times in order processing from one week to one day, and variation in lead time has dropped from up to six weeks to one week.

Another case was that of Nashua Corporation in North America, where order entry lead time has been reduced from eight days to one hour, with a 40 per cent reduction in space and a 70 per cent reduction in customer claims.

This approach has been likened to a game of rugby rather than a relay race! What this means is that a team of closely integrated colleagues runs up the field together passing the ball as they run. In the relay race no one can run until they receive the baton from the preceding person in the chain. The end result is that this vital part of the service process can be speeded up whilst simultaneously improving the quality of the output, hence a major competitive advantage is achieved.

In a manufacturing context the customer order management system must be closely linked to production planning and the materials requirements plan. Ideally all the planning and scheduling activities in the organization relating to the order and its satisfaction should be brought together organizationally.

Logistics as the vehicle for change

As markets, technologies and competitive forces change at ever-increasing rates the imperative for organizational change becomes more pressing. The paradox is that because organizational structures are rigid, even ossified, they do not have the ability to change at anything like the same rate as the environment in which they exist.

> As markets, technologies and competitive forces change at ever-increasing rates the imperative for organizational change becomes more pressing.

The trend towards globalization of industry, involving as it does the co-ordination of complex flows of materials and information from a multitude of offshore sourcing and manufacturing plants to a diversity of markets has sharply highlighted the inappropriateness of existing structures. What we are discovering is that the driving force for organizational change is logistics.

To compete and survive in these global markets requires a logistics-oriented organization. There has to be nothing less than a shift from a functional focus to a process focus. Such a radical change entails a re-grouping within the organization so that the key tasks become the management of cross-functional work flows. Hewlett Packard is an example of a company that has restructured its organization around market-facing processes, rather than functions. Order fulfilment has been recognized as a core process and so, on a global scale, there is one order management system architecture that links order entry, order management and factory order/shipment processing. This core process is supported by a common information system that provides 'end-to-'end' visibility of the logistics pipeline from order through to delivery (see Figure 8.8).

In fact it is through such breakthroughs in information technology that the type of organizational change we are describing has been made possible. The information network now defines the organization structure. In other words the information that flows from the marketplace at one end of the pipeline to supply points at the other will increasingly shape the organization – not the other way round.

Such a change will be accelerated by the trend, commented upon earlier in this book, for companies to focus on what might be termed 'core competencies' and to out-source everything else. In other words the business of tomorrow will most likely only perform those activities in the value chain where they believe they have a differential advantage, all other activities will be performed by partners, co-makers and logistics service providers. In cases such as this the need for co-ordination of information and materials flows between entities in the supply chain becomes a key priority, further highlighting the central role of logistics as a process-oriented management task.

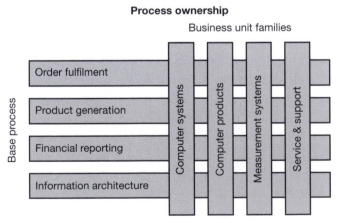

Process ownership

Business unit families

Base process

Order fulfilment

Product generation

Financial reporting

Information architecture

Computer systems

Computer products

Measurement systems

Service & support

Fig. 8.8 Global logistics co-ordination at Hewlett Packard

In this brief review of the challenges facing the organization in a changed environment we have emphasized the need to break down the 'walls' that traditionally have fragmented the organization and impeded the cost-effective achievement of customer service requirements. Clearly there is a need for 'pattern breaking' on a major scale. The only way such significant change will be achieved is through leadership from the very top of the organization. It is no coincidence that the handful of companies who have achieved excellence in logistics have been through a process of change that was driven from the top. Companies like Xerox, Hewlett Packard, IBM and Philips have experienced, and are still experiencing, often painful change as they transform themselves from functionally-based businesses to market-facing businesses. Whilst the impetus for change differs from company to company, the engine of change has been the same – the search for superior performance through logistics management.

The need for integration

Perhaps the greatest implication for the responsive organization of the challenges we have described is the priority that must be attached to integration. Not just integration within the organization but integration upstream with suppliers and downstream with distributors and customers. This integration is logistical rather than 'vertical'; in other words we do not imply ownership or domination of the supply chain but rather that there is a greater emphasis on the linkage of organizations through information.

As we saw earlier in Chapter 7, the whole nature of logistics management has been dramatically changed by the information technology revolution. Information systems have now become the driving force pressurizing companies to reconsider their relationships with customers as well as suppliers. It is no longer possible to manage the business as if it were in a vacuum with no interconnections with other organizations.

Supply chain integration implies process integration, both upstream and downstream. By process integration we mean collaborative working between buyers and suppliers, joint product development, common systems and shared information. For some companies such ideas are still unthinkable and yet the signs are clearly pointing to a future where it will be the extent and quality of supply chain integration that will determine marketplace performance.

However, in many industries the concept of process integration is increasingly accepted. For example, over the last ten years or so there has been a significant change in the way in which many car manufacturers in Western Europe have changed from fragmented, transaction-focused businesses to highly integrated and relationship-based supply chains. Companies like Rover have now embraced the philosophy of the 'extended enterprise'. In the extended enterprise the aim is to create seamless, 'end-to-end' processes so that innovative products are created and delivered to market at higher levels of quality, in shorter time-frames but at a price which in real terms is significantly less than it has ever been in the past. This is achieved through a number of means including:

1 Supply base rationalization

In the eighties Rover dealt with well over 2000 suppliers of components, materials and services. In the nineties that number was down to under 500. With the remaining suppliers Rover has established significantly closer relationships and is now looking to these suppliers increasingly to provide systems rather than components. For example, a single first-tier supplier will be responsible for supplying the complete dashboard for a particular model of car, complete with all the controls, displays and wiring ready for installation as a single unit – the whole unit being delivered on a just-in-time basis.

2 Supplier development programmes

As with the majority of companies, Rover used to view the procurement activity as primarily a purchasing function tasked with buying at the lowest price. This would typically involve using more than one vendor to supply a particular component with perhaps an element of 'playing one off against the other'.

Now, supplier development has replaced the traditional purchasing function. The idea behind this is that a cross-functional team of Rover specialists will work closely with suppliers to seek improvements in the suppliers' processes as well as in the interfaces with Rover's processes.

3 Early supplier involvement in design

Much innovation in the car industry today is supplier originated. Such developments as ABS (braking systems), engine management systems and improved suspension systems have come in large part from suppliers to the auto industry. By bringing these suppliers more closely into the new product development process it has been found that not only can innovation be continually embodied in new products but often that simpler, more cost-effective designs can be created.

It is now recognized that a significant proportion of the total cost of making and maintaining a car is 'designed-in'; the challenge today is to find ways of 'designing-out' those costs.

4 Integrated information systems

The car industry was one of the first to go 'paperless' in the sense of using IT to provide the means of enhancing the flow of information both upstream and downstream in the supply chain. The use of Electronic Data Interchange (EDI) coupled with the growing acceptance of the 'just-in-time' philosophy led to a realization that the benefits of a fully transparent information system could be considerable. Thus suppliers can now manage the flow of material into the plant on the basis of advance notification of Rover's production schedules. There are no orders, no delivery notes, no invoices – only a single source of information that provides the basis for a timely physical response which itself triggers a payment to the supplier.

5 Centralization of inventory

The extended enterprise at Rover does not only include upstream suppliers but the downstream flow of finished product through its dealer network. Traditionally dealers carried a stock of cars which may or may not have matched the requirements of their customers. If a customer demanded a colour or an option that the dealer did not have, then a 'swap' would have to be arranged with another dealer who did have that particular vehicle. Now, instead, Rover have centralized the inventory and have taken responsibility for its management. The dealers only have demonstration models, but they also have on-line access to the Rover supply system and can give the customer immediate confirmation of the availability of the car of their choice and when it can be delivered. For those vehicles that are not available from stock the dealer can enter the order directly into the Rover production schedule and the car is in effect made to order.

Managing the supply chain as a network

The new competitive paradigm that we have described in this chapter places the firm at the centre of an inter-dependent network – a confederation of mutually complementary competencies and capabilities – which competes as an integrated supply chain against other supply chains.

To manage in such a radically revised competitive structure clearly requires different skills and priorities to those employed in the traditional model. To achieve market leadership in the world of network competition necessitates a focus on network management as well as upon internal processes. Of the many issues and challenges facing organizations as they make the transition to this new competitive environment, the following are perhaps most significant:

> To achieve market leadership in the world of network competition necessitates a focus on network management as well as upon internal processes.

1 Collective strategy development

Traditionally, members of a supply chain have never considered themselves to be part of a marketing network and so have not shared with each other their strategic thinking. For network competition to be truly effective requires a significantly higher level of joint strategy development. This means that network members must collectively agree strategic goals for the network and the means of attaining them.

2 Win-win thinking

Perhaps one of the biggest challenges to the successful establishment of marketing networks is the need to break free from the often adversarial nature of buyer/supplier relationships that existed in the past. There is now a growing realization that co-operation between network partners usually leads to improved performance generally. The issue then becomes one of determining how the results of that improved performance can be shared amongst the various players. 'Win-win' need not mean 50/50, but at a minimum all partners should benefit and be better off as a result of co-operation.

234

3 Open communication

One of the most powerful drivers of change in marketing networks has been the advent of information technology making the exchange of information between supply chain partners so easy and so advantageous. Electronic Data Interchange (EDI) was an early precursor of the information highway that now exists in some industries enabling end-to-end pipeline visibility to become a reality. The textile industry in the United States has benefited tremendously from the use of shared information on sales which originates from the retail store but is then transmitted to garment manufacturer to material manufacturer to the manufacturer of synthetic fibre. With all parties 'singing to the same hymn sheet' a much more rapid response to marketplace changes is achieved with less inventory and lower risks of obsolescence. For network marketing to work to its fullest potential, visibility and transparency of relevant information throughout the supply chain is essential. Open-book accounting is another manifestation of this move towards transparency by which cost data is shared upstream and downstream and hence each partner's profit is visible to the others.

▓ British industry can save £2.4bn a year ▓

Supply chain relationships hold the key

British manufacturing companies can save £2.4bn a year by developing effective supply chain relationships with customers and suppliers. This is the conclusion of a new report, based on research for the Institute of Logistics, by A.T. Kearney, management consultants, and Manchester School of Management at UMIST. The report says that collaboration in the supply chain is not being fully exploited in the United Kingdom, with a cost penalty estimated at 6 per cent of purchased material costs each year.

Although 92 per cent of manufacturing companies say they have, or intend to have, supply chain relationships with customers and suppliers, less than a third have bothered to measure the costs and benefits associated with these initiatives. As a result, many companies are unable to develop relationships to the point where they deliver tangible results rather than rhetoric claiming 'partnership'. The difference between results and rhetoric can generate savings of up to 6 per cent in purchased material costs each year, according to Steve Young of A.T. Kearney. For a typical £100m turnover manufacturer, this would represent around £2m in lost opportunity annually.

▶

▶ The report shows that this failure to measure the 'pain and gain' of closer supply chain relationships makes it difficult to demonstrate that they have been a success in anything other than a subjective way, or to identify areas in which the relationships could be further improved. As a result, few relationships progress beyond the stage of limited co-operation at an operational level.

Development to more advanced levels is also held back by a concern on the part of suppliers about becoming over-dependent on their major customers, even though they commonly wish to increase their customers' dependence on them. The reluctance of firms to make themselves too vulnerable to particular customers acts as a constraint on the open relationships that are required to improve interfaces and share ideas on how to reduce costs and improve service and quality.

The study found that over three-quarters of the collaborative initiatives studied brought benefits to other relationships, so that developing the right relationships can be a powerful driver of change within a company overall, through the transfer of ideas and learning. This means that the idea of 'win-win' relationships needs to be treated with some caution. Some evidently successful projects appeared to entail considerable imbalances in the distribution of costs and benefits, typically with the supplier paying and the customer benefiting. However, this makes sense where the supplier transfers the learning and applies it to other areas of the business, or where the level of trust builds over time to encourage collaboration at a strategic level in areas such as market entry and product innovation.

The evidence suggests that supply chain integration is not being fully exploited. The links that exist are still fundamentally arms length, with traditional behaviours and 'them and us' attitudes. Effective partnerships rise above this to look at the extended enterprise, from raw material sources through to end customer, from a total business, rather than a narrow buyer-seller perspective.

This is not achieved overnight. The report characterizes courtship that can ultimately lead to partnership in four ways:

- Clear goals endorsed by senior management that reflect significant business objectives.
- Accurate measurement of costs and benefits allowing prioritization of effort and demonstration of success.
- Commitment of an appropriate level and quality of resources on both sides to make real progress quickly.

● Active learning processes to share best practice information across both organizations, thus leveraging individual relationships and building partnerships.

Partnerships based on this strong foundation will deliver results rather than rhetoric. Steve Young says: 'British industry needs to stop flirting with relationships and start going steady with partners who have the potential to make a difference. Each partner should expect a degree of nervousness in the other, much like marriage, if only because collaboration creates a sense of dependency.

This nervousness should be tolerated until confidence is established. It should be understood that while the customer may get immediate benefits through substantial cost savings, the supplier may suffer short-term pain before benefiting from its new competitive position.'

If there are changes in both customers' and suppliers' operations there is likely to be an equal distribution of costs and benefits – including long-term strategic advantages. However, where the changes are predominantly made by the supplier, the benefits are skewed towards the customer and the costs towards the supplier.

Source: Institute of Logistics Press Release on the publication of *Profiting from Partnership*, February 1996

Process integration and ECR

The early experiments in Quick Response Logistics – described earlier in Chapter 7 – have rapidly led to a broadening of the concept to become the basis for collaborative working in the supply chain.

In the grocery sector this development has been termed Efficient Consumer Response (ECR). ECR is an umbrella term that covers a number of related philosophies and techniques that seek to enable the delivery of superior consumer value in shorter time-frames and at less cost. The ECR Europe Executive Board – a combined manufacturer/retailer pressure group – has identified 14 elements under three broad headings where co-operation can bring significant benefits:

Demand management

● Develop strategy and capability
● Optimize assortments
● Optimize promotions
● Optimize introductions

Supply management

- Integrated suppliers
- Reliable operations
- Synchronized production
- Continuous replenishment
- Cross docking
- Automated store ordering

Enabling technologies

- Electronic data interchange
- Electronic fund transfer
- Item coding and database management
- Activity based costing

The fundamental principle of ECR is that through partnership within the supply chain, significant cost reduction can be achieved through a better allocation of shelf space in the retail store, fewer wasteful promotions and new product introductions and more efficient physical replenishment. The key to the achievement of these goals is shared information, in particular information on sales gathered at the check-out counter and transferred directly to suppliers.

Using this shared information, manufacturers and retailers can create more consumer value through the supply chain. Specifically it is suggested that benefits can be accrued in four key areas (see Table 8.1).

Table 8.1 The four pillars of ECR

New product introduction	Trade and consumer promotions	Range and assortment	Product replenishment
• Improve success rate	• Improve consumer targeting	• Match to consumer and shopper needs	• Improve on-shelf availability
• Reduce time to market	• Improve return on investment	• Reduce duplication	• Reduce cost
		• Improve return on space	• Reduce inventory
• Improve return on investment	• Co-operation across the supply chain		
• Improve quality, reduce costs			

Source: ECR Europe/Institute of Grocery Distribution

Whilst ECR brings many potential benefits to both suppliers and retailers in terms of efficiency improvements, the biggest opportunity it presents is to enable real supply chain collaboration. By sharing information it enables supply chains to become *demand chains* and in so doing to deliver enhanced customer value.

For decades, in the retail industry particularly, buyers and suppliers have acted more as adversaries than as partners. Even though commercial realities will prevail so that individual entities in the chain will still seek advantage, there now exists a framework in which they can co-operate to 'grow the cake' but compete to decide how it will be divided.

■ Supermarkets in plan to share data ■

by Peggy Hollinger

The battle for advantage in the highly competitive food sector will take a significant step forward this year with two leading supermarkets planning to share live sales data with the majority of their suppliers.

Tesco and Safeway yesterday revealed plans to extend trials sharing live information on stock levels, sales and promotional activity – currently with a limited number of suppliers – to almost all product manufacturers this year.

The move could help to cut costs substantially for retailers and suppliers. St Ivel, the yoghurt manufacturer, estimates its trial with Tesco could result in savings of up to 30 per cent on the cost of promotions alone.

Analysts said the development marked a substantial shift in the focus of competition between food retailers in the United Kingdom. Cutting prices had proved fruitless, serving only to erode the industry's margins and giving no single supermarket group any long-term advantage. 'If anyone cuts prices, the others just follow in minutes,' said one analyst.

However, building a more efficient supply chain could bring real advantages. 'It is by far the biggest area of cost and offers the biggest upside if they manage that down,' said another analyst. Costs represent about 75 per cent of sales for food retailers.

Moreover the initiatives at Tesco and Safeway signalled a significant change in the traditionally fraught retailer/supplier relationship. 'In the past it has always been easiest just to beat them (suppliers) around the head and squeeze another penny out of them,' said one analyst.

Sharing live sales information with suppliers is part of a concept known as efficient consumer response, a formula imported from the

▶

▶ United States. The success of Wal-Mart, the largest US retailer, has been attributed in part to close relationships with suppliers that have helped it to keep prices down.

Barry Knichel, Tesco's supply chain development director, said the benefits remained hard to quantify as they depended both on the type of product and the ability of a supplier to tap into the system. 'The biggest stumbling block in the past has been suppliers' system development,' he said. While Tesco hopes to offer all of its 1500 suppliers access to the live data this year, Mr Knichel said he expected about 80 per cent to take part.

Safeway said suppliers accounting for 70 per cent of its products were expected to be linked to its system within months.

Source: *Financial Times*, 28 January 1998

Co-makership and logistics partnerships

From the examples we have looked at it will be clear that the major reason for supply chain inefficiencies is the lack of co-ordination and linkage between the various parties in the chain. 'No man is an island' is a phrase which has significance for the supply chain. Indeed there is a growing recognition by many companies that partnership and co-operation achieves more than narrow self-interest and conflict. See the Toyota Case Study below.

Toyota: the power of partnership

On Monday, 3 February 1997, Japan's largest motor manufacturer, Toyota, announced that all of its Japanese assembly lines had been brought to a halt following a devastating fire at the premises of one of its affiliated suppliers, Aisin Seiki. The company supplied brake master cylinders for several Toyota models and was its only supplier of brake-fluid proportioning valves. The fire had shown up one of the weaknesses of Toyota's famous lean manufacturing system, which runs on minimum stock levels using components delivered on a just-in-time basis from a small number of linked-ownership suppliers. The fire left Toyota holding only half a day's stock of the vital components. The motor manufacturer's production lines ground to a halt soon afterwards, as did the lines of all other Toyota suppliers. This was not the first time that a catastrophic event had shut down production through-out the Toyota kieretsu. The company had suffered similar problems in 1995 when the Hanshin earthquake severed its supply lines to com-ponent manufacturers in and around the city of Kobe.

Toyota's rival Honda has long worked a policy of dual sourcing, partly because it does not have such a tightly bound network of sup-pliers, and partly to hedge against the loss of a key supplier. Honda maintains that there are advantages in retaining a degree of competi-tive rivalry among suppliers, believing that this pushes forward quality and cost improvements.

Toyota's founder Shoichiro Toyota was amongst the first to admit that his company's brand of JIT 'is still not perfect',[1] but remains con-vinced that this system is still the best available solution, when viewed in the longer term. It allows cost reductions through suppliers' economies of scale and engenders a spirit of commitment amongst the affiliates. Toyota requires that the parts makers develop the parts themselves, for a specific model while it is still at the concept stage. Given that the supplier has taken responsibility for the component's development, there is no question that the same supplier would not be given the manufacturing work. Only when such unfortunate incidents as the Aisin Seiki fire do occur, is the company likely to turn to other sources. In this instance around 20 of Toyota's other affiliated sup-pliers were asked to rally round, and they immediately set about re-tooling, retaining employees and setting up new production lines in a co-ordinated effort to provide the missing components. Reports indi-cated that by Friday, 7 February, Toyota had restarted assembly lines at all of its plants, successfully restoring output to 90 per cent of its usual level. Full production was resumed by the following Monday.[2]

References
1. Nakamoto, Michiyo (1997), 'Toyota Slams on the Breaks', *Financial Times*, 7 February, p. 12.
2. Reitman, Valerie (1997), 'Toyota Stabilizes its Production Levels in Japan on Suppliers' Weekend Efforts', *Wall Street Journal Europe*, 11 February.

The importance of co-operation is well illustrated by the often quoted example of the 'prisoner's dilemma'. The scenario is that you and your partner have been arrested on suspicion of robbing a bank. You are both put in separate cells and not allowed to communicate with each other. The sheriff tells you both independently that you will be leniently treated if you confess, but less well so if you do not!

In fact the precise penalties are given to you as follows:

Option 1:   You confess but your partner doesn't.
Outcome: You get one year in jail for co-operating but your partner gets five years.

Option 2:   You don't confess but your partner does.
Outcome: You get five years in jail and your partner gets only one year for co-operating.

Option 3:   Both of you confess.
Outcome: You get two years each.

Option 4:   Neither of you confess.
Outcome: You both go free.

These options and outcomes can be summarized in the matrix in Figure 8.9.

What is the most likely outcome? If neither you nor your partner really trust the other, particularly if previous experience has taught you to be wary of each other then both of you will confess. Obviously the best strategy is one based upon trust and hence for neither party to confess!

This simple example provides a good analogy with the real world. The conventional wisdom of purchasing has tended towards the view

	You Confess	You Don't confess
Partner Confess	2,2	1,5
Partner Don't confess	5,1	0,0

Fig. 8.9 The prisoner's dilemma: penalty options (years in jail)

that multiple sources of supply for a single item are to be preferred. In such situations, it is argued, one is unlikely to become too reliant upon a single source of supply. Furthermore we can play one supplier off against another and reduce the cost of purchases. However such relationships tend to be adversarial and, in fact, sub-optimal.

One of the first things to suffer when the relationship is based only upon negotiations about price is quality. The supplier seeks to minimize his costs and to provide only the basic specification. The buyer in situations like this will incur additional costs on inbound inspection and re-work. Quality in respect of service is also likely to suffer when the supplier does not put any particular priority on the customer's order.

At a more tangible level those customers who have moved over to JIT manufacturing with the consequent need for JIT deliveries have found that it is simply impractical to manage inbound shipments from multiple suppliers. Similarly the communication of orders and replenishment instructions is so much more difficult with multiple suppliers.

The closer the relationship between buyer and supplier the more likely it is that the expertise of both parties can be applied to mutual benefit. For example many companies have found that by close co-operation with suppliers they can improve product design, value-engineer components, and generally find more efficient ways of working together.

This is the logic which underlines the emergence of the concept of 'co-makership'. Co-makership may be defined as:

The development of a long-term relationship with a limited number of suppliers on the basis of mutual confidence.

The benefits of co-makership relationships are typically found to be:

- Shorter delivery lead times
- Reliable delivery promises
- Less schedule disruption
- Lower stock levels
- Faster implementation of design changes
- Fewer quality problems
- Stable, competitive prices
- Orders given higher priority

The basic philosophy of co-makership is that the supplier should be considered to be an extension of the customer's factory with the emphasis on continuity and a 'seamless' end-to-end pipeline. As the trend to out-sourcing continues so must the move towards co-makership. Nissan Motors in the United Kingdom have been one of the leading advocates of this concept. A key element of their approach is the use of 'supplier development teams' which are small groups of Nissan specialists who will help suppliers to achieve the requirements that Nissan places upon them. The overall objective of the supplier development team is to reduce the costs and increase the efficiency for both parties – in other words a 'win-win' outcome. Because the cost of materials in an automobile can be as high as 85 per cent, anything that can reduce the costs of purchased supplies can have a significant effect on total costs.

Figure 8.10 depicts a not-untypical situation where a car manufacturer's purchased materials are 85 per cent of total costs. This is then exploded further where it is shown that the material costs of the component supplier are a figure closer to the average for manufacturing industry of 40 per cent. Of the remaining 60 per cent ('supplier value-added'), 80 per cent of that figure might be accounted for by overheads of which typically 30 per cent or so would be accounted for by the supplier's logistics costs (i.e. inventory, set-up costs, transport, warehousing, etc.).

What this implies is that approximately 12 per cent of the cost of materials to the car manufacturer are accounted for by the supplier's logistics costs (i.e. 85 per cent x 60 per cent x 80 per cent x 30 per cent). When it is realized that a proportion of the supplier's logistics costs are caused by the lack of integration and partnership between the

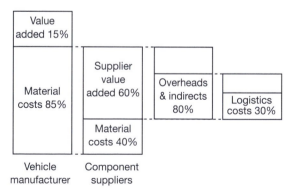

Fig. 8.10 The impact of suppliers' logistics costs on the costs of a car

car manufacturer and the supplier, it becomes apparent that a major opportunity for cost reduction exists.

Under the traditional adversarial relationship the vehicle manufacturer would seek to reduce his material cost by squeezing the profit margin of the component suppliers. The co-makership approach is quite different – here the vehicle manufacturer seeks to reduce a supplier's costs, not his profits. Through collaboration and closely integrated logistics planning mechanisms the two parties seek to achieve a situation where there are benefits to both parties. Companies like Nissan Motors in the United Kingdom have shown that this is not a Utopian dream but can be a practical reality.

The principle of co-makership can be extended in both directions in the supply chain – upstream to suppliers and downstream to distributors, retailers and even end users. The prizes to be won as a result of successful co-makership potentially include lower costs for all parties through reduced inventories and lower set-up costs as a result of better schedule integration. The implications for competitive strategy

> **The new competitive paradigm is that supply chain competes with supply chain and the success of any one company will depend upon how well it manages its supply chain relationships.**

are profound. The new competitive paradigm is that supply chain competes with supply chain and the success of any one company will depend upon how well it manages its supply chain relationships.

Table 8.2 summarizes the differences between the conventional approach to supplier relations and the co-makership concept.

Supplier development

Mention was made earlier of the idea of 'supplier development teams'. The purpose of these teams is to seek out, with suppliers, ways in which the relationship between the two parties can be made mutually beneficial.

There are many advantages to taking a pro-active approach to supplier development, not only in terms of cost reduction but also from a marketing perspective. For example, many companies are finding that an increasingly valuable source of innovation is the

Table 8.2 Comparisons of conventional purchasing with co-makership

Purchasing dynamics	Conventional purchasing	Co-makership
Supplier/buyer relationships	Adversarial	Partnership
Tenure of relationships	Variable	Long-term
Tenure of contract	Short	Long
Order quantity	Large	Small
Transportation strategy	Full truck load of a single item	JIT delivery
Quality assurance	Inspect and re-inspect	No incoming inspection
Means of communication to supplier	Purchase order	Verbal release
Frequency of communication	Sporadic	Continuous
Impact on inventory	An asset	A liability
Number of suppliers	Many; the more the better	Few or single
Design process	Design the product, then ask for quote	Ask for supplier ideas, then design the product
Production quantity	Large lots	Small lots
Delivery schedule	Monthly	Weekly or daily
Supplier location	Widely dispersed	As compact as possible
Warehouse	Large, automated	Small, flexible

Source: Adapted from Giunipero, L.C., *Guide to Purchasing*, National Association of Purchasing Management, USA, 1986

supplier – either for product innovation or process innovation. These companies are finding that by getting suppliers involved in the product development process at an early stage a new perspective is introduced which frequently leads to innovative solutions. One car manufacturer found that by working closely with a carpet manufacturer that supplier was able to suggest an improved specification which reduced the need for costly and heavy sound insulation material in the rest of the car.

Supplier development should also extend to analyzing how the vendor's own systems and procedures can be streamlined and integrated more closely with the customer's. Bearing in mind the fact that competitive advantage is increasingly a function of supply chain efficiency and effectiveness it will be apparent that the greater the collaboration, at all levels, between supplier and customer, the greater the likelihood that an advantage can be gained.

In selecting suppliers, and also in seeking criteria for reducing the supplier base, the organization needs to look for vendors who are able to accept the concept of co-makership. Typically today's sophisticated buyer is looking for assurance that the supplier can consistently meet pre-determined quality standards. Usually this will entail the supplier gaining certification through the appropriate standard setting body such as the International Standards Organization (ISO) or the British Standards Institute (BSI). Because the customer will no longer conduct inbound quality inspection and because they will more than likely be operating on some version of just-in-time inventory management, the need for total quality assurance from the supplier is imperative.

Again, we frequently encounter organizations who, on a regular basis, formally appraise their suppliers according to carefully defined criteria. This is the system often known as vendor evaluation. Ideally, vendor performance measurement should be a continuing process whereby regular feedback is presented to management of both parties to ensure that opportunities for improvement are recognized and acted upon.[2] An example of a Vendor Evaluation protocol is given in the Appendix to this chapter.

Many major manufacturers now encourage their suppliers to come together in the form of a 'supplier association'. The purpose of these associations is to share best practice and to seek to identify further ways in which process integration within the supply chain can be enhanced.

Co-operation rather than confrontation in the supply chain is the business model that is bringing results in industries as diverse as aerospace and grocery retailing. An impressive body of evidence exists for the tangible financial benefit that can be derived from supply chain integration. It can indeed be claimed with some justification that 'supply chains compete, not companies'.

Summary

Responsive supply chains are by definition highly integrated. They are internally integrate across functions and they are externally integrated with upstream suppliers and downstream customers. Many companies are impeded in their attempts to become more agile and responsive because of an entrenched functional structure. They manage functions rather than processes and hence have a fragmented approach to the marketplace. It is also difficult for such firms to contemplate external integration when they lack internal integration.

Those companies that have succeeded in breaking down the functional 'silos' are now looking to forge ever closer linkages with their supply chain partners. A key to supply chain integration is the open flow of information from one end of the pipeline to another. By sharing information, supply chain partners are able to respond more rapidly to known demand and to do so with less inventory in the system as a whole and hence at lower cost. Such thinking is now revolutionizing retailing for example, as the growing implementation of ECR highlights.

References

1. Schonberger, R.J., *Building a Chain of Customers*, The Free Press, 1990.
2. Harrington, C., Lambert, D.M. and Christopher, M.G., 'A Methodology for Measuring Vendor Performance', *International Journal of Business Logistics*, Vol 12, No 1, 1991.

Appendix: example of a vendor evaluation system

1 Rate the supplier's interest in developing a partnership

1	5	10
Little interest shown in developing relationship. Releases no information on production costs.	Some attempt made to improve relationship. Keeps us informed of corporate developments.	Values long-term relationship. Significant senior management interest. Prepared to share long-term plans. 'Open-book' pricing.

2 Rate the supplier's delivery performance

1   2   3   4   5   6   7   8   9   10
Percentage on-time delivery against agreed delivery dates:
Less
than
75% 80% 85% 90% 95% 96% 97% 98% 99% 100%
on time

3 Rate the supplier's pricing against the market

1	5	10
Consistently above market price.	At market price.	Below market price. 'Never knowingly undersold'.

4 Rate the supplier's cost savings initiatives

1	5	10
A few cost saving ideas have been put forward with limited results. Reluctant to pass lower market prices.	Makes a number of suggestions and we routinely achieve savings of 2–3 per cent of annual spend.	Consistently plans for cost savings. Will actively support investigations and trials of alternatives. Will actively pass on market price reductions. Programme achieves 5 per cent cost savings per annum.

249

5 Compare lead time against industry norm

1	5	10
Long lead times. Supplier complacent. Little flexibility in coping with criticalities.	Average lead time. Supplier has no real plans to improve. Will help with criticalities.	Consistently less than competitors. Makes constant efforts to reduce lead time. Willing to respond to critical requests.

6 Rate the supplier's achievement of defect-free deliveries

1	5	10
Several rejections recorded. Recurring defects still present.	An isolated rejection where the fault was unlikely to lead to further losses. No evidence of systematic faults.	No rejections.

7 Rate the supplier's ability to avoid complaints

1	5	10
Five or more referrals. Persistent faults found 'on-line'.	Up to two referrals, promptly dealt with. Isolated 'on-line' difficulties.	No referrals. Materials trouble-free 'on-line'.

8 Rate the supplier's response to quality problems

1	5	10
Supplier offers little or no help. May tackle symptom, not cause.	Supplier will undertake investigation but lacks responsiveness and resolution of a 'zero-defect' company.	Immediate, in-depth investigation. Corrective action effective. Appropriate compensation offered.

9 Rate the supplier's certificate of conformity/analysis

1	5	10
Serious omission on certificates. Certificates often late. Extra charge levied.	Certificates generally acceptable or not requested. Sometimes needs chasing. No charge levied.	Certificates very comprehensive and always on time. No charge levied.

10 Rate the quality of delivery documentation

1	5	10
Misses vital information. Poor presentation.	Contains all basic information, i.e. item code and order number.	Contains comprehensive information including lot numbers, lot weights, etc.

11 Rate acceptability of palletization/presentation

1	5	10
Some broken pallets. May be poorly stacked. Some labels face inwards. Multi-lot deliveries.	Adequate presentation. Occasional traffic claim. Acceptable lot sizes. No traffic claims.	Excellent pallets. Goods presented well. Clean, well stacked and stable.

12 Rate the quality of account representative

1	5	10
Inappropriate frequency of contact. Has little knowledge of supply market. Slow response to enquiries. Unable to influence his company's approach. Does not relate to our current business needs.	Basically sound in all aspects but could achieve better results if allocated more resources to our account.	Always well prepared. Very positive approach. Available when needed. Fast response. High quality, reliable market information. Can effect in-house changes. Highly professional.

13 Rate the supplier's local call-off co-operation

1	5	10
Supplier does not support scheme. Many queries and operational problems exist.	Some attempt at building factory relationship. Queries quickly resolved.	Excellent support supplier builds good relationship with factory. Genuine desire to make call-off work. Good exchange of information for mutual benefit.

14 Rate the efficiency of the supplier's administration system

1	5	10
Many price queries. Rebates and credits consistently late.	Genuine attempts to minimize price queries. Credits and rebates acted upon.	No price queries generated. Credits and rebates speedily dealt with.

15 Rate the efficiency of the supplier's sales office

1	5	10
Never volunteers information on due dates. Seems unaware of order status. Delays or difficulty in placing orders. May accept orders which cannot be honoured.	Routinely passes progress information. Occasionally requires prompting. Order details checked quickly and necessary action taken.	Speedy and accurate transmission of order progress information. Always knows status of each order. Honours order details or immediately agrees alternatives.

16 Rate the supplier's booking-in procedures

1	5	10
Hardly ever books in. Drivers turn up at any time.	Books in goods but timing sometimes ignored by driver.	Always books in. Always in good time for delivery.

17 Rate the supplier's track record in bringing in new ideas

1	5	10
Other customers given priority. Few innovative ideas.	Some innovations brought to us. Supplier primarily working for his own benefit.	Many innovations incorporated. Willing to work closely on research projects.

18 Rate the supplier's assistance in solving technical problems

1	5	10
Poor ability to solve problems. Little interest shown.	Assistance given, but some reluctance to allocate resources to solve problem.	Fast response, correct level of expertise brought to bear.

19 Rate supplier's adherence to agreed development schedules

1	5	10
Hopeless response. Samples, tooling, out-turns, etc, often not on time. Displays inflexible attitude.	Some slippage may occasionally be seen. Finds it difficult to respond to change.	Programmes maintained vigorously to agreed time scale. Reacts favourably to change.

20 Rate abilities of the day-to-day technical representation

1	5	10
Representative has little technical knowledge.	Has average technical knowledge but will readily call upon specialists when needed.	Excellent technical knowledge, backed up by specialists when needed.

Leading-edge logistics

This chapter:

Identifies the characteristics of companies currently believed to be at the forefront of logistics development.

•

Reflects on the nature of the new organizational paradigm, looking at the new tools, methods and relationship management strategies being developed to enable the firm to respond to the demands of a changing environment.

•

Focuses on some of the most far-reaching changes currently underway in the field of supply chain management, including the arrival of the extended enterprise, the virtual supply chain and the use of postponement to reconfigure the value chain.

•

Discusses the role and impact of on-going developments in information networks.

•

Provides an in-depth case study of how one company has successfully overhauled its entire approach to supply chain management in order to meet the needs of its changing marketplace.

Throughout this book the emphasis has been upon the achievement of competitive advantage through logistics excellence. Many of the ideas presented are relatively untried and still, for the majority of companies, the area of logistics and supply chain management is unexplored territory.

However, an increasing number of organizations can be identified in which logistics is quite clearly recognized as a major strategic variable. Companies like Xerox, Dell, Nissan, Benetton and 3M have invested significantly in developing responsive logistics systems. Whilst their success in the marketplace is due to many things there can be no doubting the role that logistics has played in achieving that success.

A study carried out in North America for the Council of Logistics Management sought to identify the characteristics of companies that were at the leading edge in logistics. The main findings are summarized in the box below and overleaf but the essential features of these organizations seemed to be that they:

- Exhibit an overriding commitment to customers
- Emphasize planning
- Encompass a significant span of functional control
- Commit to external alliances with service suppliers
- Have a highly-formalized logistical process
- Place a premium on operational flexibility
- Employ comprehensive performance measurement
- Invest in state-of-the-art information technology

■ How the leading-edge companies manage logistics ■

Concerning organization structure, leading-edge firms:
- Have had formal logistics organizations longer
- Are more apt to have logistics headed by an officer-level executive
- Adopt a more fluid approach to logistics organization and encourage frequent reorganization to take advantage of opportunities that arise

▶

257

- Tend to favour centralized control
- Are becoming more centralized as they adapt organization structure to mission
- Are responsible for more 'traditional' staff and line functions
- Are more apt to execute boundary-spanning or externally-oriented logistics functions
- Tend to manage more 'beyond' or extended functional responsibilities not traditionally considered to be part of logistics.

Concerning strategic posture, leading-edge firms:
- Have a greater tendency to manage logistics as a value-added process
- Reflect a stronger commitment to achieving and maintaining customer satisfaction
- Place a premium on flexibility, particularly in regard to accommodating special or non-routine requests
- Are better positioned to handle unexpected events
- Are more willing to use outside service providers
- Place a greater premium on how well the service company performs in managing itself and its service to clients
- Are more apt to view service/provider relationships as strategic alliances
- Anticipate greater use of outside services in the future.

Concerning managerial behaviour, leading-edge firms:
- Expend more effort on formal logistics planning
- Are more apt to publicize their performance commitments and standards by issuing specific mission statements
- Are more apt to have chief logistics officers involved in business unit strategic planning
- Respond effectively to non-planned events
- Regularly use a wider range of performance measures, including asset management, cost, customer service, productivity and quality
- Are more significant users of data processing technology and enjoy a higher quality of information systems (IS) support
- Typically have more state-of-the-art computer applications and are planning more updates and expansions
- Are more involved in new technology such as electronic data interchange (EDI) and artificial intelligence (AI).

Source: *Leading Edge Logistics: Competitive Positioning for the 1990's*, Council of Logistics Management, Oakbrook, Illinois, USA, 1989

The new organizational paradigm

It will be apparent that to achieve success in all of these areas will require significant change within the company. It requires a transformation that goes beyond re-drawing the organization chart and entails a cultural change that must be driven from the top. In fact the basic principles which have traditionally guided the company must be challenged and what is required is a shift in the basic paradigms that have underpinned industrial organizations for so long.

Fundamental business transformations

Most of us work in organizations that are hierarchical, vertical and functionally defined. The organization chart for the typical company resembles a pyramid and provides a clear view of where everyone fits in relation to each other and will also normally reflect reporting relationships. In essence, the conventional

> Most of us work in organizations that are hierarchical, vertical and functionally defined.

organization structure is little changed since the armies of the Roman Empire developed the precursor of the pyramid organization.

Whilst there can be no doubting that this organizational model has served us well in the past, there are now serious questions to be asked about its appropriateness for the changed conditions that confront us today. Of the many changes that have taken place in the marketing environment, perhaps the biggest is the focus upon 'speed'. Because of shortening product life cycles, time to market becomes ever more critical. Similarly, the dramatic growth of just-in-time (JIT) practices in manufacturing means that those companies wishing to supply into that environment have to develop systems capable of responding rapidly and flexibly to customers' delivery requirements. Indeed, the same is true in almost every market today as organizations seek to reduce their inventories and hence a critical requirement of a supplier is that they are capable of rapid response.

The challenge to every business is to become a *responsive organization* in every sense of the word. The organization must respond to changes in the market with products and services which provide innovative solutions to customers' problems; it must respond to volatile demand and it must be able to provide high levels of flexibility in delivery.

259

What will be the distinguishing features of the responsive organization? One thing is certain: it will not resemble today's functionally focused business. There will be many differences but the major transformations will probably be:

- From functions to processes
- From profit to performance
- From products to customers
- From inventory to information
- From transactions to relationships

To consider each of these in turn:

1 From functions to processes

Conventionally, organizations have been 'vertical' in their design. In other words businesses have organized around functions such as production, marketing, sales and distribution. Each function has had clearly identified tasks and within these functional 'silos' or 'stovepipes' (as they have been called), there is a recognized hierarchy up which employees might hope to progress.

The problem with this approach is that it is inwardly focused and concentrates primarily upon the use of resources rather than upon the creation of outputs. The outputs of any business can only be measured in terms of customer satisfaction achieved at a profit. Paradoxically, the achievement of these outputs can only be achieved by co-ordination and co-operation *horizontally* across the organization. These horizontal linkages mirror the materials and information flows that connect the customer with the business and its suppliers. They are, in fact, the *core processes* of the business. In the horizontal organization the emphasis is upon the management of processes. These processes, by definition, are cross-functional.

The justification for this radically different view of the business is that these processes are in effect 'capabilities' and it is through capabilities that the organization competes. In other words the effectiveness of the new product development process, the order fulfilment process and so on, determines the extent to which the business will succeed in the marketplace.

2 From profit to performance

Whilst there can be no arguing that, long term, sustained profit has to be the goal of any commercial organization, there is a growing realization that if profit is the end, then we should spend more time examining the means whereby it is achieved. Many management boards begin their weekly meetings with a review of the financial position. In other words, before anything else gets discussed, revenues will be examined and costs detailed at some length. Ratios, capacity utilization, production efficiencies – these are the currency by which the conventional business is measured and hence controlled.

There is a saying that 'what gets measured, gets managed', implying that it is through the choice of performance measurement that behaviour is determined. Thus, in a marketplace where employees are required to 'clock' in and out of work each day, punctuality may be improved but their willingness to work more than the agreed hours may be reduced. Hence the importance of understanding what the critical performance criteria are and therefore what should be measured.

The underlying logic of this viewpoint is that performance drives profitability. Therefore, if we get the right performance then profit will follow.

Many of these new performance indicators will be non-financial. That is, they will focus management's attention upon such things as customer satisfaction, flexibility and employee commitment. Thus the management meetings of the near future may begin their agenda not with the financial review – that will come later – but with a review of such non-financial performance indicators as:

Customer satisfaction
- Customer retention
- Brand preference
- Dealer satisfaction
- Service performance

Flexibility
- Set-up times
- Commonality of components and materials
- Reduction of complexity

People commitment
- Employee turnover
- Suggestions submitted and implemented
- Internal service climate and culture
- Training and development index

Within each individual organization the key performance indicators will necessarily be different. But the principle of focusing upon the drivers of profitability is paramount.

3 From products to customers

Even though the marketing concept has gained widespread acceptance across industry, there is still an underlying tendency to manage products rather than customers. This emphasis is reflected in job titles such as 'Brand Manager', 'Product Group Manager' and in accounting systems that can provide precise information on product profitability but that are incapable of measuring the profitability of customers.

Because customer satisfaction has to be the ultimate objective of any commercial organization it is imperative that the management structures and the measurement systems also mirror this. In organizational terms the requirement is to create a means whereby markets, channels and customers can be managed and appropriate accounting and control procedures can be implemented. 'Demand management' is emerging now in some leading-edge companies as an integrating, cross-functional approach to servicing customers.

Such approaches need to be supported by accounting systems that can better identify the costs of servicing customers and hence their profitability. In the same way that 20 per cent of a company's products will generate 80 per cent of its profits, so, too, do 20 per cent of its customers generate 80 per cent of the profit. The problem in the past has been that traditional accounting systems have not been able to provide accurate measures of the 'cost-to-serve'. Now, using 'activity based costing' and 'throughput costing', it is possible to identify the aspects of service that create cost and hence, where necessary, to modify the service package, customer by customer.

In marketing terms, this transformation will also require greater emphasis to be placed on 'customer value' and not just 'brand value'. Essentially, this means that the supplying organization must focus its efforts upon developing an 'offer' or 'package' that will positively impact customers' perceptions of the value that they derive through ownership of that offer. The argument that is increasingly being voiced is that a critical component of such customer value is service. In a sense, we are approaching the time when logistics and marketing need to be managed conjointly.

4 From inventory to information

One commentator has suggested that 'uncertainty is the mother of inventory', meaning that because organizations are unsure of future demand they must carry inventory to buffer themselves against that uncertainty. It follows that if uncertainty can be reduced then so, too, can the inventory that is carried to cover it. The conventional solution to the problem of uncertainty has been to make a forecast.

However, the inaccuracy of forecasts has led many to believe that they are only right by chance and that it is self-defeating to rely on a forecast since, by definition, the degree of error embodied in it will directly influence the need for stock. Instead, if information on actual customer usage of a product could be linked directly into the logistics system, then the need for the forecast could be much reduced.

This is the concept of 'substituting information for inventory'. Benetton, the Italian fashion manufacturer, has achieved its strong position worldwide not just through innovative styles and its strong brand, but through the speed with which it can respond to changes in the market. Even though trends in styles and colours will differ from one corner of the globe to another and even though fashion life cycles are short and fickle, Benetton can usually match the market requirement through its advanced logistics systems. By capturing information at the point of sale and swiftly transferring details of what is selling back to the point of production, whole weeks are taken out of the total response time. Combined with the flexibility in manufacturing for which Benetton is renowned and with state-of-the-art, computerized, global distribution systems, this gives Benetton the ability to get a product into the retail store within weeks of the order being placed. Traditionally, in that industry, it will take months to meet a replenishment order, if indeed it can be achieved at all.

5 From transactions to relationships

One of the primary goals of many companies is market share. However it can sometimes be the case that a blind pursuit of market share will emphasize more the 'winning' of customers than the 'keeping' of them. What matters is not so much the absolute level of market share but rather the quality of it. In other words, does our market share comprise a large number of customers who are transitory or promiscuous – who will drift from one supplier to another? Alternatively, are the majority of our customers loyal and committed to us as a supplier?

More and more, research is suggesting that the longer customers stay with us, the more profitable they become. The longer a customer stays with a supplier the more they are likely to treat it as a preferred supplier. The trend towards customers seeking to reduce their supplier base and to move towards 'single sourcing' is gathering speed. The benefits of such an approach include: improved quality, innovation sharing, reduced costs, integrated scheduling of production and deliveries. Underlying all of this is the idea that buyer-supplier relationships should be based upon partnership.

An increasing number of companies are discovering the advantages that can be gained by seeking out mutually beneficial, long-term relationships with suppliers. From the supplier's point of view, such partnerships can prove formidable barriers to entry to competitors. One powerful route to developing partnership relationships is through superior logistics. Logistics in this context becomes the thread that connects the inbound and outbound flows of channel partners.

Managing the supply chain of the future

If these business transformations are to be successfully achieved then not only must the organization be open to change, but the skills available to it must be significantly enhanced.

It has been said that if the external environment is changing faster than the internal environment then there is a good chance that the company will soon be in trouble. Creating a climate that welcomes change should be one of the prime tasks of any business leader.

Since it is through people that change is created, attention must be paid to how the organization develops a set of skills and competencies that are appropriate to the constantly changing external environment. Table 9.1 suggests that the management skills and competencies needed to cope with the business transformations we have described are much broader than those traditionally encountered in the business.

> Since it is through people that change is created, attention must be paid to how the organization develops a set of skills and competencies that are appropriate to the constantly changing external environment.

Table 9.1 Managing the supply chain of the future

Paradigm shift	Leading to	Skills required
From functions to processes	Integral management of materials and goods flow	Cross-functional management and planning skills
From products to customers	Focus on markets and the creation of customer value	Ability to define, measure and manage service requirements by market segment, i.e. 'perfect order achievement'
From revenue to performance	Focus on the key performance drivers of profit	Understanding of the 'costs-to-serve' and time-based performance indicators
From inventory to information	Demand-based replenishment and quick response systems	Information systems and information technology
From transactions to relationships	Supply chain partnership	Relationship management and 'win-win' orientation

The extended enterprise and the virtual supply chain

The nature of business enterprise is changing. Today's business is increasingly 'boundaryless', meaning that internal functional barriers are being eroded in favour of horizontal process management and externally the separation between vendors, distributors, customers and the firm is gradually lessening. This is the idea of the *extended enterprise* which is transforming our thinking on how organizations compete and how value chains might be reformulated.

265

Underpinning the concept of the extended enterprise is a common information 'highway'. It is the use of shared information that enables cross-functional, horizontal management to become a reality. Even more importantly it is information shared between partners in the supply chain that makes possible the responsive flow of product from one end of the pipeline to another. What has now come to be termed the *virtual* enterprise or supply chain is in effect a series of relationships between partners that is based upon the value-added exchange of information. Figure 9.1 illustrates the concept.

The notion that partnership arrangements and a mentality of co-operation are more effective than the traditional arms-length and often adversarial basis of relationships is now gaining ground. Thus the supply chain is now becoming a confederation of organizations that agree common goals and bring specific strengths to the overall value creation and value delivery system. This process is being accelerated as the trend towards out-sourcing continues. Out-sourcing should not be confused with 'subcontracting' where a task or an activity is simply handed over to a specialist. In a way it would be better to use the term 'in-sourcing' or 're-sourcing', when we refer to the quite different concept of partnering that the virtual supply chain depends upon. These partnerships may not be for all time – quite possibly they exist only to exploit a specific market opportunity – but they will be 'seamless' and truly synergetic.

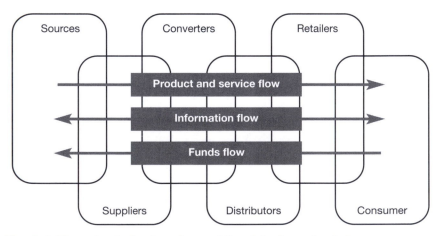

Fig. 9.1 The extended enterprise and the virtual supply chain
Source: A.T. Kearney

In the same way that organizations have dramatically reduced the number of suppliers they do business with, even moving to single sourcing, so too have many of those suppliers focused on serving fewer customers – but doing more for them. This could be termed a 'vertical' growth strategy rather than the traditional 'horizontal' growth strategy which seeks out more customers to whom to sell the same product or service. The automobile industry provides a good example of vertical strategies where first-tier suppliers or 'lead' suppliers are now taking on responsibility not just for supplying components but supplying complete systems. See the Mercedes/Swatch Smart Car Case Study below.

The smart car and the virtual supply chain

The Geneva Motor Show is one of the biggest events in the automotive manufacturers' calendar, a showcase for the newest and best that the industry has to offer. At the 1998 show, the car that everyone wanted to see was not the newest, sleekest offering from an established marque with an illustrious past. Instead it was the eagerly-awaited 'Smart Car', the tiny, cheap, two-seater run-around, produced by Micro Compact Car (MCC) in an unlikely joint venture project between Germany's Daimler-Benz and Swiss watchmakers, SMH. Designed to appeal to the young urban drivers of continental Europe, it forms part of a wider urban mobility concept that includes space-saving parking, pool leasing and networking with public transport systems. In short, the innovative little car is destined to be unlike any other car currently on the road. The public were intrigued by both the concept and the car's appearance, but other carmakers were much more interested in the MCC's manufacturing systems. Smart Car could be built in only seven and a half hours, some two and a half hours less than the time taken to build a car by the industry's leading performers.[1] The difference in performance is due to the fact that MCC is a very different kind of car company with a radically different approach to vehicle development and manufacturing.

The cars were to be produced in a region with no previous history of automotive manufacturing, at a single site factory complex at Hambach in eastern France. At the heart of the complex is a large cruciform building housing the main assembly line. Radiating off each arm of the cruciform are a number of smaller structures, containing one or another

▶

267

of MCC's seven first-tier suppliers or 'system partners' – a multi-national collection of specialist companies, subcontracted to undertake large portions of the assembly process. The systems partners are responsible for around 70 per cent of the engineering work on the car and have been involved in its development right from the concept stage.

The car is constructed around an integral body frame, known as the 'Tridion', to which a variety of subassemblies or modules can be attached. These include five main 'super modules' – chassis, power-train, doors and roof, electronics and cockpit – supplied to the production lines in sequence, by the systems partners who are fully integrated into the assembly process.[2] Their involvement in modular subassemblies reduces the carmaker's capital costs and reduces the amount of MCC's working capital tied up in stocks, as suppliers are only paid once the modules are used. Some of the modules, such as the powertrain and cockpit, contain complex subassemblies, assembled in advance by the suppliers. In all, the seven systems partners supply around 50 per cent of the car's components or subassemblies (by value), the rest are to be supplied by a further 16 non-integrated suppliers, some located at quite a distance from the plant.

Smart Car's integrated manufacturing site is the next logical extension of the 1990s trend that saw clusters of first-tier suppliers opening dedicated facilities in industrial parks adjacent to large automotive customers' plants. It is also indicative of a trend towards integrated suppliers actually installing parts on the line, which totally blurs the distinction between the car manufacturer's own employees and those of its systems suppliers.

At Hambach, ownership of the factory buildings and the site's facilities management is out-sourced to specialist providers. In addition, programme management and information technology operations have all been passed over to Andersen Consulting on a long-term contract. Andersen will also develop and implement the business and vehicle production processes and oversee Smart Car's introduction to the market.[3] The cars will be sold through a network of dealerships located in special 'lifestyle centres' within shopping complexes or other frequently visited urban locations. There, multi-media systems will allow customers to order on-screen individually configured vehicles. The cars will then be delivered to the dealership on a one-day lead time, via one of five European regional distribution centres. To retain maximum flexibility, some elements of product customization will take place at the distribution centre, where stocks of easily interchangeable modules and body parts will be held, so that features can be changed or added as required. Likewise, the modular construction of the vehicles means that they can easily be upgraded or reconfigured at any point during the lifetime of the car by simply replacing easily detachable subassemblies or body parts. This changes the nature of the product itself from a fixed consumer durable to a much more flexible, renewable product, with associated benefits in terms of reverse logistics and recycling.

In practice the Smart Car and the organization that builds it represent a curious blend of out-sourcing and reintegration. MCC has secured the expertise and full commitment of leading manufacturing specialists and service providers, while spreading the investment and financial risks associated with this ground-breaking project. If the public do take to the little car, then despite a long set-back when the prototype failed a crucial high-speed stability test,[4] Smart Car's makers could still recoup their DM 1.8bn investment, as originally planned, during the car's first five to six year production cycle.[5] If this is so then Smart Car could be set to redefine the processes of car manufacturing and ownership.

References

1. Simonian, Haig (1997), 'Carmakers' Smart Move', *Financial Times*, 1 July.
2. Van Hoek, Remko and Weken, Harm (1997), 'How Modular Production can Contribute to Integration in Inbound and Outbound Logistics', *Proceedings of the Logistics Research Network Conference*, University of Huddersfield, 16–17 September.
3. Reuter News Service (1997), 'Andersen Consulting joins Smart Car Project', *Reuter News Service – Western Europe, Reuter Textline*, 18 February (Q2:23).
4. Reuter News Service (1997), 'Smart Car Fails the Elk Test', *Computergram, Reuter Textline*, 19 December (Q2:18).
5. Miller, Scott (1997) 'Kohl, Chirac see Smart Car as a European Symbol', Reuter *News Service – Western Europe, Reuter Textline*, 27 October (Q2:55).

Reconfiguring the value chain through 'postponement'

One of the distinguishing characteristics of a virtual supply chain is that the final product or offer is not created until the last possible moment. The idea is that maximum flexibility is achieved if there

269

can be a postponement in the creation of what has been termed 'time, place and form utility'.[1] Time and place postponement occurs when the organization centralizes its inventories to enable both a reduction in the total inventory in the system and an improvement in product availability. The latter is achieved because it is generally easier to forecast aggregate requirements than, say, individual country requirements.

The search for time and place postponement has led many companies in Europe, for example, to create European Distribution Centres (EDCs) from which they service a wider demand. The problem with this strategy, widely adopted though it is, is that it can lead to a significant increase in transport costs, there may also be considerable differences in local requirements (e.g. local language, packaging) and the product is held as finished inventory with commensurately high holding costs.

It is at this point that the third type of postponement becomes attractive – the postponement of the final form of the product.

Conventionally it has always been thought that production should take place in the factory and that often those factories should be centralized and make standard products to a forecast. The problem with this model is that in a fast-changing market the risk of committing to a specific configured product ahead of knowing actual demand can be considerable. As we have already noted, in many high-tech, fashion or seasonal markets, short life cycles are leading to increased levels of obsolescence and stock write-offs.

The alternative option in the virtual supply chain is to substitute information and agility for inventory. If information on actual end user requirements can be rapidly transmitted upstream and shared between supply chain partners and if, through flexible manufacturing and postponement, the final product can be made on demand, then clearly a significant competitive advantage would accrue. How then can this desirable state of affairs be achieved?

The first requirement is that the value chain must be redefined to include the value chain of upstream and downstream partners – the value chain for the extended enterprise in effect. Figure 9.2 illustrates the concept.

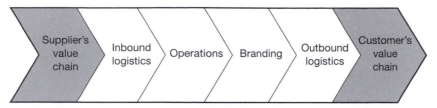

Fig. 9.2 The extended value chain

The question now is where in the chain should the various elements of final customer value be created? The challenge is to delay the final configuration as long as possible and hence reduce the risk. To achieve this will often mean a complete rethink in product design. Can the product be modularized, can it be designed so that localization can be performed at a later stage? Hewlett Packard have made the idea of 'design for a localization' a fundamental element of their product development philosophy.[2]

Often the final assembly or finishing of the product may be performed by another partner in the supply chain. Many logistics service providers are now acting as value-added partners in an extended, often global supply chain.

Whilst the unit costs of manufacturing under a postponement strategy may be higher than under the traditional mass production model, the overall cost/benefit will often be considerable as inventory holding costs fall, obsolescence reduces and customer service improves. In many ways the concept of postponement is making redundant the conventional wisdom of the economies of scale.

The role of information in the virtual supply chain

Leading organizations have long recognized that the key to success in supply chain management is the information system. However, what we are now learning is that there is a dimension to information that enables supply and demand to be matched in multiple markets, often with tailored products, in ever-shorter time-frames.

This extension of the information system beyond the classical dimensions of simple planning and control enables time and space to be collapsed through the ability to link the customer directly to the supplier and for the supplier to react, sometimes in real-time, to changes in the market. Rayport and Sviokla[3] have coined the term 'marketspace' to describe the new world of electronic commerce, internets and virtual supply chains. In the marketspace, customer demand can be identified as it occurs and through CAD/CAM and flexible manufacturing products created in minimal batch sizes. Equally, networks of specialist suppliers can be joined together to create innovative yet cost-effective solutions for complex design and manufacturing problems. The way that Boeing and Airbus now design and assemble their advanced aeroplanes, for example, would not be possible without the use of global information networks that link one end of the value chain to the other.

The Internet has perhaps provided one of the biggest breakthroughs of the late twentieth century when its potential impact upon supply chain management is considered.

The Internet provides a perfect vehicle for the establishment of the virtual supply chain. Not only does it enable vast global markets to be accessed at minimal cost and allow customers to reduce dramatically search time and transaction costs but it also enables different organizations in a supply chain to share information with each other in a highly cost-effective way. These *extranets* as they have come to be termed are revolutionizing supply chain management. Organizations with quite different internal information systems can now access data from customers on sales or product usage and can use that information to manage replenishment and to alert their suppliers of forthcoming requirements.

The example opposite highlights how one of Britain's major retailers, Tesco, is using an extranet to link with its suppliers. At the same time the company is already trialing a home shopping and delivery system for consumers over the Internet. Within the business too *Intranets* are being constructed that enable information to be shared between stores and to facilitate communication across the business. We are probably even now only scraping the surface in terms of how the Internet and its associated technologies can be leveraged to further exploit the virtual supply chain. Figure 9.3 highlights some of the current applications of Internet-based concepts to supply chain management.

Customer service
- Information and support products and services
- Electronic help desk
- Mass customization and order processing

Marketing channel
- Public relations and advertising
- Market research and test
- Electronic malls and catalogues

Information retrieval
- Online news
- Statistics, reports and databases
- Data mining
- Competitive analysis

Supplier relationships
- Logistics
- Product search
- Electronic data interchange
- Ordering and payment
- Supply chain integration

Financial transactions
- Selling and payment
- Managing accounts
- Credit card payments

INTERNET
INTRANET
EXTRANET

Building strategic alliances
- Newsletters, bulletin boards, discussion databases
- Sharing knowledge and experience

Electronic distribution
- Product, data, information

Internal communications
- Complete internal, external, vertical and horizontal communications
- Groupware
- E-mail
- Collaboration
- Knowledge transfer
- Telecommuting

Human resources and employee relations
- Job opening posting
- Expert search
- Employee training and support
- Distance learning

Sales force automation
- On-site configuration and order processing
- Sales process transformation

Fig. 9.3 Internet applications and the supply chain
Source: A.T. Kearney

■ Tesco links up to extranet ■

Retailer Tesco is building closer links with suppliers by setting up the Tesco information exchange 'extranet' to help implement efficient consumer response (ECR) techniques to reduce waste and increase product availability for customers. It is anticipated that the scheme will eventually cover the majority of Tesco's suppliers.

Tesco, GE Information Services which is one of its biggest information technology suppliers, and foods group St Ivel have developed an interactive process for the management of price promotions which offers better communication with the producer and allows the sharing of basic supply information. In a typical Tesco store between 5 per cent and 10 per cent of products are on promotion at any one time. Estimating consumer response is therefore often difficult and can sometimes carry unexpected costs.

The extranet will help at all stages of promotion. This starts from initial proposal through business planning and supply chain management, execution and finally evaluation.

Suppliers will gain access to Tesco sales data and can therefore track their products. The early trials with seven suppliers have shown that suppliers gain significant benefits in their day-to-day business.

Introducing a new product will be both quicker and more efficient as specifications for new lines will be made available electronically. Joe Galloway, Tesco divisional director, says the system has already shown its worth enabling the firm to estimate stock levels to fulfil promotions.

'We are now engaged in trials with other suppliers,' he says. Paul Chadwick, of GE Information Services' retail supply chain operation, says the extranet solution will deliver real business benefits to the whole supply chain.

Source : *M.T. Logistica*, March 1998

Making change happen

As we have seen, the task of creating and implementing integrated supply chains to deliver greater customer value at less cost is daunting. Not only must a clear vision of the role of logistics in the organization be articulated but significant organizational change will also be necessary. New ways of working with upstream and downstream partners must be forged and the underpinning information systems put in place.

Is all of this possible? The answer has to be in the affirmative because without the fundamental transformations discussed in this chapter the organization is unlikely to prosper in the future. The good news is that many companies are

> **New ways of working with upstream and downstream partners must be forged and the underpinning information systems put in place.**

finding that, given the leadership, major change can be effected. Also the climate is now far more conducive for breaking down the boundaries both within the business and between businesses. Companies that in the past were hierarchical are now much flatter, those same companies that maintained adversarial relations with suppliers are now talking about partnership and there is a new and re-vitalizing focus on customer value creation.

A good example of a company that recognized the need for change as it faced unprecedented levels of competition in terms of quality and service is provided by Xerox.

Xerox recognized that it would have to fundamentally change the way in which it addressed its various markets and it set about a worldwide change programme that was to have significant implications for logistics and supply chain management. It therefore makes a fitting conclusion to this book to end with a summary of the way in which Xerox has achieved significant improvement in their competitive position through reengineering its approach to logistics and supply chain management.

Implementing an Integrated Supply Chain: the Xerox example

This section is written by Matthew Stenross and Graham Sweet of Xerox Corporation, USA, and is reproduced with their kind permission.

Xerox is a large global company with interests in financial services and document processing. This discussion is concerned with how Xerox's document processing business is improving its logistics performance through supply chain integration.

The primary mission of Xerox's document processing business is to develop, manufacture, market, and service a broad range of document processing products including large scale electronic printers, duplicators, copiers, work stations, engineering products, telecopiers, and supplies associated with those products. The products are marketed in over 130 countries by a direct sales force

▶

275

▶ of 15 000 and a network of dealers, distributors and agents. The after sales service process is backed up by a service force of 30 000 technicians worldwide.

Xerox manufactures on a global basis with 22 major manufacturing facilities located in Europe, North and South America and in the Far East. These plants ship to marketing organizations which are responsible for the customer interface for sales and after sales support. The marketing organizations cover the total product array and are geographically organized. Customers in Europe and Africa are supported by Xerox Europe; US customers are supported by the United States Marketing Group; Canadian, Latin America and South American customers are supported by the Americas Operation; and Customers in Japan and the Pacific Rim are supported by our Fuji Xerox affiliate. Within each of these marketing organizations are sales, service and distribution groups.

Xerox corporate goals helped to frame the overall direction of what was needed to be accomplished within the supply chain. The goals are:

- Customer satisfaction
- Return on assets
- Market share
- Employee satisfaction

Since Xerox is, for the most part, a vertically-integrated company, directly manufacturing, selling and servicing our products, the supply chain is defined as illustrated in Figure 9.4. As may be seen, the Xerox supply chain is a closed loop. New material purchases are balanced by recycling returned parts and equipment to provide a significant portion of the asset requirements for spare parts and machines. This environmentally sound practice will grow in the future.

In 1989, the corporation examined its inventory performance in relationship to other diversified electronics firms based in the United States (see Figure 9.5). This benchmarking effort highlighted to Xerox senior management the gap against leading companies. An opportunity existed to provide the corporation with cash needed for new product development through the reduction of cash needs for inventories. It was

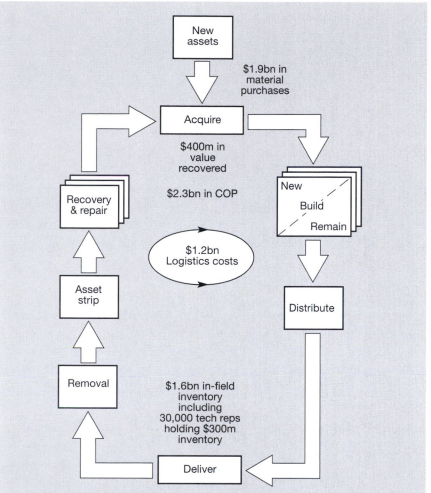

Fig. 9.4 The Xerox supply chain

also recognized that existing distribution, logistics, materials and manufacturing organizations were working hard. Their performance was not the issue. It was rather that functional operating unit objectives and goals limited the overall inventory performance of the company.

In 1989, the Central Logistics & Asset Management group was established to improve the asset management performance across the supply chain, rather than in individual organizational components of the chain. The group's mission as 'change agents' was to provide business sponsorship for inventory and logistics management through the development and implementation of integrated

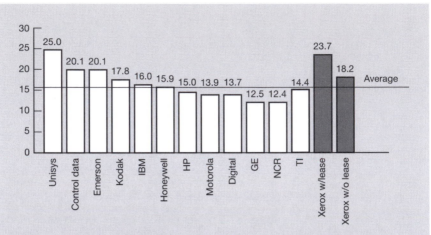

Fig. 9.5 Xerox's inventory performance in relation to other electronics

strategies and processes. The group is not just a staff organization, as it shares with the line organizations the responsibility for ongoing, year to year, achievement of improvements in customer satisfaction, logistics cost, and inventory reductions. So two things occurred: one, the mission became more than a mere inventory reduction campaign and tied into the overall corporate objectives; and two, short and long term activities needed to be balanced.

The approach taken consisted of several elements. First a vision had to be created. Integrating the supply chain could create a competitive advantage for the corporation; the goal was to be the best in service level, asset utilization and logistics cost. This vision would be detailed through the development of a strategic route map, identifying specific targets for critical supply chain measures of customer satisfaction, asset utilization and logistics cost. New integrating concepts would be tested first in 'showcases', then fine tuned prior to implementing them on a broad scale. To monitor the overall progress, supply chain performance measurements would be integrated. Lastly, the lessons learned would be incorporated into process reengineering efforts which in turn could lead to revising the information system base.

Route map

One of the first activities was the development of a route map of performance improvements. This chart comprehended current state and future state and identified yearly goals for performance improvements by fac-

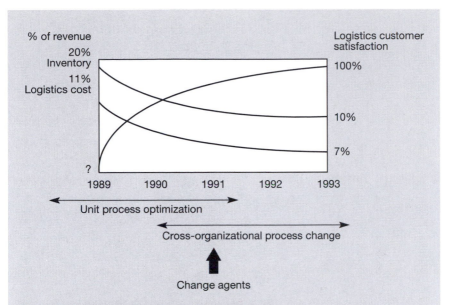

Fig. 9.6 Integrated supply chain – route map

toring in what changes were being undertaken with supply chain processes. The route map is illustrated in Figure 9.6. The goals were set for four years out and were based on benchmarking both performance and process. This provided management and employees with a picture of the four year plan. It also helped explain the new measures which were not in use before. For example, previously each organization measured its inventory performance based on its outflow of material in relationship to how much it had on hand. This was changed to a total supply chain measure of inventory as a percentage of revenue for all organizations, both marketing and manufacturing. Likewise, logistics costs had always been viewed as the cost of distributing product and was reported to be in the 4–5 per cent range. Taking a total supply chain view, and including costs such as transport, the cost of money for inventory and duties, the total cost of operating the supply chain became closer to 11 per cent. Traditionally, service levels were based on internal factors, how long it took to pull, pack and ship an order in a warehouse, for example. Through some focus groups with customers that were held by the US logistics group, the customer requirement was defined as the reliability of our delivery to an agreed date. Questions inserted into Xerox's ongoing customer satisfaction survey allowed information to be collected regarding how the customer really perceived the supply chain performance.

▶ The goals were aggressive; Xerox set about to get 100 per cent satisfied customers with the logistics process and at the same time halving the inventory requirements – a $1bn reduction – and reducing the logistics spend by 4 percentage points, a $300–400m reduction. It was not a question of trading off service level with cost. Xerox needed to reengineer its supply chain and thus needed to change culture, performance measurements, reward systems, relationships and behaviours within the company. Planning began with incorporating operating unit process optimization efforts. Some of these efforts were 'home grown', while others were the result of bringing in ideas from operating companies in different parts of the world. By understanding where the supply chain was going in each organization the group could then interact with the components of the supply chain, and as change agents, begin the cross-organizational process changes that would provide the integration needed.

Unit process optimization

An effort this large does not happen overnight. Each part of the company had a different experiential base, and were at differing levels of sophistication in their supply chain processes. A great deal of benefit was achieved through these operational groups improving their processes aided by sharing of practices among the operating units. A multinational cross-functional team had been in existence since 1986, but through the focus on integrating the supply chain, its role was strengthened. People who owned the inventory, customer delivery, and manufacturing/supplier processes participated in the team. But it wasn't limited to only logistics and materials people. Product design, marketing, quality, finance and information management people played a large role in the team.

This cross-functional team became the guardians and key stakeholders in the development and implementation of the strategies. This forum created the opportunity for line management buy-in to the integration strategy under development. Through their work, ideas that were proven in one organization could be shared and promoted in another. It also helped ensure that individual unit projects fitted into the overall direction, and were not being duplicated. Improvements to customer dissatisfiers from the customer satisfaction measurement system were put in place and high level measures were translated into more easily managed measures by operating personnel, such as percentage of orders delivered by the customer-requested delivery date. In Europe and America, teams worked to remove inventory echelons through the use of improved transport. Information was provided to promote the sharing of inventories among the operating units, and asset recycling practices were shared and encouraged among the units.

In parallel with the work being done with the supply chain, the corporation was developing its overall business architecture model. The emphasis of this effort was to re-orient Xerox to a cross-functional process view focusing on the customer and ultimately reengineering the company's business processes. One of the business areas that was viewed as high priority was inventory management and logistics. While this did not encompass all the business processes involved in the supply chain, it was sufficient to use as a lever to promote the integrated supply chain and helped provide more momentum to the efforts.

Process vision

The principles of the overall process vision were exploded into elements of the detailed functions within the inventory management and logistics area. This helped to provide the detail necessary to frame actions. Figure 9.7 contains the overall vision principles and how they affect process elements within the logistics area. These principles became the basis for the development of strategic actions in each of the process areas. These process areas are not organizationally-oriented, but rather focus on the activities which are performed. The sequencing of the processes is key. First, the satisfaction of customer orders, and the concomitant internal movements of material, is of primary importance using a common language throughout the supply chain to describe offerings to the customer, and its component pieces. Processes for planning had to be demand-driven to provide flexibility all the way from the customer through manufacturing. The supply chain was designed as an integrator for the entire company. Finally, the emphasis was to manage the flow of assets, not manage the stock in warehouses.

By comparing the vision to current state and incorporating the activities already underway in the operating units the changes required could be identified. This was done for each of the basic asset types in Xerox – equipment, supplies for the equipment, and spare parts for the equipment. The marketing channels and asset flows for each of the asset types are different. Spares are for the most part used by service

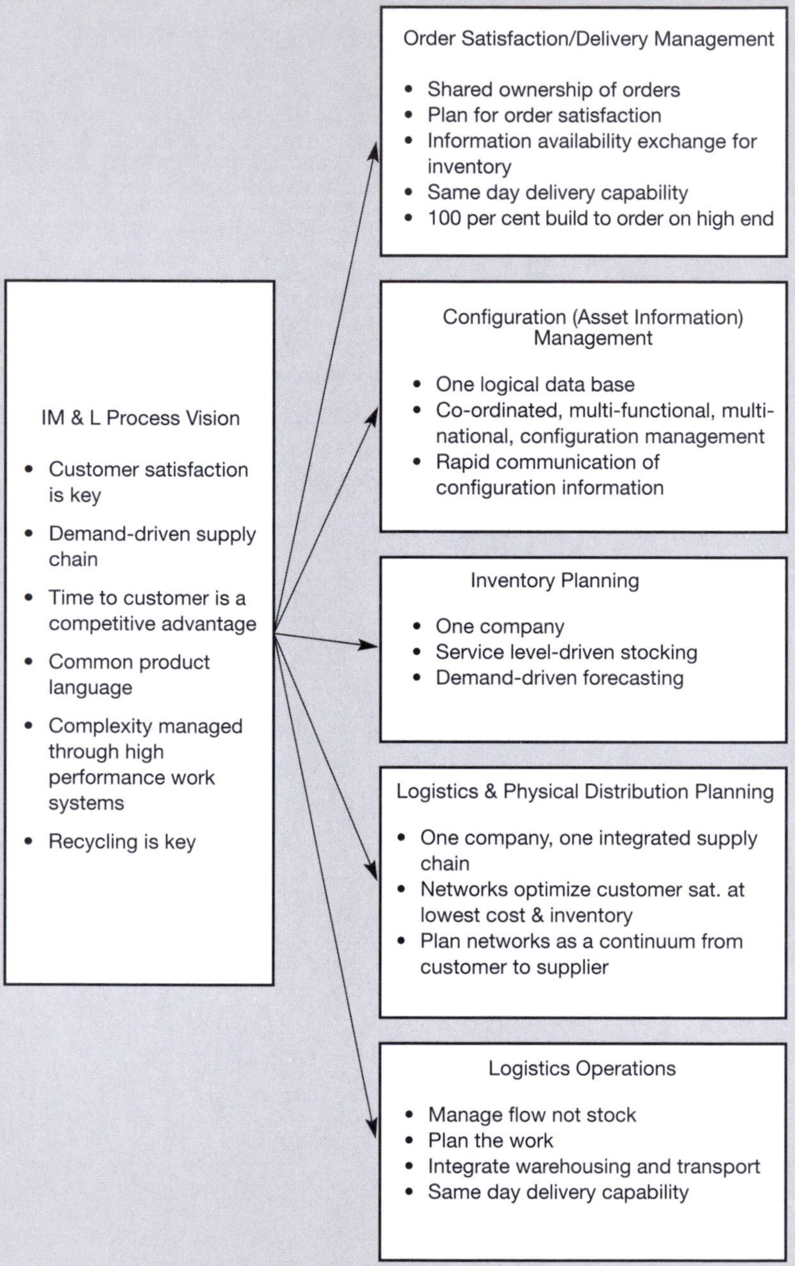

▶

Order Satisfaction/Delivery Management

- Shared ownership of orders
- Plan for order satisfaction
- Information availability exchange for inventory
- Same day delivery capability
- 100 per cent build to order on high end

Configuration (Asset Information) Management

- One logical data base
- Co-ordinated, multi-functional, multi-national, configuration management
- Rapid communication of configuration information

IM & L Process Vision

- Customer satisfaction is key
- Demand-driven supply chain
- Time to customer is a competitive advantage
- Common product language
- Complexity managed through high performance work systems
- Recycling is key

Inventory Planning

- One company
- Service level-driven stocking
- Demand-driven forecasting

Logistics & Physical Distribution Planning

- One company, one integrated supply chain
- Networks optimize customer sat. at lowest cost & inventory
- Plan networks as a continuum from customer to supplier

Logistics Operations

- Manage flow not stock
- Plan the work
- Integrate warehousing and transport
- Same day delivery capability

Fig. 9.7 Inventory management and logistics process vision

technicians in response to customer service calls. The flow of spare part assets is to the technician's stock. Supplies do not normally require special handling and are typically offered through telemarketing channels. Equipment does require special handling, due to its sensitive electronic and mechanical components. It also requires some degree of enabling at the customer's site, although not for the smallest products.

Much work had been accomplished in the spares and supplies chain in the 1980s and Xerox was at or near benchmark levels. This was effected in large part through the sharing of the best practices among the operating units and encouraged by the multinational cross-functional team. Although improvements in both these areas would continue, the focus of the Central Logistics and Asset Management group is on equipment. It was here that the greatest improvements could be made. These improvements also required changes in processes that cut across more than one organization and operating unit. It was here that the co-ordinating role of the CL & AM organization could best impact the business.

The integrating strategy resulted in the development of the envisioned equipment network for the corporation. The process would be reengineered to meet the customer requirements for each of the types of equipment marketed. The commodity type products, personal, small office copiers and telecopiers need to be designed to be easily installed so that the customer can receive them when desired. On the high volume end of the product spectrum (measured in copies per month – not number of units sold), the desire is to have 100 per cent build to the customer order. To accomplish this within the customer-required time frame will require Xerox to exchange information for inventory.

This strategy integrates distribution of product with the manufacture of product and the supply of components for manufacturing. It requires a continuing influence on the development of individual organizational practices, the construction of systems to support the practices, the design of new products, and has set the management style. This strategy is illustrated in Figure 9.8.

Process improvements in process

Xerox has made good progress towards the full implementation of an integrated supply chain; but still has much to do. Cross-functional process implementation has changed the mind sets of people in the supply chain. This change permits us to go further. Current work focuses

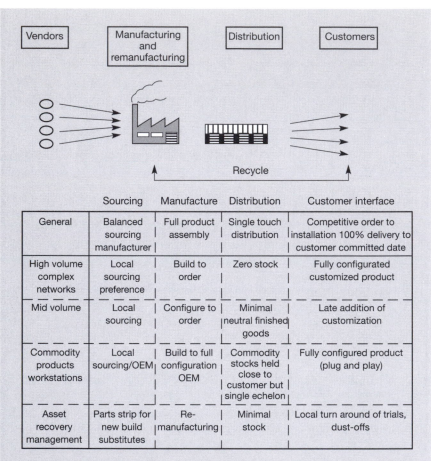

	Sourcing	Manufacture	Distribution	Customer interface
General	Balanced sourcing manufacturer	Full product assembly	Single touch distribution	Competitive order to installation 100% delivery to customer committed date
High volume complex networks	Local sourcing preference	Build to order	Zero stock	Fully configured customized product
Mid volume	Local sourcing	Configure to order	Minimal neutral finished goods	Late addition of customization
Commodity products workstations	Local sourcing/OEM	Build to full configuration OEM	Commodity stocks held close to customer but single echelon	Fully configured product (plug and play)
Asset recovery management	Parts strip for new build substitutes	Re-manufacturing	Minimal stock	Local turn around of trials, dust-offs

Fig. 9.8 Envisioned equipment network

on the manufacturing processes and the ability to be more flexible to meet demand in the marketplace. In an environment where you can accurately predict customer demands, the manufacturing processes can be quite inflexible. What is needed in today's environment is a balance between forecast accuracy and the ability of manufacturing to adjust its production to meet current demands. This requires a significant culture change in terms of responsibilities, reward structures, factory layouts and systems. It will not happen overnight. It also requires the sourcing patterns for components to be examined, and looking beyond first-tier suppliers to their suppliers and so on to gain the most benefit.

Order satisfaction processes need to be streamlined from the field all the way through manufacturing and Xerox is currently engaged in a reengineering effort to accomplish this. To support the order process, improvements are needed in information flow to allow people in the supply chain to communicate effectively and efficiently with each other. This requires that we begin the conversion to a common product language, understandable from salesforce to manufacturing and supplier. Future capability means intercepting the new product planning process to ensure that goals such as manufacturing and logistics flexibility are built into the products.

Management of change

The biggest change is to internalize the congruent goals that have been established. Each initiative goes through stages in its implementation. Initially, the objective is to convince people that change is necessary and get them to understand the change required. The next phase requires converting that understanding to a positive perception, and leading it into implementations in pilot and expansion. The last phase is to get ownership of the change into the hands of the people affected most by the change so that they believe that it is the only way of accomplishing the task. An environment that allows people to understand the change agenda and to react positively can speed the implementation.

Xerox is currently in the process of taking a major step into integration of the supply chain through this means. The performance measures of the senior managers of the marketing units and the manufacturing units have been changed to include the total assets in the supply chain. This moves from functional measures to cross-functional measures. Marketing, manufacturing and development managers are now measured on total supply chain inventory as a percentage of revenue and total customer satisfaction. As these measures become part of the way of doing business within the company, the next stage will be to measure logistics costs in the same way, as costs incurred across the supply chain in the process of delivering a document solution to the customer, not as costs that affect only one cost centre. This will allow a focus on the total impacts of supply chain activities and not treat them as separately attainable goals. This goal structure is illustrated in Figure 9.9.

Some keys for success

The performance improvements achieved so far, and scheduled for the next few years, have been helped by several fundamental factors. The

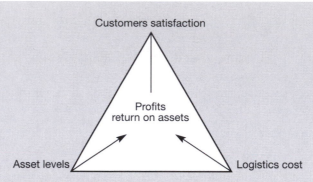

Fig. 9.9 The logistics triangle

effort has been cross-functional with a joint ownership of the problem and its solution by people involved in the supply chain. We have had strong and consistent senior management support. The corporation's quality culture with its emphasis on benchmarking, problem solving and quality improvement processes, along with the encouragement of cross-functional team work provided a favourable environment to effect change. It allows people from different parts of the company to use a common language to describe, analyze and improve our processes. And perhaps the most important element was the commitment to deliver benefits early in the implementation of the strategy through short term process changes and operating unit optimization. This has not allowed senior management to become impatient with the pace of change.

The implementation is not complete. Significant supply chain process improvements are yet to be accomplished. We have made major strides, and we realize that like most strategic goals, we are in a race without a finishing line.

Summary

To achieve leadership through logistics requires the organization to go through a number of fundamental transformations. The first of these is to make the transition from a functional or 'vertical' orientation to a process or 'horizontal' orientation. The second issue focuses upon performance measurement. It is critical that key performance indicators of the business are 'horizontal' not 'vertical', i.e. they should reflect the new orientation of the business. The third transformation is a switch in emphasis from product management to customer management, reflecting the fact that it is through the creation of customer value that firms compete.

The fourth transformation is at the heart of logistics and supply chain management. This is the concept of 'substituting information for inventory' enabling the business to become demand driven rather than forecast driven. Finally, and perhaps most importantly, the key business transformation is to recognize the need to change from a 'transaction' mentality to a 'relationship' mentality. It is through the management of relationships in the supply chain that the business gains and maintains competitive advantage.

References

1. van Hoek, R.I., Commandeur, H.R. and Vos, B., 'Reconfiguring Logistics Systems through Postponement Strategies', *Journal of Business Logistics*, Vol 18, No 2, 1998.
2. Lee, H.L., Billington, C. and Carter, B., 'Hewlett-Packard Gains Control of Inventory and Service through Design for Localisation', *Interfaces*, Vol 23, No 4, 1993.
3. Rayport, J F. and Sviokla, J.J., 'Managing in the Marketspace', *Harvard Business Review*, November–December 1994.

Index